This book is to be returned
the last date stamped b

Supp
Stude
in Online, Open
and stance Learning

Open and Distance Learning Series

Series Editor: Fred Lockwood

open &
distance
learning
series

Supporting
Students

in Online, Open
and Distance Learning

Second Edition

Ormond Simpson

**KOGAN
PAGE**

First published in 1999 as *Supporting Students in Open and Distance Learning*
Second edition published in 2002

Kogan Page Limited
120 Pentonville Road
London N1 9JN
UK

Stylus Publishing Inc.
22883 Quicksilver Drive
Sterling VA 20166–2012
USA

British Library Cataloguing in Publication Data

A CIP record for this book is available from the British Library.

ISBN 0 7494 3740 5

Typeset by JS Typesetting, Wellingborough, Northants
Printed and bound in Great Britain by Clays Ltd, St Ives plc

To my daughters, Anina and Leila, who gave the best kind of support

I was at the Mathematical School, where the Master taught his Pupils after a Method scarce imaginable to us in Europe. The Proposition and Demonstration were fairly written on a thin wafer, with Ink composed of a Cephalick Tincture. This the Student was to swallow upon a fasting stomach, and for three Days following eat nothing but Bread and Water. As the Wafer digested, the Tincture mounted to his Brain, bearing the Proposition along with it. But the Success hath not hitherto been answerable, partly by some Error in the Quantum of Composition, and partly by the Perverseness of Lads: to whom this Bolus is so nauseous, that they generally steal aside; and discharge it upwards before it can operate; neither have they been yet persuaded to use so long an Abstinence as the Prescription requires.

Jonathan Swift, Part Three – A Voyage to Laputa, Balnibarbi Luggnagg, Glubbdubdrip and Japan, *Gulliver's Travels*

Contents

Series Editor's foreword

Prior to the first edition of this book, three things had happened to me that combined to have a significant impact on the way I approached my work and that would be likely to make me a better teacher and tutor.

Firstly, I read a book chapter describing an experimental distance learning course. It involved adult learners within a multinational company who were using a particular Virtual Learning Environment; a computer software system that allows an institution to teach online and enables students to download course materials, take part in electronic discussion groups, submit assignments and so on. The wizardry of the computer system was impressive but the evaluation revealed daunting demands on the learners and their need for advice, assistance, guidance and support during their studies.

Secondly, I chaired an examination board at which student performance on the course was assessed and awards determined. Many of the students did extremely well and we awarded several distinctions – wonderful news for these students. However, about 7 per cent of the original group had dropped out of the course before the end and about 3 per cent failed. My feeling of shared pleasure for those who were successful was marred by what I could imagine was the effect on those who had dropped out and failed. I felt I had personally failed those students.

Thirdly, the British Government released 'Performance Indicators' for each university in the country. It distinguished between full-time and part-time students, noted the proportion of students categorized as coming from disadvantaged groups and recorded drop-out rates in the first year against various benchmarks. It marked the start of what will undoubtedly be a lively debate on the value of these Performance Indicators, on the methodology adopted, on a whole range of issues – but hopefully they will be a way in which we can improve the learning experience of our students and increase their success.

Upon reading the first edition of this book by Ormond Simpson I realized that advice and assistance could readily have been provided on the online learners in the multinational company, that I could have done more to provide academic and non-academic support for my learners, and that we can all do more to recruit learners, support and retain students so as to increase their eventual success – whatever their course of study.

This second edition of *Supporting Students in Online, Open and Distance Learning* is broader in scope with all sections updated. In addition, the need for learner support in the use of different media and particularly in online learning and computer conferencing is addressed. Whether you regard yourself as a teacher or trainer, manager or administrator, tutor or counsellor, I believe there will be something in this book for you and thus for your learners. The author adopts a style that is informal yet informative; it is comprehensive in its coverage whilst flagging those areas outside the scope of a single book. It addresses a broad range of issues from learning skills development to supporting difficult students, from face-to-face support at a distance, from addressing theory to the problems posed by difficult students. Throughout, Ormond Simpson draws from his own substantial experience and provides numerous concrete examples and case studies that serve to illustrate and reinforce the points he makes. I suspect that you will find all the sections in the book valuable. However, I also suspect that its main success will be in sensitising you to the needs of the learners and what we can do to support them, and that you, like me, will gain much from this book for the benefit of your learners.

Fred Lockwood

Preface to the second edition

It was very gratifying to be told by the publishers of the first edition of *Supporting Students in Open and Distance Learning* that it had been well received by reviewers and readers and that a second edition was now appropriate. On the other hand re-reading it has been a salutary experience both stimulating the question 'Did I really write that?' and the realization of how fast things move in this field.

This second edition has been substantially broadened in scope although the perspective remains firmly on ODL. Nevertheless I hope that there will be useful material in it for anyone working in student support in almost any context, from full time to flexistudy students, and from Internet highway institutions to developing world organizations who rely on older (but possibly equally effective) technologies.

All sections have been revised and updated with particularly substantial additions to reflect current concerns in ODL with tuition in different media, student retention, structures and quality assurance, staff development and especially online support and computer conferencing. At the same time I have tried to retain the practical nature of the book that was popular with readers and I hope that there is still material in it that can be simply pulled out, re-edited to suit, and used directly with students and support staff.

My grateful thanks are due to my assistant Anna Cribb who has now typed more drafts of this text than she cares to remember.

Introduction

Open and distance learning (ODL) is more than 150 years old and dates back perhaps to the early days of one social revolution – the 'Penny Post' (the ability to send a letter anywhere in the UK at a standard rate of one old penny) with Isaac Pitman's correspondence courses in shorthand. Some people claim St Paul's Epistles as the first open and distance learning package consisting of both correspondence and a face-to-face element.

Now many revolutions later, but particularly the information technology (IT) revolution, there is an explosive growth in open and distance learning worldwide. There are nearly 30 open universities operating in developed and developing world environments and countless other organizations working at non-higher education levels. Many conventional institutions have perceived the 'sunrise industry' potential of ODL and have set up subdivisions to develop it. Indeed, it is probable that ODL now represents the fastest growing sector in education worldwide.

This book is about one specific but vital aspect of ODL: student support. In some ways, student support has not received the attention it has deserved. This may be because it is seen as less glamorous than other activities in ODL or peripheral to the real business of developing materials. Perhaps it may be that (as suggested by Paul, 1988) institutions believe that students' personal issues are a far greater factor in drop out than any institutional factors and therefore beyond the institution's control. Or perhaps the managers of ODL programmes have not often been in the position of new and unqualified learners on a distance education course and find it hard to empathize with how highly such learners value support. Now, with a tighter focus on retention rates in ODL, the introduction of IT into student support and developing interest in student outcomes, there is increased interest in student support in ODL and the role it plays.

The definition of open and distance learning

This has been the subject of much debate: I shall use the simplest terms. An open learning system is one that has no entry requirements apart from very broad ones such as age. A distance learning system is one in which the courses and support are supplied by various distance media such as correspondence although there may be face-to-face elements.

Obviously open learning is not necessarily at a distance, or distance learning open. Nevertheless, they present very similar challenges in terms of student support. Those challenges in turn are similar to those posed 'on campus' where students are physically present on campus but studying largely independently – a response to the increasing numbers entering higher education for example.

Thus the target audience for this book is a wide range of staff either currently on ODL schemes or about to start. They may be tutors, advisers and counsellors working directly with students or administrators and managers organizing student support. They may be working in this country or abroad, in either the developed or developing world. They may work in a variety of institutions, some purely operating at a distance, some in a mixed mode, some in 'campus mode' with full-time students, some open and some with entry requirements.

The term 'student support' will cover as complete a spectrum of activities as possible, from the organizing and management of student support including staff development through to direct interaction with students as tutors, advisers, mentors and other roles.

Approach of the book

This is grounded in theory as far as possible. Nevertheless, the intention above all is to produce a practical resource of immediate use. I hope for example that it will be of help to people with needs as various as:

- running a face-to-face session on developing study skills with a group of new students;
- managing student support staff;
- designing materials for student support.

As such, the book contains elements that can be extracted and adapted both for direct student support and for staff development. It need not be read from cover to cover but can be dipped into wherever your interest lies.

Resources for further study

Books

There are a number of books listed in the references that would be helpful reading, particularly Gibbs (1981), which has a very useful survey of research into the development of learning skills, and McGivney (1996), which surveys issues to do with student retention. Other books containing interesting articles in the area are Thorpe and Grugeon (1987), Tait (1999) and Morgan (1993).

Web sites

The most important of a number of useful Web sites are:

- International Centre for Distance Learning, http://www-icdl.open.ac.uk, which has a searchable database of articles containing more than 500 items in the category of student support at the time of writing.
- International Extension College, www.iec.ac.uk, which is particularly useful in a developing world context with reviews, resources and information on courses in distance education.
- International Research Foundation for Open Learning (IRFOL), www.col.org/irfol, which undertakes research again particularly in the developing world. Research reports can be downloaded from this site on topics like cost-effective delivery systems in basic education.
- Distance Education Clearing House at http://www.uwex.edu/disted. This site has links to many other sites – one provides access to bibliographies on distance education and within this a link to sites related to issues about student support.
- Distance Learning channel, at www.ed-x.com, which offers news and course descriptions about degree programmes on the Web.
- American Center for the Study of Distance Education (ACSDE), at http://www.ed.psu.edu/acsde, which offers a link to an online symposium on distance education.

Newsgroups

Newsgroups come and go but there is one which might be worth subscribing to. Distance Education Online Symposium (DEOS), run by the ACSDE, has over 1300 international subscribers. To subscribe, go to the ACSDE site above.

Journals

There are a number of specialist journals with useful articles:

- *Open Learning*, co-produced by the UK Open University and Carfax Publishing. Titles often reflect particular interest in student support. (Web site: http://www.tandf.co.uk.)
- *Distance Education*, published by Carfax Publishing for the Open and Distance Learning Association of Australia (ODLAA).
- *American Journal of Distance Education*, published by Pennsylvania State University. Generally only contributions relating to the Americas.
- *Journal of Access and Credit Studies*, published by the National Institute of Adult and Continuing Education (NIACE), Leicester; a new journal that promises to be eclectic in its approach to open learning.
- *'Open Praxis'* – bulletin of the International Council for Distance Education www.icde.org.
- *British Journal of Educational Technology*, particularly on information and communication technology. See http://www.blackwellpublishers.co.uk.

Online journal

- *European Journal of Open and Distance Learning (EURODL)*, a relatively new on-line venture. (Web site: www.nks.no/eurodl.)

Chapter 1

Models and definitions

Models of ODL systems

There are many structural models of open or distance learning. The simplest possible model envisages a straight transfer of material between institution and student in a kind of chemical reaction:

Student + Teaching materials = Successful student.

This model may be varied with perhaps some feedback from student to institution.

Few ODL institutions now operate such a simple model, although there are some institutions in developing countries that are forced to start up this way. Now the most common model envisages a 'catalytically assisted reaction' where a third element enters the equation:

Student + Teaching materials + Student support = Successful student.

There are other metaphors for the elements that have been used. The first is the 'sales' (course production) and 'after sales service' (student support) model. The terminology of this model has been recently updated into 'production' and 'customer care' and indeed the vocabulary of customer care may offer some interesting analogies, as we shall see later. A little more cynically, some of my colleagues refer to course production as the cavalry (who dash in to push back the lines of ignorance) and student support as the infantry who actually have to occupy the territory subsequently.

Regardless of the preferred model, student support is generally seen as encompassing tuition and a miscellany of activities with names like counselling, guidance and advice. In fact, the range of activities that comes under the heading of 'student support' is enormously varied. I have kept track of 'student support' actions that I have taken recently. Without trying to categorize, I have done the following:

- talked with a student who is demoralized by a poor exam result and tried to help him put it in perspective;
- arranged for an elderly student in a remote village to get a small grant for fares to take a taxi to tutorials in the nearest town;
- written to some part-time tutors to see if they would be willing to set up a voice mail notice board for their students;
- lobbied a university working party to put some software on its Web site to allow students to calculate their course grades more accurately;
- organized a small graduation ceremony in a local prison;
- written a bid to fund a student mentoring project;
- placed some staff development materials on a computer mediated conferencing site;
- arranged payment and thanks for a part-time tutor who has just undertaken some extra work with a student on numeracy;
- written to the widow of a student who had just died;
- helped a colleague edit a taster pack of materials designed to give new students a taste of a course;
- written to a student who has been taking courses for three years without passing any of them;
- explained (by phone) the concept of kinetic energy to a student on an introductory science course.

If you have any experience of ODL then I have little doubt that you will have a similar, probably even more varied list – and it is very difficult to classify this cavalcade of activities in any way that makes sense.

Definitions in student support

The confusion of this cavalcade is reflected in terms used to classify different areas of student support. Words like 'guidance', 'advice' and 'counselling' have all been used in different ways by different organizations. For example, the phrase 'educational guidance' that used to refer to all student support other than strict tutorial work has become more closely attached only to advisory work carried out with enquirers or registered students before their courses start. The term 'counselling' was originally used by the UK Open University to refer to all non-tutorial support, but has always carried unhelpful connotations of psychotherapy and has been replaced by the more general term 'student support'.

It is important to try to keep the terms as clear as possible. In this book, I define student support in the broadest terms as all activities beyond the production and delivery of course materials that assist in the progress of students in their studies.

I suggest it falls into two broad areas. The first is academic (or tutorial) support – which deals with supporting students with the cognitive, intellectual and knowledge issues of specific courses or sets of courses. This will include, for example, developing general learning skills, numeracy and literacy. The second is non-academic or counselling support – the support of students in the affective and organizational aspects of their studies. There are further sub-divisions within these two divisions.

Academic support consists of:

- defining the course territory;
- explaining concepts;
- exploring the course;
- feedback – both informal and formal assessment;
- developing learning skills, such as numeracy and literacy;
- chasing progress, following up students' progress through the course;
- enrichment: extending the boundaries of the course and sharing the excitement of learning.

The first two items in the list above may well be the responsibility of the course material rather than the tutor in a distance education environment. The challenge there, as we shall see later, may be to move tutors away from traditional explicative modes of working in order to emphasize the other facilitative modes.

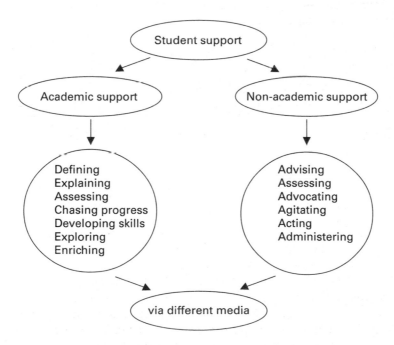

Figure 1.1   *Structure of this book*

Non-academic support consists of:

- advising: giving information, exploring problems and suggesting directions;
- assessment: giving feedback to the individual on non-academic aptitudes and skills;
- action: practical help to promote study;
- advocacy: making out a case for funding, writing a reference;
- agitation: promoting changes within the institution to benefit students;
- administration: organizing student support.

You will notice that of this list, only the first three are work directly with students. Much student support activity may not necessarily occur directly at the student–institution interface. There is clearly much overlap between these divisions as we shall see in chapter 2 ('support categories') and to some extent the division is artificial and arbitrary but helpful.

The structure adopted by this book appears in the form shown in Figure 1.1.

The term 'guidance' (where used) will refer to non-academic support activities undertaken in the period before the start of a course.

In my experience, this type of diagram is most helpful in retrospect. However, it is useful in defining the terms we shall be using (even if rather arbitrarily) throughout the book. I am also not happy with the terms 'academic' and 'non-academic' support, but such phrases seem preferable to using terms which may be used differently elsewhere or have unhelpful connotations. If you can think of better terms you should use them!

Chapter 2

Background to student support

Reasons for student support

There are many reasons for ensuring that student support is a vital element in any ODL scheme. These fall into three main categories.

Practical reasons for student support

Retention

One characteristic of ODL is its association with high drop out rates (at least in comparison with conventional institutions). Woodley (1987), in a survey of 3000 UK evening course students, found a 21 per cent drop out rate by the end of term, followed by a massive 58 per cent failing to re-enrol subsequently. Clearly there will always be some drop out; less clearly, we do not know what minimum is achievable, in any particular situation – see chapter 13.

There are implications for institutions as governments everywhere take an increasingly instrumental view of education and start to link funding to outcomes. Institutions will become less able to rely on recruiting large numbers of new students in the hope that some will get through, and will need to develop more sophisticated ways of increasing retention. Some improvements will be possible by redesigning course materials but much more will have to be achieved through enhancing and developing student support.

Students' demands

As ODL provision grows, so competition mounts. The UK Open University was once the only distance learning provider in the town in which I work; now it is possible to study at a distance through a local university, a further education college and a sixth form college. With the development of the Internet competition can now be worldwide. Where students have a choice they will judge institutions by the quality of the materials they produce and – probably even more – by the standards of student support they offer.

Theoretical reasons for student support

Student isolation

Clearly, studying through ODL is often a very isolating experience; students are isolated from other students, their tutors, the institution and sometimes their own family and friends. Such isolation must inhibit if not prevent entirely any possibility of dialogue in their studies. Yet education – at least as perceived in traditional thought – is essentially a process of dialogue. Can we claim to be offering any kind of education if we do not offer our students the opportunity for dialogue at the same time? Moreover, is it possible to offer dialogue only through course materials? If overcoming isolation through dialogue is important for us, then this can only realistically take place through the process of student support. In addition, and more practically, it has been suggested that isolation is probably the most important factor in drop out; students who fail to establish support networks are more likely to withdraw.

Democracy versus authoritarianism

It has been argued that ODL can be potentially a very authoritarian educational system with pre-packaged course material that can present only a particular perspective (Tait, 1989). Student support offers the student some choices and some chance to challenge orthodoxies.

Moral reasons for student support

This heading may seem a little strange but there is a moral aspect to ODL as there is in any educational activity. There ought indeed to be a kind of educational 'hippocratic oath'. If one justification for student support is to help students progress their studies, there is a higher moral imperative that sometimes conflicts with that – assisting students to do what is right for them in whatever situation they are currently experiencing.

Clearly there are situations where a student support adviser or tutor will have irreconcilable demands. Typically there will be students who are experiencing difficulties – illness, divorce or bereavement – or who are simply struggling with the intellectual demands of a course. There is a fine line between encouraging and supporting such students to continue at whatever personal cost and allowing them to withdraw – perhaps prematurely – becoming drop out statistics and leaving them with a sense of failure. That line can only be drawn if we have sophisticated and clearly thought out student support policies and procedures.

With increasing emphasis on student retention, may this kind of conflict become more common? All we can do is to flag this as an issue that may become more important. For the moment we rely largely on students' abilities to know when they have had enough; what might happen when there are higher rewards (and penalties) attached to their decision remains to be seen.

Balance between course production and student support

None of the suggestions above will help you to set a balance of resources between course production and student support. There will always be those who argue that the attractions of placing resource into multimedia course production outweigh the need for a quality student support service. It seems difficult to devise research that can compare the effects on student retention or satisfaction of either another CD ROM or an extra face-to-face tutorial on any particular course. Asking students what the balance should be is one way, but as we shall see later in this book different students will give different answers. The debate between course production and student support will always be complex.

Student support: who your students are

The obvious way to start thinking about student support is to think about your students and potential students – who are they and what do they need? You might like to ask yourself the question, 'What skills, personal qualities and values does anyone need to become a successful student in open and distance learning?' I have brainstormed this question as an introductory exercise on a number of occasions with different groups of distance educators and there is surprising unanimity about the resulting list. Our list looks like this.

To succeed as a student in ODL a person needs:

Intelligence	Ability to deal with job pressures
Numeracy	Ability to handle demands of family
Literacy	Ability to manage the paperwork
Motivation	Ability to create a good study environment
Ability to ask for help	Ability to prioritize among study demands
Self-confidence	Ability to accept constructive criticism
Sense of humour	Ability to handle stress of being assessed

You may well have other items on your list, and you would be entitled to say that these qualities are what anyone needs to succeed at almost anything, and you would be right. But what is most interesting about this list is the following:

● The relative importance of items on the list: for example, is motivation generally more important than self-confidence? If so, what are the implications for student support?
● The difference between a quality and a skill – for example, how far is motivation an innate quality or can it be enhanced? If so, how far can a tutor or adviser develop a student's motivation and by what means?
● We can attempt to classify items on the list in some way that might give us some ideas about how student support could be structured. One such way is to group sets of items and label them as shown in Figure 2.1.

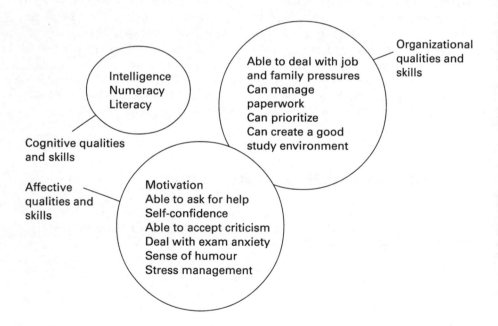

Figure 2.1 *Classifying qualities and skills*

This might suggest a 'phrenological' theory of student support (see Figure 2.2). Although this is not a serious suggestion, nevertheless if you carry this image in your head it may act as a reminder of the need, when talking with students, to consider more than just an appeal to their intellect.

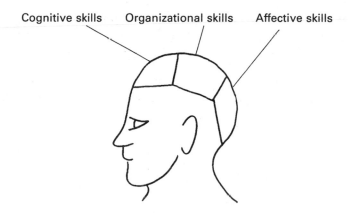

Cognitive skills   Organizational skills   Affective skills

Figure 2.2   *A 'phrenological' theory of student support in ODL*

Support categories

The phrenological model also offers a way of classifying student support into two main modes: supporting cognitive development, as a result of academic support; and supporting affective and organizational development, through non-academic support.

These two areas are not entirely distinct, of course; tutors working with students may move effortlessly and unconsciously from one mode (academic) to another (non-academic) as they move from a discussion of 15th-century Italian art into how the students will manage to submit the following week's assignment. Nevertheless, it is a distinction that remains useful in many student support activities. For example, as tutors move from one mode to another they will be using a slightly different set of qualities and skills as they do so. Many of the skills will be similar, but the emphasis will be different as shown in Figure 2.3.

There can be arguments over what skills should appear precisely where. Chapter 3 will look at them in more detail. For the moment consider this set of queries that have crossed my desk recently. Are these academic or non-academic issues? How relevant is the distinction?

- A student says that he is getting behind in the course because he is finding it hard to concentrate. 'Is there some way of increasing powers of concentration?' he asks.
- A student e-mails you: 'Hello – it's me again! I can't get this essay in on time either. Can I have my usual extension? About three weeks, okay?'
- A student phones: 'I broke my wrist last week and I'm finding it hard to write. What can I do?'
- A student just cannot handle algebra.
- A student asks if it is okay to discuss the next assignment in a self-help group with other students.

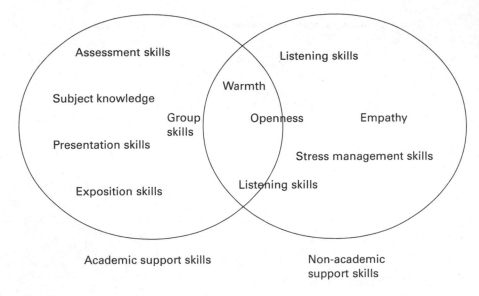

Figure 2.3 *Support skills*

- You write to a student who has not submitted his very first assignment and he replies that he finds the course very demanding. This is his first ODL course and he has not done any introductory study.
- A student whose grades have been average approaches you and says that he is getting well behind and asks whether he could put in the next assignment late. He sounds rather depressed.
- You receive a letter from the husband of one of your students to say that his wife has had to go into hospital for an operation. She is okay but is likely to be unable to work for several months.
- A student e-mails you and says – 'I'm sorry – I just can't face sitting the exam. I'm terrified of exams and just go to pieces.'
- A student approaches you and says she wants to talk about some problems at home. She tells you her husband is being difficult about her studies. Suddenly she bursts into tears.
- As an adviser you receive a letter from a student that says, 'I'm really not happy with the grade the tutor gave me on the last assignment. I just can't see why he's given me a "D". Would you have a look and see what you think?'
- A very anxious student phones you for the second time this week for a reason that strikes you as really rather trivial.
- A student who attends tutorials sometimes has been putting in poor assignments. They show some knowledge but are rather jumbled with many irrelevancies and do not really answer the question.
- You phone a student who fails to submit an assignment. He tells you, 'I'm going to have to drop out. Frankly I just don't seem to be able to find enough time.'

- One student in your tutorial group is very talkative and others do not contribute.
- A student writes to say she is pregnant and the baby is due in about six months.
- A student phones you and says that he just can't get the computer conferencing software to work properly.

It may be thought that this list was contrived but there are few queries in it that fall into a clear distinction between academic and non-academic issues. Even the query about algebra may have more to it than there seems at first sight. Unless we try to categorize to some modest extent we may be either overwhelmed by the complexity of the problems students raise, or worse we may tend to be just tutors or advisers and forget the need to be both. So, this arbitrary distinction is maintained when the activities of academic and non-academic support are looked at in more detail in chapter 3.

Chapter 3

Non-academic student support: advising

This chapter looks more closely at the various categories of student support defined previously. We shall start with non-academic support and particularly the area of advising, because there are general principles that can be drawn that apply to other areas of student support.

Advising activities

It may be helpful to see advising as encompassing three basic activities: informing, commending and exploring.

- **Informing** is the process of giving accurate, timely and appropriate information to students about any aspects of their studies: 'That course starts in September and you still have time to enrol.'
- **Commending** may seem a slightly curious word to use but it means the process of outlining a range of options to a student while suggesting that one or more may be the most appropriate: 'There are three introductory maths courses you could take but with your background I would suggest that "Maths for Returnees" is the most appropriate.'
- **Exploring** is the process of helping students clarify the options open to them in such a way as (ideally) to enable them to come to a decision for themselves: 'I am so sorry to hear of your daughter's illness: let's talk it through and see whether it's best to drop out now or carry on.'

These activities form a 'spectrum' of student advice:

Figure 3.1 *The 'advice spectrum'*

The activities are not clearly differentiated from each other – you may well be selective in the information you offer so that you are effectively commending a course of action, or you may commend some consideration as part of an exploring process.

You may well move from one part of the spectrum to another and back again in one interview. You may start by exploring an issue with a student, and then offer a piece of relevant information because of that exploration which in turn will allow you to commend a particular way forward. Alternatively, a query that is presented as a straight information request may need exploring before the correct piece of information can be given.

Spectra have non-visible elements at either end. Maybe beyond the 'exploring' end of this spectrum there is the ultra-violet area of counselling and psychotherapy that will not be ventured into except to set our boundaries (see chapter 16).

Manipulation

Before looking at each of these areas in turn, it may be useful to look at Figure 3.2, which shows a different presentation of the same spectrum in which the axes are as follows.

Horizontal: the student is included in the solution to the issue (the solution is very much dependent on the student's particular characteristics and needs) versus the student is excluded from the solution to the issue (the solution may be an item of information that is completely independent of the student).

Vertical: the process concentrates on the issue versus the process concentrates on the student.

This leads us to the same three activities as in the spectrum: for example, giving an item of information is independent of the student (in the sense that the item will be the same regardless of who the student is) and the process does not involve the student apart from the posing of the initial question. However, interestingly this presentation indicates the existence of a fourth mode of student advising where the process ostensibly centres on students but the solution actually excludes them. This is 'manipulation' where advisers attempt to get students to accept their solutions by apparently including them in the discussion of the problem.

There could be debate about whether manipulation ever has a part to play in student support. I concede that on rare occasions in the past I have perhaps tried to get students to accept solutions to their problems that suit me rather than them. However, I suspect that these aims have never been achieved and that manipulation as a process is not only unethical but also ineffectual. However, it is a continuous temptation to guard against.

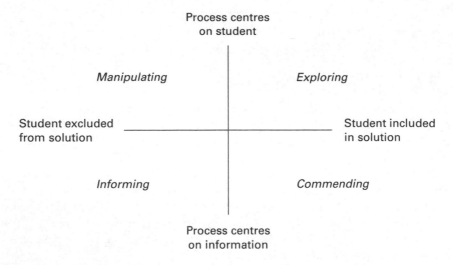

Figure 3.2   *Manipulation (adapted from R De Board, Counselling People at Work)*

Selecting

A different question might be asked at this point compared with the student questions at the end of chapter 2: 'If this question is a non-academic issue is it an informing, commending or exploring issue? Or is it likely that I may have to operate in two or three different modes in order to try to help this student?' It should be remembered that it may be as frustrating for a student who is only requesting a straightforward piece of information to be subjected to the exploring mode as it is for a student whose issue needs exploring to be fobbed off with a piece of information.

Informing

In many ways, giving information is the Cinderella activity of non-academic student support. It is not glamorous, taken for granted and often seen as a clerical level task. Yet it is a vital activity in student support and needs much more careful attention.

The challenges are considerable: institutions are becoming steadily more complex as different programmes develop and require their own information resources. Information becomes spread out and lurks in numerous different places. Many institutions are now far too complex for one individual to comprehend, and there is an increasing tendency to refer students on to different sections of the organization. Yet students are increasingly used to 'one stop shopping' of the kind provided by insurance companies and banks. Therefore the structure of our student support services needs to be considered (see chapter 15).

Of course, the development of information and communication technology (ICT) may come to our rescue. Students will be able to surf the Internet to find the information they need, but anyone who has tried to recover a specific item of information from the Internet will know that this is not always easy and can be very time consuming. There is evidence to suggest that students find it hard to see where they are going on the Internet and are easily confused by it (see chapter 7).

There are institutional problems too. Where information is seen to be important to recruit new students then considerable resource is put into it. Where information is only for current students then it has a much lower profile. The contrast in my own institution between the Introductory Brochure – colour, pictures, designer layout – and the Student Handbook – no colour, no pictures, ring binder format – could hardly be more marked.

In addition, there will be institutional differences as to what information should be in the student domain. I am currently engaged in an argument with my own organization's exams office over the level of information that should be available to students on its assessment policies. I prefer greater openness; they argue that if students know more precisely what they need to do to pass, they will lower their sights when the best advice should still be to do their best. How information is supplied to students and what information is supplied are difficult areas that need research and negotiation.

Commending

It is unusual to commend a particular route for a student very early in an advisory session. Commending usually follows informing or exploring.

It is a truism that people only take the suggestions that it suits them to take. Indeed, it is an everyday experience that students will only take particular recommendations on board when they arise from a process in which they persuade themselves that those recommendations are right.

One of the great temptations of student support is the tendency to recommend particular courses of action to students without allowing them to take on self-persuasion. It is not surprising that recommendations given like that are subsequently ignored. In my own institution, this becomes particularly obvious in the area of guidance when advising new students what course to take. New students appear to persist in taking courses that appear superficially attractive despite advice that those courses are in fact out of their reach because of their academic or time demands.

Clearly there are attractions in giving early recommendations and there has to be some element of *caveat emptor* (let the buyer beware) when working with adults. However, it is very tempting to make a recommendation quickly so that the organization is in the clear without having to take time to help the student think through the implications of the recommendation. If a recommendation is to be effective there will often need to be some exploration.

Exploring

Exploring is actually a minority activity in ODL. I estimate that of the student support I undertake directly with students some 50 per cent is giving information, 30 per cent is recommending, and only 20 per cent (if that) is exploring in any sense. Yet because it is a more challenging activity, there is much more to say about the processes, the skills and qualities involved.

Advising qualities and skills

Student support advisers will express a range of personal qualities and use a variety of skills in their work. The suggestions made by Rogers (1951) about psychotherapeutic counselling may still provide an appropriate framework for the study support context (see chapter 14).

Personal qualities in student support

Rogers suggested a list of personal qualities that should be expressible by a counsellor. The qualities he suggested were:

Warmth

Warmth (or 'non-possessive warmth' in Rogers' terms) is the ability to be appropriately friendly and approachable. Interestingly, in a small-scale survey of UK OU tutors of what qualities students most valued in a tutor, being friendly and approachable was second in a hierarchy of skills and qualities (Gaskell and Simpson, 2000).

This survey was of tutors operating by phone and face to face. It is interesting to note that this hierarchy of skills and qualities may be different for tutors on-line and in any case may not be the criteria by which tutors are selected.

Table 3.1 *What students value in tutors*

Priority	What students most value in tutors
1	Knows subject
2	Is approachable
3	Gives good feedback in face-to-face tutorials
4	Gives good feedback on assignments
5	Can help develop study skills
6	Is easy to get hold of
7	Marks promptly
8	Understands students' problems
9	Can help with time management
10	Can explain grades clearly

Empathy

This is the skill of understanding other people's feelings without 'taking them over' in any way. This is not always easy; for example, most of the people working on student support in an institution have been successful students in the past. It may be difficult for them to understand the feelings of a student who is experiencing failure or exam stress.

Case study 1

I took a call recently from a student. He started by asking, 'Can you help me?' and continued to explain his rather complex query. However, he seemed confused and aggressive as I tried to clarify his query. He kept saying, 'I don't know if you can help me.' Suddenly I realized that I had to respond to the anxiety in his voice and I dropped the rather bureaucratic mode into which I had slipped. 'Look, I can feel that you're really quite worried about this and actually I don't know if I can help you,' I said, 'but I will have a very good try if you can tell me your problem.' I must have hit a note of empathy because he seemed to relax and our interview immediately continued more easily.

Acceptance

This is the quality of non-prejudice, of accepting other people's values and background and of not expressing criticism of them. This looks simple but again is not always easy. For a start, there is a sense in which criticism is the lifeblood of the educational process. Of course, this is (or should be) criticism of their work rather than of them.

The problem is that expressing criticism directly or indirectly that can be interpreted personally will usually shut down any useful dialogue, especially where students already lack confidence. Students' diffidence in contacting tutors may be due partly to feelings that they will be the subjects of criticism, expressed or unexpressed, as a result.

The issue of values is also important. Educators probably hold a raft of values that are not always held to the same extent by their students: values to do with the worth of education, the importance of working hard and the pre-eminence of the intellectual. It is not obvious which values have to be held by students in order to progress in their studies.

Another aspect of acceptance (or rather non-acceptance) is prejudice in various forms such as:

- ageism: for example assuming, probably unconsciously, that older students will be too slow or younger students insufficiently committed to study;
- racism: unexamined assumptions about the influence of ethnic background on learning are difficult to eradicate from even the best-intentioned staff;

Case study 2

I remember trying to work with a tutor who had very strong ideas about the value of punctuality, precision and order. She was increasingly unable to deal with the disordered work lives of her students and particularly the difficulty they had of getting work in exactly on time. She finally found the job intolerable and resigned.

Another of the most frustrating cases I had was of a student with very tightly held perfectionist values. He would only undertake work which he believed was of the highest standard and if he was not convinced of its worth he would refuse to submit it. I was quite unable to persuade him that it was necessary to cut corners sometimes and put in work that was slightly less than perfect. Eventually the stress of holding such values was too great for him and he withdrew.

- sexism: assumptions about students based on their sex;
- elitism: an -ism to which educators are particularly prone perhaps; it is still not uncommon to come across cases where a tutor has unconsciously dismissed a student's chances because of that student's socio-economic or educational background.

However, this concept of acceptance may seem altogether too fuzzy and soft. What do we do when we find someone's views or behaviour quite intolerable – for example, someone who is behaving in a racist way in a tutorial? Rogers (1961) suggests that it should be possible to draw a distinction between accepting people and not accepting their behaviour, but the difference may be hard to draw in practice.

It will be important that any ODL institution has clear Equal Opportunities guidelines in place. Such guidelines will need to address all aspects of student support as well as its course materials.

Openness
This is the quality of honesty, of not being into authority roles or the 'white coat' syndrome. It means also not making promises that cannot be kept but sharing one's inadequacies where appropriate and admitting one's limitations.

Skills in student support: establishing dialogue

The function of bringing these qualities to bear on the student–supporter interaction is to develop and maintain a high level of dialogue between the student and supporter. Someone who is warm, accepting, open and empathic will have

---

Case study 3

I recently oversaw a computer conference where a student made a comment that the tutor thought was sexist. The tutor immediately deleted the comment from the conference and sent a sharp e-mail to the student telling him what he had done. The tutor had been irritated previously by the student's apparent lack of engagement with the course and his response was a reflection of that. However, in effect that response was not just to the student's behaviour but also to the student himself, and that was not helpful. Had the tutor reflected a little longer he might have found a way of making it clear that it was the student's comment that was unacceptable without putting down the student as well. As it was, the student made a formal complaint about the episode which took a good deal of work to resolve.

Case study 4

Several years ago, a student approached me for advice. She addressed me as Dr Simpson and was clearly and quite unduly overawed by what she perceived to be my authority and expertise. Sadly, I got off on this fantasy myself and delivered some well-meant but wholly inappropriate advice that she took away and subsequently very sensibly ignored.

---

set the groundwork for dialogue, but it will still be necessary to use both listening and interview structuring skills to carry the dialogue forward.

Listening skills

Effective listening skills can seem very simple especially when they are laid out, as here, as a set of techniques. Yet analysis of the breakdown of student support – students losing faith in their tutors, students becoming alienated from their studies – often shows that the reasons are not to do with systems faults or inadequate theoretical stances but because students were not listened to adequately. Perhaps these simple listening skills are not as obvious as they might be. The skills include:

Reflection or mirroring
This means reflecting to students what they have said but in such a way as to reassure them that they have been heard, to clarify their statements and to carry the dialogue forward. For example:

Student: 'I'm dropping out because I'm bored by this course.'
Adviser: a) 'But you've only been on the course a month', b) 'Some parts of the course are rather boring', c) 'You feel the course doesn't interest you any more.'

Response a) of course is non-accepting and faintly critical. Response b) is better but does not really take the dialogue forward. Response c) is a simple reflection. It tells students that they have been heard and will encourage them to continue and clarify their feelings.

Open-ended questions
This means using questions that do not have a simple yes or no answer where possible. Such questions encourage further exploration of the issues rather than bring discussion to a full stop. For example:

Student: 'I was thinking of switching to that music course.'
Adviser: a) 'You like music then?', b) 'What is it about studying music that attracts you?'

Response a) just invites a yes/no answer but b) is an open-ended question which invites a more considered response.

Acknowledgements
This involves simply acknowledging students' statements without responding with a further question. This encourages students to continue with their train of thought. For example:

Student: 'I don't know, I just want to get out of sales.'
Adviser: 'Mmm?'
Student: 'I'd like a job that was really worthwhile.'

Acknowledgements are particularly important on the phone where there are no visual clues to reassure callers that they are being heard.

Silences
This means being able to endure silence in a dialogue. This can be quite difficult: advisers might feel that they have to fill gaps in the conversation. However, if it is clear that someone is struggling to articulate a difficult concept then an interruption, no matter how well meant, can be disruptive of that process.

Selecting skills

Of course, no amount of reflecting, acknowledging and other kinds of response will help develop the dialogue unless the responses are appropriate. It was suggested earlier in this chapter that there were three activities in advising: informing, commending and exploring. It was also suggested that one of the important skills for an adviser was to select which response is appropriate to a particular statement. This also applies to the responses in the process skills below: choosing a challenging response inappropriately may well close a dialogue down rather quickly for instance.

Process skills

There is a process of moving through various stages in any dialogue and different activities at different stages. Those stages that seem the most important are:

- **Clarifying**: helping a student clarify a need or feeling probably through a process of repeated reflection. 'Ah so what you're saying is that you've lost your motivation?'
- **Checking**: going back occasionally to check that you are getting a reasonably accurate overall picture of the problem or issue. 'So there are really two issues here, are there? You've lost your motivation but there's also a problem to do with finding the time because of your new job responsibilities?'
- **Contextualizing**: placing students' concerns in a wider context or pattern. 'Actually in my experience a lot of students run into this same kind of problem at this time of year.' This can be reassuring to students who may need to know that their particular position is not unique and may indeed be quite common. Perhaps there is a sense in which contextualizing legitimizes a problem as an appropriate one to have and for which there are time-tested responses.
- **Conceptualizing**: offering theories or explanations or pointing out patterns in a problem. 'Might you be finding it hard to concentrate on your essay because you're worried about what the tutor might say when she reads it?' Conceptualizing appeals to both advisers and students because it sometimes offers a kind of intellectual insight into problems rather in the way that rational–emotive therapy purports to do (Ellis, 1962). At the same time there is a danger of an adviser using conceptualizing to take over a student's problem, to become a white-coated dispenser of prescriptions which may be inappropriate: 'Yes I've come across this problem before – it happens a lot. What you need to do now is. . . .' Conceptualizing must therefore be used sparingly and carefully.
- **Challenging**: pointing out hidden issues or inconsistencies. 'I understand that you feel you've run out of time to do the course. However I also note that you've taken on a lot of extra voluntary work. Could it be that actually the course is less important to you?' Alternatively, perhaps more obviously, 'You tell me that you're very keen on the course but I see you've not actually been able to complete any assignments on it. Can you tell me why you've not been able to do that?' Challenging is obviously a difficult technique to use; if used inappropriately it is likely to feel like non-acceptance by the student and the dialogue will close. Clearly, challenging is an important part of a tutor's skills but there is a danger that it can leak inappropriately into an advisory

environment. There are substantial differences between challenging statements in a student's essay and challenging a student's personal thoughts.

- **Consequent action**: agreeing jointly at the end of the dialogue the action to be taken by the student, the adviser or both. 'OK then, you'll look into the resources at your local careers office and I'll see what information we've got in our library.' Sometimes such consequent action agreements are like a contract that binds both sides thus involving students intimately in the resolution of the issues they have raised.

Not all of these activities will be present in every session, of course. A simple informing or commending activity may only involve a brief clarification followed by a consequent action, or not even that. On the other hand, you may need to go through two or more cycles of the activities – see Figure 3.3.

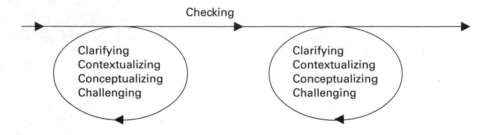

Checking

Clarifying
Contextualizing
Conceptualizing
Challenging

Clarifying
Contextualizing
Conceptualizing
Challenging

Figure 3.3 *Advising processes*

It is very easy to talk about such qualities and skills in abstract but less easy to illustrate them. The following is an exercise designed to help new advisory staff reflect on the issues involved in this section that you might like to try. The scoring system is for amusement only.

NON-ACADEMIC STUDENT SUPPORT: VALUES AND RESPONSES EXERCISE

This exercise is designed to evaluate your values and responses in a student support environment. At the end of the exercise, which takes about 10 minutes, you can score it and get some feedback on your perceptions and skills.

SECTION I

Below are a number of statements about the educational advising of students. Please ring the number that most clearly corresponds to your natural reaction to each statement.

Table 3.2   *Statements about the educational advising of students*

	Agree strongly	Agree	Disagree	Disagree strongly
The main job of an adviser is to get students through their courses	1	2	3	4
Students with problems just need clear advice on what to do	1	2	3	4
It is all right for advisers to show their feelings	1	2	3	4
The trick to advising is to get people to think they found your solutions for themselves	1	2	3	4
Advisers can only help students if they have experienced the problems themselves	1	2	3	4
Advising is mainly about helping students clarify their needs	1	2	3	4
An adviser needs to be able to probe and analyse people	1	2	3	4
An adviser never gets impatient	1	2	3	4
Students who fail can be helped by advising	1	2	3	4
Advising is just listening	1	2	3	4

SECTION I: COMMENT

Statement I: Disagree 2, Strongly disagree I

The main job of an adviser is to help students make the right decision for themselves; that may not always be to continue study. Obviously an adviser will explore what help might be appropriate in overcoming obstacles but not to the extent of manipulating a student to continue whatever the cost or exacerbating a student's feelings of failure.

Statement 2: Strongly disagree 2, Disagree I

Students with problems need help in clarifying and understanding those problems. Sometimes because of that clarification it will be appropriate to give information or advice. However, advice is only effective when it is mutually agreed and arises naturally out of the exploration.

Statement 3: Agree 2, Strongly agree 1

Advisers are not distant white-coated authorities; they have feelings and will share them as they feel appropriate.

Statement 4: Strongly disagree 2

Advising is not about manipulation in any form.

Statement 5: Disagree 2, Strongly disagree 1

People's problems may be similar but the solutions are unique to them. An adviser working from his or her experience may well attempt to impose solutions on the student.

Statement 6: Strongly agree 2, Agree 1

This is probably the best definition of advising of any kind.

Statement 7: Strongly disagree 2, Disagree 1

While insight and empathy are important skills for an adviser, the image of an adviser as detective, interrogator or psychoanalyst is unhelpful. It implies an unequal relationship between counsellor and client (and is likely to put any client on the defensive).

Statement 8: Disagree 2, Strongly disagree 1

An adviser is just a human being and every human being feels impatient with others occasionally. An adviser will find a non-aggressive and non-critical way of expressing that feeling if appropriate.

Statement 9: Strongly agree 2, Agree 1

Students fail for many reasons, many of them non-academic such as time, motivation and assessment anxiety. Advising may well help such students. Even those students who cannot handle the academic demands of a course may be helped by advising on referral and coming to terms with their position.

Statement 10: Disagree 2, Agree 1

The essence and main activity of advising is indeed active perceptive listening. However, a good adviser will also use his or her experience and skill to help the student clarify and conceptualize the issue or problem, as well as challenging the student's perceptions when appropriate.

SECTION 2

Below are a series of statements from a student, each with a range of responses from an adviser. Ring the letter of the response that is closest to the response you would make as an adviser.

Mary is a new student and has been studying for a couple of months.

1. Mary   I have to be honest with you, Jean/Jim. I just don't think the course is for me.
   Adviser   a)   Oh, goodness, Mary, it's a bit early to be deciding that! Give it another week or two at least.
                 b)   I'm sorry to hear that, Mary. But that's how it goes sometimes.
                 c)   Why, what's wrong with the course?
                 d)   You feel the course isn't what you wanted?

2. Mary   I just can't get started on it.
   Adviser   a)   I have that problem sometimes!
                 b)   Tell me what happens when you try to study.
                 c)   It's a question of will power, Mary. You've just got to force yourself to get down to it.
                 d)   Well, what's stopping you exactly?

3. Mary   It's my concentration really. I can study quite well for a while but then my mind starts to wander.
   Adviser a)   Some bits of the course are rather boring.
                 b)   Well, it's like I just said. You can't get away from the need to exercise simple will power.
                 c)   You're distracted by something?
                 d)   Mmm?

4. Mary is silent for a while and then sighs heavily.
   Adviser a)   You seem to be easily discouraged.
                 b)   Sorry, I don't seem to be helping you much.
                 c)   Would you like to tell me how you're feeling?
                 d)   What are you thinking?

5. Mary   The fact is that my family never really wanted me to do the course.
   Adviser a)   You're under a lot of pressure from them?
                 b)   That sounds pretty tough.
                 c)   Families are often like that.
                 d)   You know, it's your life – you should tell them exactly what's what.

6. Mary   I just can't talk to them about it.
   Adviser a)   They don't want to listen to you?
                 b)   What do you think will happen if you do?
                 c)   Yes, I know it's difficult but you're going to have to sometime, aren't you?
                 d)   It might be easier than you think.

7. Mary   They just don't understand why I'm doing this.
   Adviser a) I do know how you feel. But I'm sure if you tried to tell them again they'd understand.
           b) You know there are times when you just have to stand up for yourself.
           c) It's difficult getting your feelings across, isn't it?
           d) You've not been able to make them understand?

8. Mary   So tell me what I do?
   Adviser a) What do you think you ought to do?
           b) Well, you know what I think.
           c) I can't tell you, but I'd be happy to discuss it with you further if you like.
           d) That's a tough one – you're in a very difficult position, but there's no hurry, we can talk some more.

9. Mary   Look, I know you're busy and I really don't want to take up more of your time.
   Adviser a) No, that's all right. That's what I'm paid for.
           b) I'm glad you've been able to tell me this.
           c) It is getting late. Let's discuss this again.
           d) Do stay – I've plenty of time.

10. Mary   I just don't feel able to decide anything at the moment anyway.
   Adviser a) OK. But I'd like to have another chat if that would be all right with you. Would next Tuesday do?
           b) It's a difficult decision. Let's have another chat sometime.
           c) I'm sure it will all be for the best.
           d) Well, don't let it go for too long. You need to get it sorted out soon.

SECTION 2: COMMENT

Most responses to statements can be categorized as:

Directive   or   non-directive
Closed   or   open
Non-reflective   or   reflective

Directive responses

These tend to push the client into a particular course of action: for example, Statement 1, Response (a) – 'Oh goodness, it's too early for that! Give it another week or two at least!' Directive responses can often sound faintly critical and are seldom effective as they rarely deal with the real issues.

Non-directive responses

These leave the student to decide on direction: for example, Statement 1, Response (b) – 'I'm sorry to hear that, Mary. But that's how it goes sometimes.'

Closed questions

These invite yes/no or similar specific responses: for example, Statement 2, Response (d) – 'Well, what's stopping you exactly?'

Open questions

These invite the student to expand and explore the issue: for example, Statement 2, Response (b) – 'Tell me what happens when you try to study.'

Reflective responses

These mirror back the student's statement to students in such a way as to clarify the statement, reassure them that they have been heard and encourage them to explore further: for example, Statement I, Response (d) – 'You feel the course isn't what you wanted?'

Non-reflective responses

These do not attempt to mirror the student's feelings or statements: for example, Statement I, Response (c) – 'Why, what's wrong with the course?'

Advisers generally use non-directive, open, reflecting responses as far as they can to encourage students to explore, clarify and move towards a resolution of an issue for themselves.

Statement I

Response (a) Score 0 – directive and unhelpful.
Response (b) Score I – non-directive and non-critical but not particularly helpful in exploring the issue.
Response (c) Score 0 – faintly defensive and unlikely to encourage the dialogue.
Response (d) Score 2 – a clear open reflection.

Statement 2

Response (a) Score I – friendly and non-directive but the counsellor is 'taking over' the problem with his/her own experience, which is not always helpful.
Response (b) Score 2 – not a reflection but an appropriate non-directive and open response.
Response (c) Score 0 – directive and faintly critical.
Response (d) Score 0 – closed and rather impatient.

Statement 3

Response (a) Score 0 – a kind of reflection but quite inaccurate and unhelpful.
Response (b) Score 0 – directive and possibly unhelpful.
Response (c) Score I – reflective and helpful but possibly a little closed.
Response (d) Score 2 – all that is needed at this point really.

Statement 4

Response (a) Score 0 – something of a put-down however sympathetically said.
Response (b) Score 0 – not likely to encourage confidence.
Response (c) Score 2 – gives student permission to go on in a non-directive way.
Response (d) Score 1 – as above but not so well put.

Statement 5

Response (a) Score 2 – a reflection.
Response (b) Score 1 – all right but putting words into the student's mouth.
Response (c) Score 0 – could be worse but not particularly helpful. The counsellor is taking over the problem again.
Response (d) Score 0 – directive and rather censorious.

Statement 6

Response (a) Score 1 – a good try at a reflection but not what she said.
Response (b) Score 2 – a little better than above as it moves forward more.
Response (c) Score 0 – rather critical.
Response (d) Score 0 – irrelevant to the student's feelings.

Statement 7

Response (a) Score 0 – well meaning but probably of no use.
Response (b) Score 0 – considerably worse.
Response (c) Score 1 – helpful.
Response (d) Score 2 – is slightly better.

Statement 8

Response (a) Score 0 – not a good reflection, just a counsellor feeling that he or she is on the spot and bouncing the question straight back.
Response (b) Score 0 – directive.
Response (c) Score 2 – open and honest but leaving the door open.
Response (d) Score 1 – not as honest as (c) as it implies that the counsellor may be able to offer a solution at some future point.

Statement 9

Response (a) Score 0 – it makes it sound as though the counsellor is under some rather tedious obligation.
Response (b) Score 2 – a small validation for the student's courage in getting so far.
Response (c) Score 1 – honest but also slightly dismissive.
Response (d) Score 0 – could sound insincere.

Statement 10

Response (a) Score 2 – a clear commitment to give more help if the student wants it.

Response (b) Score 1 – rather vague and no clear commitment to follow up.
Response (c) Score 0 – woolly and pathetic?
Response (d) Score 0 - directive.

Your scores (but don't take this too seriously . . .)

Score 30–40: you clearly have excellent qualities of empathy and openness. It may be that you will want to be just a little more directive in your work sometimes!
Score 20–30: you have a good feel for the skills and qualities of an adviser. You may occasionally be judgemental so watch out for that.
Score 10–20: you would still make a good educational adviser but you should be careful not to be too directive. Allow your students a little more space to find their own solutions sometimes.
Score 0–10: you probably have many fine qualities and skills but being an educational adviser may not be among them!

Non-academic support: advising categories

As well as seeing non-academic support as a range of activities, it may be helpful to categorize it into two broad types: developmental support and problem solving support.

Developmental advising

This support helps students towards particular goals. Examples are:

- vocational advising – helping a student towards a particular career or career change;
- course choice advising – helping a student choose a particular course or study programme;
- learning skills advising – helping students develop appropriate skills for their studies;
- general motivational counselling.

We shall be returning to aspects of these but perhaps it is worth just explaining the inclusion of the last item. Motivation is an essential of student progress. It is probable that some of the issues raised by students are to do with their losing touch with what has been driving them up to that point. So it seems useful to explore a student's motivation in the hope that it will both clarify and restore that driving force. We will return to this when we look at the process of re-motivating students at particular points in their study.

Problem solving advising

This support helps students overcome barriers and hazards that are affecting their progress. Examples are:

- institution-related problems – falling foul of rules and regulations; fee problems;
- study problems – learning skills generally such as concentration, assignments and exams;
- time problems – getting behind or being disorganized;
- personal problems – domestic and other problems that have impinged on study.

Again, the distinctions are arbitrary and the distinction between study and time problems is made because they reflect to some extent the distinction that was made in the 'phrenological' metaphor between affective issues and organizational issues. Nevertheless, it often seems that there is a link between students who profess that problems of concentration affect their study where stress seems to be a factor, and those admitting to organizational difficulties where time management is important. We will look at this in more detail in the section on developing learning skills in chapter 11.

Personal factors are much more difficult and, as was said earlier, are strictly outside the scope of this book. However, it would be a poor student support system that did not make some effort to try to support students through the many events that can disrupt their lives. There are four points worth considering:

- **'Holding'.** For some students their studies are a lifeline, something that sustains them when the rest of their lives is in dreadful shape. There are examples of students who have continued to study despite apparently quite appalling personal problems such as divorce, bereavement and severe physical and mental disability. There is a concept from counselling theory that seems to be of use here, 'holding'. This is specifically about not attempting to solve people's probably long-standing, complex and difficult problems, but providing a background of support for them which enables them to continue their lives or their studies. Such support may be no more than a slightly increased level of contact or expressions of encouragement and support. However, it may also be rather more, in which case the support staff may need to be considered.
- **Staff who get involved.** Managers of student support staff may find themselves in a position where they become concerned that students are making too great demands on their staff. The demands may not be specific; their staff may become involved of their own volition and want to do more for someone whose situation is particularly harrowing. At what point they may need to encourage them to reduce their level of support may be very tricky to judge.
- **Dealing with distress.** In some workplaces, there is a high chance of being contacted at some point by a student who is in considerable distress. In the end there is one resource that should be available and it is just common humanity: trust your own feelings and do what feels right without the white coat.
- **Ensuring there is a good referral system** – see chapter 10.

Non-academic support: assessment, action, advocacy, agitation and administration

To some extent, there is less to say about the remaining activities in non-academic student support since they are very institution dependent. The kind of actions that can be taken, the cases that can be advocated, and the causes that can be agitated about will be very dependent on the institution in which one works. However, there are some general issues that will be worth looking at.

Assessment

Assessing can be defined as the gathering, processing (and usually feeding back) of information about students' skills, knowledge and interests in order to support them in making appropriate choices.

This book maintains the distinction between academic and non-academic assessment. Academic assessment encompasses not only assessment of a student's academic progress on a course but also pre-course assessment that might involve, for example, numeracy and literacy diagnostic tests. That still leaves the issue of assessing students' non-academic development in a course, for example their progress in developing learning skills, as well as a broad field that takes in vocational and other diagnostic activities. One way to categorize such activities is sequentially.

Pre-course assessment

Course and programme choice
Assessing the student's interests, aptitudes and motivation in order to commend particular courses and programmes is a very important part of any pre-course advice.

Learning styles
This is much less obvious but may be worth considering. There is considerable interest in using tests of various kinds to determine students' preferred learning styles, for example *StudyScan* (see chapter 7). Another example is *The Manual of Learning Styles* (Honey and Mumford, 1986) which claims to distinguish activist, reflector, theorist and pragmatist styles. Even if these distinctions are soundly based in theory, it is not as yet clear how a particular style relates to learning success in ODL. The greatest value of such tests seems to be in situations when dealing with students with very little confidence. For such students to be told 'you are an activist learner' enhances their self-esteem as up until now they had not seen themselves as any kind of learner at all. Possibly the most these tests will be used in the near future will be to see if dyslexic students can be identified at an early stage in their studies so that special help can be given.

In-course assessment

Learning skills

There seems to be value in undertaking informal assessment of learning skills development during a course in the expectation that a student who sees his or her skills increasing may develop self-confidence as a learner much faster than in the absence of such feedback. Such assessment is often fruitful in group work when peer evaluation will generally reveal that students share common progress.

Vocational assessment

Assessing students' interests, abilities and skills has been a part of the careers adviser's armoury for a long time. Relatively sophisticated computer assisted programs have been developed such as Gradscope, CASCAID (Computer Assisted Careers Aid) and JIIG-CAL (Job Interest and Information Generator – Computer Assisted Learning). Such programs mostly work by comparing students' responses with previously calibrated responses from workers in particular careers, producing suggested matches for the students to particular careers. Students can then refine their responses if the suggestions do not seem appropriate. See chapter 7 for more detail.

Self-assessment

It should be remembered that, for many if not all students, assessment can have negative associations. It is associated with competition, past failures and exams. In recent trials of externally assessed pre-course diagnostic materials in my own institution, there was only a 20 per cent return rate, despite the fact that it was made clear that there was no connection between the assessment and the offer of a place. In addition, of course, the returns came overwhelmingly from students who were perfectly competent in the skills assessed. Thus there may be some value in the concept of stand alone self-assessment materials which encourage students to reflect on their own needs, aptitudes and motivations without any external assessment of any kind. This is an excerpt from a booklet called *Taking Off* which used to be sent to new students in my own institution.

SECTION 1: HOW DO YOU FEEL ABOUT BEING A NEW STUDENT?

We hope that working through *Taking Off* will answer a few questions and provoke a few thoughts about your decision to study. You may already have a number of mixed feelings.

Tick those feelings below that seem to correspond to any of yours:

● I am not sure whether I will be able to find the time for study.
● I am not clear what university courses are like.

- I am not sure I can cope with a specific topic, eg maths, essay writing etc.
- I have not done any serious studying for a long time.
- I feel excited about belonging to a university.
- I think I'll meet some interesting people.
- I expect the course to be interesting.
- I hope I shall become more intellectually competent and confident.
- I hope I shall prove to myself that I am cleverer than I thought.
- I want to be better qualified and get into a different line of work.

SECTION 2: HOW READY ARE YOU?

To study you are going to need various skills, some of which may be rusty and need development. For instance, it may be some time since you had to read a piece of non-fiction (book or article) in order to learn something from it.
  Rate yourself on the skills below:

Table 3.3 *How ready are you?*

	Yes, I can do that	No, I shall need some practice
Reading something to learn from it		
Planning and writing essays		
Being able to concentrate for sustained periods		
Summarizing, criticizing and commenting on other people's ideas		
Accepting constructive criticism of your own ideas and work		
Using simple statistics, reading graphs (maths and science courses)		
Managing family, job, and study demands all at once		

If you have honestly answered 'yes' to all these questions then you are already an exceptional (and unusual) student. If, on the other hand, you have answered 'no' to some of them, then you might find it helpful to practise these skills between now and when you start a course. See our brochure for some ideas and have a look at the suggestions for 'Getting Prepared' in the next section of this booklet.

The problem in using materials like these is that it is very hard to assess their value. Do students seriously undertake the activities? Do they seriously reflect on the results? Do they draw useful conclusions about themselves whatever those may be?

Personal development plans (PDP)

The use of materials like these is now increasing, with some institutions introducing personal development or learning plans designed to encourage students to reflect on their learning. While they may be useful before a course starts, it is not clear that such materials are popular with students once a course is under way, and their overall effect is yet to be fully assessed.

Action

Sometimes the simplest possible student support is the most effective. Arranging a lift home, putting two people with similar needs in touch, phoning up a dilatory section of the institution and asking for some outstanding item to be sent, setting up a special face-to-face meeting with a tutor – these are all simple actions that can have disproportionate success.

Although the different sorts of action that can be taken in any institution will depend on that institution, there are certain requirements that must be in place:

- **Closeness and immediacy.** Action often arises out of a student's immediate needs, so there must be support as close to the student as possible and response as speedily as possible.
- **Empowerment of staff.** This means that the staff nearest the student must have some power to undertake action (within certain guidelines) without having to refer. For example, if the student support nearest the student is a part-time tutor then that person must have some power to take action (such as offer some extra one-to-one time) and know that he or she will be supported by receiving compensation for that time.
- **Guidelines.** In such a situation there must of course be clear guidelines as to the extent to which empowerment applies. There will need to be clear staff development about the boundaries of empowerment and the reasons for empowerment.

Advocacy

Advocacy has always been a very distinct part of student support in ODL with several aspects:

References: for jobs, further courses and funding

A characteristic of ODL is that the institution may know very little about its students, so it will be necessary to set up systems for overcoming these difficulties. These might be forms for requesting information from students for particular purposes, as well as a format for references that does not disadvantage ODL students against their colleagues from conventional institutions.

Appeals against the institution's rulings

This can be a very difficult area. Perhaps because its students are more remote from the institution than in a face-to-face organization, it may be easier for conflicts and misunderstandings to arise. In addition, in any conflict between institution and student there is heavy weighting towards the institution with its resources, stamina and ability to be the final judge in many cases. But this picture is changing: first, with the introduction of, or increases in, student fees there seems to be an increasing assertiveness on the part of students and an increasing tendency to resort to litigation. Second, the anomaly of institutions acting as judge and jury in their own cases has been noticed. In the UK the Dearing Report recommended that internal complaints procedures should reflect 'natural justice' and the National Union of Students is currently campaigning for an independent and uniform system of appeals.

This can leave a student support adviser in a very difficult position. How far can or should he or she act as a mediator between the institution and a particular student who appears to have had a bad deal? There is no easy answer to this, especially in the light of increasing employment insecurity and the use of short-term contracts for staff.

Example

This is an extreme example of the problem. A student who had failed to get an answer from one of the offices in my own institution had contacted me. Her request for a response seemed reasonable and indeed, on my first contact with the office on her behalf, they indicated that they would indeed write to her. Some six months later, despite at least four reminders from me, they had still failed to do so. At that point, I wrote to the office saying I would have to take the final recourse of any citizen faced with an unresponsive bureaucracy. This was to hold a peaceful demonstration outside the office concerned. I said that I would appear on a certain date armed with a placard and leaflets. I got my response (at the cost of continuing frosty relations with the office concerned – a consequence that is not unimportant). However, it is extremely unlikely that I would have taken that risk if I had not been tenured staff. I like to think that such a situation would be unlikely to arise now with prescriptive complaints procedures in place, which require answers within certain time scales, and a clear Student Charter – see chapter 15.

Agitation

Agitation and advocacy are ultimately linked. A rather arbitrary distinction is that whereas advocacy has sometimes to do with changing the institution's procedures for a single student, usually as a one-off, agitation is changing the institution's procedures for all students, permanently.

The term 'agitation' is being used slightly tongue-in-cheek, of course, yet sometimes when one sees how institutions in which one has worked have changed, it seems more as a result of random muttering, underground movements and individual insistence than as a result of rational debate and due committee processes. That being said, there have to be such processes through which student support staff can represent their experiences and work for changes in institutional policies. Again, there seem to be a number of issues:

- ODL institutions tend of necessity to be heavily managed. The administration tends to play a larger role than in conventional organizations, and tends to have more power and can be resistant to change.
- Institutions that cater for very large numbers prefer to treat their customers as a single entity where possible in order to keep costs minimized. Customizing the institution to meet students' various needs – 'post-Fordism' – is expensive.
- Academic standards. Uniquely in the service industries, educational institutions have to maintain standards that quite deliberately set hurdles that their customers have to overcome. If too many exceptions are made, if regulations become too student-friendly, there is an argument that academic standards may be compromised. Indeed, that argument is already made in respect of both universities and schools where improved pass rates are sometimes interpreted not as the result of improved standards of support but as the result of decreasing academic standards.
- Short-term non-tenured contracts. There has been a substantial increase in the last few years in the use of short-term contracts in some ODL institutions. While such contracts provide flexibility for the institution in rapidly changing environments, staff who are on such contracts are less likely to want to take on entrenched interests within the institution. If they are hoping for a renewal of their contract then a low profile and an aversion to trouble may be their natural policy.

In the light of these opposing forces, it seems extraordinary that institutions do actually adapt to students at all. Nevertheless, there are a number of positive trends – several of them already mentioned:

- The increasing assertiveness of students as previously mentioned (my own institution has recently been sued successfully through a small claims court by a student).
- Pressure on institutions to develop their appeals and complaints procedures.
- And in particular, competition between institutions.

The role of student support advisers in agitation

So where does this leave the role of student support advisers? They need to be sure of the following:

- That their institution has clear processes for taking on board student demands.
- That there are clear complaints and appeals procedures. If those procedures have some independent involvement so much the better.
- That the representation of the coal-face student support workers must be prioritized by the institution's senior management. The world is littered with examples of commercial enterprises that failed to stay in touch with their customer base despite their customer service workers actually knowing where the service had failed – they simply lacked the representation to say so.
- That student support advisers should be able to take modest risks. There will be circumstances when it will be useful to remember one of *The Intrapreneur's Ten Commandments* (Pichot, 1986): 'it is easier to ask for forgiveness than for permission'.
- That they are prepared to refer and use the institution's student charter. Clarify the perceptions of their role by the rest of the institution. Are they to be trench war defenders of the institution, mediators between the institution and its students, or knights on chargers on behalf of students? If it is to be the second then there will need to be clear and well-defined skills development in mediation.

These issues of course all arise in connection with quality assurance in ODL, which will be looked at in chapter 15.

Administration

The administration of student support will depend on the structure of the institution. Some underlying principles may be true of any institution and are covered in chapter 15.

Chapter 4

Academic support: tuition

Although 'academic support' is the more accurate description for the activities described in this chapter, the term 'tuition' is so widespread that it could be used. However, there are reservations, as tuition implies certain activities more relevant to face-to-face learning than ODL. The transition from conventional tuition to ODL tuition is not always easy.

Tuition activities

Like non-academic support, tuition covers a wide range of activities. Perhaps again they fall into a spectrum shown in Figure 4.1, running from those which are very strictly course material related to those which depend much more on the tutor.

Defining the course territory	Explaining the course	Assessing: formal and informal	Chasing student progress	Developing learning skills	Exploring the course	Enriching the course

Figure 4.1 *Tuition activities*

Defining the territory

In most ODL systems, the course content – the syllabus – is defined by the course material. There are exceptions to this – institutions where the territory is negotiated between the student and institution such as the Empire State University of New

York – and it could be argued that courses with projects leave some of the territory up to the student.

Nevertheless the definition of territory in ODL is generally much more specific than in conventional educational settings where even a set syllabus still allows the tutor some control over the detailed content. This is both a weakness and a strength: a weakness because the tutor is teaching to someone else's material and may not be as committed to it as the originators; and a strength as for the same reason a tutor will not be committed to the defence of that material at all costs. (You may recognize this as the argument previously adduced for student support as a democratizing influence in ODL.)

Explaining the course

Again, in most ODL courses, the essential explication of the course is carried out by course material. This material may be in print, online, CD ROM, video, audio or other media so that the explanations come from different sources and may be from different perspectives but the principle remains.

Of course, there is still a substantial role for the tutor in providing alternative explanations of particularly difficult points but there are also dangers, particularly for tutors from conventional institutions new to ODL. Familiar with situations where they are entirely responsible for the explication of a course, they may try to replicate that, forgetting that that is the business of the course material. Such misunderstandings may become apparent when they complain that they have insufficient time to cover the course.

Assessment: informal and formal

Informal assessment

Informal assessment means feeding back to students some sense of the progress they are making in a course. Some of that activity is carried out by course material, and certainly no distance education package used to be complete without its sets of self-assessment questions and answers (SAQs) scattered in the text, although there was always some doubt as to how far students actually used them. There is some evidence that this kind of passive feedback attempt might even be harmful: students (the majority) who skipped the SAQs still felt guilty about doing so, and felt less competent as students as a result.

This makes the tutor's role in informal assessment all the more important. After all, it is much harder to dodge a tutor's questions than SAQs in a text. And a tutor can interact with an answer, clarify it and phrase the next question in appropriate relationship with it without damaging a student's self-confidence.

Formal assessment

Computer assessment

Formal assessment can be carried out by the course material through assignments that are marked by computer. There are now intelligent programs that not only mark answers as right or wrong but can also provide standard feedback depending on the wrongness of the answer.

Tutor assessment

Nevertheless, formal assessments carried out by tutors are very important in ODL; for many students such feedback is the most substantial teaching contact they have with their tutor. For some it may be the only contact. Giving such feedback is a difficult task: too kind or elliptic and students will not understand where they are and what they need to do to improve; too direct and unvarnished and they may be so discouraged that they will drop out inappropriately. It may be easiest to illustrate this with an example.

Case study I

Carol was a new student on a physics course. She had very little background in the subject and found mathematics difficult. Her main aim in taking it was as grounding for some earth science courses in which she was interested. Her first assignment on the course was a borderline pass but she put a lot of work into it. The tutor wrote to her as follows:

Well done, Carol, you made a very good attempt at something that I appreciate must have been particularly difficult for you.
Q1 – A clear account. You lost some marks because you misunderstood how to measure the length – see my comments on the script.
Q2 – Well laid out and clearly calculated. Again, you lost some marks because of one particular slip – confusing the difference between average and final speed.
Overall, a very sound beginning. You have some problems with maths but they can be overcome – we'll talk about them in the next tutorial. Keep this up and you'll do fine!

This is a good example of a 'feedback sandwich': the bad news is sandwiched between positive opening and closing comments.

If a student's work is clearly a fail then the task must be approached even more carefully. If this student has failed, it might be better to break the news to her by phone if possible. Alternatively, when I worked as a tutor I used to insert a simple leaflet along with my comments on a low-grade assignment.

NOT DONE AS WELL AS YOU HOPED ON YOUR ASSIGNMENT?

I'm sorry that you've had a low grade for your assignment or that you've not done as well as you wanted. This little leaflet is designed to help you put your grade into perspective and to enable you to do better next time.

Put it into perspective

The very first thing to remember is that it's not you that's failed – it's just your assignment and it's not personal! The second thing is that a low grade isn't a catastrophe for your course. One failure or poor grade won't ruin your chances of passing your course.

Keep going

So the important thing is to keep going. Don't let one fail grade knock you off course – there's still all to play for.

What went wrong?

Obviously, if you do keep going, you'll want to know what went wrong. Do read the comments on your assignment. It's tempting when you get an assignment back only to glance at it and put it away. But I've tried to give useful advice, so do make the most of it.

Did you answer the question?

This must be the most common reason for not doing as well as you expected in assignments and exams. It may be because you're not yet used to the 'style' of the course: what is meant by words like 'discuss', 'report', 'describe' in the context of this particular course. This may be especially true if you've not written assignments for some time. (See 'Getting it right next time' below.) Or you may be subject to 'assessment stress' (most of us are!). Feeling stressed about a task sometimes means that you lose concentration and are unable to tackle the task methodically.

Can you see why you lost marks?

If not, then you should seek clarification straight away. Phone or write to me as soon as you can. This isn't as easy as it sounds, I know, but I'll be keen to help you.

Do you think I got it wrong?

Mistakes do happen, tutors are only human, and if you think there's an error, or I've missed something or not given you proper credit, or if you just can't see where you failed, then do contact me straight away. If we don't agree, you can appeal and there'll be no hard feelings. (See 'Appealing against an assignment grade' below.)

Did you run out of time?

And so were unable to submit a complete assignment or had to make it a rush job? If you are having difficulties managing time, then there's a leaflet I can send you called 'Getting Behind' which you might find helpful.

Were you affected by illness, accident, bereavement or something similar?

That can't be taken into account in marking your assignment, of course, but at the end of your course you should tell the Exam Board and then your difficulties can be taken into account.

Getting it right next time

Perhaps the best thing to do is to kiss off this assignment and to get your next one sorted. I can help here in at least two ways: if you're not clear what the next question means, do consult me. Obviously I can't answer the question for you, but I can clarify the question and ensure that you're not misinterpreting it or barking up the wrong tree. If appropriate, then you may be able to send a brief outline plan of your answer well before the due date. I can then check that you are answering in the right way before you write up the assignment.

Appealing against an assignment grade

If you do want to appeal against an assignment grade, then:

● Return your assignment to me with a note explaining why you think your grade might not be accurate. Obviously the more clearly you explain your reasons, the better your chance of a new grade.
● If I agree, I'll re-grade the assignment.
● If I don't, your assignment will be returned to you with an explanation of why the grade should stand.
● If you are still unhappy you can then send your assignment to the Centre, again giving reasons.

Good luck for your next assignment!

Progress chasing

This may seem an odd activity to have under 'tuition', with its connotations of an industrial production process. Perhaps 'Student progress monitoring and follow up' would be more accurate. Whatever it is called it is one of the key activities of a tutor in ODL, far more so perhaps than in conventional education. At its simplest, progress chasing means a tutor checking on the progress of his or her students at appropriate intervals – possibly around assignment submission dates – in order to see where they have got to and to take proactive action if they appear to be falling behind.

Progress monitoring is particularly important as it is one of the few student support activities that directly addresses the complex but vital area of student motivation – one of the qualities that was mentioned at the outset. It could be referred to as 'student motivation management'.

Case study 2

For a number of years I supervised a group of tutors teaching the same course. There were two in particular who seemed to be in vivid contrast. Peter was quite elderly, a rather dry, punctilious man with an occasionally acerbic touch. His face-to-face teaching was competent and uninspired and his main characteristic was that nothing seemed to worry him, no organizational catastrophe (and I inspired quite a number) seemed to throw him. He eventually told me that he had landed with the first wave of troops in Normandy on D-Day and that – as he put it – 'Nothing has ever really worried me much since.'

Jeff was Peter's opposite: young, dynamic, charismatic, he was a gifted teacher who could make his subject come alive and enrich his students' studies.

I kept track of their students' results and noticed that they were in contrast too. Consistently year after year one of them got better results than the other.

There would be no point to this anecdote if the answer was obvious. It was old Peter who out-performed young Jeff every time. And the answer was simple: if I phoned Peter up and asked him 'How's that pregnant student of yours getting on?' he'd immediately answer, 'I spoke to her last week – everything's fine.' Jeff would have scratched his head and said, 'I've not heard from her for a while so I can't really tell you.'

Learning skills development

There is a very substantial role for a tutor in developing the learning and study skills of his or her students. Some students will already be effective learners when they begin their studies, but it is the nature of ODL – particularly open learning – that there will be many students who come from educationally disadvantaged backgrounds and do not have effective or appropriate learning skills for the courses they are about to take. For example, a recent study in my own institution (Datta, 1998) revealed that up to a third of new students embarking on an introductory course had reading skills and comprehension below the readability levels of parts of the course. Clearly, in a situation like this, the course materials themselves – already too difficult for many students –- are unlikely to be very successful in developing learning skills among those students.

Therefore, the burden of helping those students develop survival skills at the beginning of courses will fall very particularly on their tutor. We shall look at learning skills in more detail in chapter 11.

Exploring, enthusing and enriching

Finally, there is a role that only a tutor can play which is enormously important for developing and maintaining motivation among students. This role is where a tutor can encourage students to study in depth, to push beyond the boundaries of the course and to develop a sense of excitement about their learning and progress. Most tutors can easily think of examples of exploration and enrichment from their own experience – visits to galleries and concerts, suggestions for outside reading, discussions on current newsworthy topics, examples, demonstrations, experiments, presentations on the tutor's specialist topic and many others.

There are no fixed recipes for these activities; you can remember teachers who fired your imagination in different ways through their own enthusiasm, commitment and encouragement. The excerpt below from a student's letter captures a little of the sense of inspiration that tutors can sometimes inspire in students.

> I'm very grateful to all the tutors on all my courses. But it was S— on my first course who really made it all work for me. She was very supportive and always helpful but she had a particular enthusiasm for the psychology side of the course – I didn't know what it was but she really caught my interest because she was so encouraging – I wrote a lot of crap sometimes which she couldn't let me get away with but she also made me feel that I got things right on the button sometimes too. Therefore, I'm now studying to work in psychology full time!

Balance between activities

It is impossible to lay down where the priorities in these activities will lie. Clearly, the implications are that in a distance education system the tutor will spend little time defining the course. Priorities in the other activities will be set by students' needs and expectations, the institution's organization and policies, and above all by the time and resources available to the tutor.

Students' needs will depend on both their current knowledge and skills base and on the stage they have reached in their studies. Perhaps explaining and learning skills development will be particularly important in the start and pre-start stages. In the mid-course stage, a tutor's assessment and progress chasing skills will be particularly needed, and towards the end of the course, perhaps there will be space for exploring and enrichment.

The institution's needs may have to do with academic credibility, quality assessment activities and retention requirements. These are not necessarily entirely compatible – for example academic credibility may involve emphasis on (say) face-to-face tuition which could be at the expense of progress chasing and retention activities carried out at a distance.

It is expected that there will be an increasing emphasis on access and retention as the competitive environment grows. This may mean a move towards learning skills development and progress chasing activities, possibly at the expense of explaining, exploring and enriching.

Tuition styles

There are different styles of approach in all the various activities that a tutor undertakes. It is possible to distinguish between two extremes, the didactic and facilitative (Wright, 1987).

Didactic: the tutor is very much in the formal lecturer role, explaining and presenting.

Facilitative: the tutor facilitates the student's own exploration of the course.

Again, this is not a clear distinction but a spectrum as shown in Table 4.1.

Table 4.1   *Didactic versus facilitative activities*

Didactic	Facilitative
Tutor explains to students	Students find out
Students dependent on tutor	Students are independent
Process controlled by tutor	Process controlled by students
Course and knowledge centred	Skill and process centred
Authoritarian?	Democratic?

Clearly, the extremes are fairly theoretical, and even in conventional education most tutors operate somewhere in between and vary their style. However, given the points previously made about the tutor not having responsibility for course content or definition, and the theoretical considerations outlined in chapter 14, it is not surprising that there is considerable emphasis in ODL on using facilitative modes of tuition. So tutors are often expected to have large elements of discussion or group work in their face-to-face activities. Thus, a typical facilitative face-to-face tutorial might have:

- a group discussion on economic theories, the tutor facilitating the discussion, but involving students as much as possible;
- students working on papers on mathematical problems, the tutor working with different pairs in turn;
- groups tackling an experiment with the tutor occasionally interrupting to ask questions.

In each case, the intention is to involve the students in the activity of the tutorial rather than make them passive participants.

Of course there will be other activities in a tutorial from time to time – a short presentation on some topic of particular interest or an explanation to the whole group of something that has confused many of them. See chapter 6 for a fuller discussion.

Student expectations of tuition

At this point tutors – particularly those from conventional educational systems – sometimes raise the issue of 'What do students want?' Often the answer suggested is that what students want are purely didactic teaching methods, lectures and formal presentations and that they are happiest sitting in rows, the passive recipients of the tutor's knowledge and skill.

It is easy to see how this perception can arise. Certainly in the first face-to-face tutorial for a course, it is hard for students to take an active role for reasons of embarrassment, lack of knowledge and general uncertainty. It is therefore not surprising that a tutor will want to take the initiative and start by delivering a talk. General questions directed to the students will not always elicit much in the way of answers for similar reasons, and so the tutor is reinforced in his or her perceptions.

In fact, what research there is suggests that students want structure; they need to feel some confidence that tutors know what they are doing in terms of both their course knowledge base and the teaching skills they bring to their work. After that, the students want to feel a sense of progress and interaction with the tutor and with other students (Thorpe, 1988). It looks as though most students prefer a style that is predominantly facilitative, that allows them interaction with the tutor and other students and some influence over direction and content too. Within that framework, didactic elements are clearly acceptable. Being authoritative is fine, being authoritarian is not.

Tuition in practice

This chapter has merely outlined some of the principles underlying academic support in ODL. These ideas are developed in subsequent chapters by examining how they apply in different media.

Chapter 5

Delivering student support at a distance

Introduction

We shall see in chapter 8 that student support in ODL can come from various sources. The next three chapters look at student support from the institution or its agents and the media which can deliver it.

One of the most striking characteristics of ODL has been the startling growth in the variety of media that it uses. The basic postal correspondence of the past has now become a multi-media operation using:

- written media;
- phone;
- face to face;
- audiotape;
- video;
- computers;
- radio;
- television;
- and mixed media such as videophones and streaming video.

Student support also uses all these media although the use of broadcast radio and television for student support is now relatively rare in the developed world. However, it is interesting to note that the appearance of cheaper batteries and clockwork radio have given radio a new lease of life for distance education in the developing world, especially in nomadic education.

Within each medium, there are different types of use: for example, written media covers letters, leaflets of various kinds, problem pages and so on.

Student support in writing

There can be no doubt that the balance of activity within particular media of student support has changed in the last few years. A considerable amount of time was spent by support staff 20 years ago dictating individual letters to individual students for a secretary to type and send. Now a lot of personal correspondence is done by word processor and at least as much time is spent on the telephone or sending e-mail messages. In addition, of course, few people now speak of 'correspondence courses'. Yet there is still much strength and advantage to written materials which can appear either as letters to individuals, standard letters or problem pages, or as leaflets which are straightforward, self-assessment or experiential texts.

Individual letters (including standard letters)

Letters are still often used in student support and they tend to have very specific purposes. Letters are usually about serious matters; they form a permanent record and can communicate complex information. The use of word processing and mail merge means that even standard letters can be tailored to the recipient to some extent.

Therefore, letters still tend to be used for answering complicated queries, communicating serious recorded information such as exam results and dealing with complaints. Nevertheless, there is still a world of difference between a well-written and effective letter and the stilted formality that can still overcome otherwise literate teachers when dealing with difficult issues.

An effective letter often naturally follows the outline structure suggested for any exploring activity – clarifying, checking, conceptualizing, contextualizing, challenging and consequent action – and uses the usual qualities of warmth and empathy. Take the example below that I wrote recently to a student.

Dear Mr G . . .

Your Course Result [*an immediate clarification – this was what his rather confused and rambling letter was about*].

Thank you for your query about the discrepancy between your continuous assessment and exam grades – I can appreciate your disappointment at the difference between them [*checking and some empathy*]. In fact, discrepancies like this are very common and I am sure many students feel like you do [*contextualizing*]. Unhappily, it is University policy not to give feedback on exam papers because of the considerable cost implications. However, I would be happy to ask your tutor to go through the paper with you if you think that would be helpful. Perhaps you would let me know [*consequent action*].

Yours sincerely

Ormond Simpson

This will seem an obvious example. Yet some of the letters that students receive from my institution are tactless, defensive and lacking in clarity, and it is not surprising that sometimes students respond negatively. Perhaps the most important thing that letter writers can do is to use their empathy and ask how they would feel about receiving the letter they have written.

Problem pages

Problem pages in magazines have a long history and seem as popular as ever. If an institution has some kind of newsletter for its students, then a problem page may be worth considering as an item. The excerpt below is taken from *Open Learner*, the magazine of the UK National Extension College.

Q I really want to study, it's just that I keep finding something else to do that seems more important. I try and settle down to work but my mind keeps wandering to all the household tasks I've left undone and I begin to feel guilty. The next minute I find that I simply can't concentrate. I end up leaving my studies (feeling by this stage that it's hopeless anyway) to get on with something else. Finally I feel both a martyr and a failure – I almost wish I hadn't enrolled for my course! Do other students experience the same problems and is there a solution?

A Many – in fact the majority – of our students are busy people working or bringing up a family. The difficulty in finding the time to study is a natural consequence of a busy lifestyle. Many students may be failing to give themselves permission to study. Perhaps you feel it is selfish of you to devote time to your course when other members of your family demand your attention. However, everyone has a right to their own time and recognition and acceptance of this is essential – especially vital for the home study student. It can seem that without the routine of more traditional teaching methods you are 'not really studying properly'. You need to banish these ideas as nonsense and be aware that if you are taking an examination it will provide the same qualification – and demand the same input – as for those attending classes or lectures. Time is so precious that the daily tasks that fall regularly to most of us are enough to keep us busy until it is time to sink exhausted into a chair! This 'end-piece' of time is not appropriate for study purposes when your brain needs to be at its most active.

It is impossible to provide a single, foolproof 'solution' because each case is different. Comments like 'don't give up' and 'continue with your studies' are not helpful because you need to learn to manage your time. In recognition of this common problem, NEC has produced two publications that should help. They are *How to Study Effectively* (2001a) and *How to Manage Your Time* (2001b).

The problem with problem pages, as the example above may illustrate, is that it is hard not to fall into over-directive styles of response.

Leaflets

Despite the advance of so many kinds of communication, there is still a strong case to be made for the use of leaflets on student support. They have many advantages:

● cheap to produce and despatch;
● permanent record and reference;
● can be reworked into other forms such as Web pages and audiotapes.

It is noticeable that many other support providers, such as Social Services and medical hospitals, use leaflets. My wife has just returned from the local Casualty Unit after bumping her head, clutching a leaflet entitled *Your Head Injury: What to do now*. Undoubtedly the doctor there had told her what to do but, at a time when her memory skills were not at their best, the leaflet was a useful (and permanent) reference.

   Of course, there is also the problem that it is easier and cheaper to fob off patients with leaflets rather than allow them to talk to a doctor, but overall leaflets are a valuable element in any student support system.

Types of leaflets

It may be useful to distinguish between types of leaflets: straight text, self-assessment and experiential.

Straight text
Many leaflets are written as straightforward text without requiring particular responses from the student. This is a simple example from my own institution aimed at students who appear to be falling behind with their studies.

GETTING BEHIND? CATCHING UP WITH YOUR STUDIES

Are you getting behind with your studies? Or are things piling up so much that you feel you're about to?
   Don't give up! There are various things you can do to help yourself including managing your time more effectively and adopting 'strategic learning' approaches.

Catching up or bailing out?

So you're behind with your studies? Are you wondering whether to cut your losses and withdraw now or keep plugging away? Think about it carefully – some students withdraw sooner than they need.

If you'd like to carry on there are two things you can consider – strategic study and time management.

Strategic study

There seem to be two basic study methods – deep and surface. Most students would prefer the deep, thorough approach if possible and get stressed if they feel themselves forced to take the surface, skimming approach. But there may be a third approach – strategic – deciding what needs to be done to catch up or to attain a specific outcome such as a clear pass if not a distinction.

There are several ways to adopt a strategic approach:

- Remember everything you do counts. Even a failed assignment takes you closer to your target – it doesn't drag you back. So always put in any assignment you've done even if it's incomplete or you're dissatisfied with it. Your tutor would rather have it than not.
- Consult your tutor. He or she may be able to suggest parts of the course to skim or miss out and other appropriate strategies.
- Go to tutorials. Don't persuade yourself that you'll look silly for being behind. It's almost certain that you'll find others are in the same position – there's nothing like finding others in the same boat for getting you rowing again . . .
- Don't be a perfectionist. Everyone likes to do the best they can but in this case perfectionism is the enemy of progress. Remember that strategic study is a temporary expedient until you catch up and can study more thoroughly again.

Time for study

Time is almost always a problem for students – 40 per cent of students say it is their principal study problem and 60 per cent of withdrawing students say it was the reason why they dropped out.

Students also say that they find time in various ways – some in bits and pieces, studying 'on the hoof' and grabbing 15 minutes here and there. Others are more systematic and set aside tranches of time without interruption. There doesn't seem to be a single right way to find the time – experiment to find the best way of managing your time for yourself.

Time – how much? We suggest a figure of X hours' study a week to cover all activities – reading, going to tutorials and writing assignments. Obviously this average figure varies depending on:

- The stage of the course: the beginning and pre-exam periods may well be more time-consuming than other parts of a course.
- Your previous background and work on a course: experienced students always say how useful it is to get some course reading done before it starts.
- Your personal pressures: there will be weeks when it'll be impossible to spend this time because of family, work and health demands. It's important not to allow yourself to get stressed as a result of missing periods of study – you can catch up better if you're not panicking about getting behind.

Time management

There seem to be two ways of organizing time:

Time planning

Set up a schedule of regular study periods negotiated with family and stick to it as far as possible.

For example (try completing this yourself):

Table 5.1   *Time planning*

Day	Times Example	Hours Your schedule
Sun	8.00–12.00 pm	4
Mon	9.00–11.00 pm	2
Tues	9.00–11.00 pm	2
Wed	off	–
Thurs	9.00–11.00 pm	2
Fri	9.00–11.00 pm	2
Sat	off	–
Total	12 hours	

This requires quite a lot of discipline but if it suits you it does give a structure that family and friends can understand and go along with.

Time finding

Look at your current activities and see what might be eliminated or reduced. For example try completing this chart:

Table 5.2   *Time finding*

Activity	Hours per week now	Revised allocation
Watching TV		
Socializing		
Time with partner		
Child care		
Housework		
DIY		
Hobbies		
Others		
Totals	(A)	(B)
Extra study time available		
A–B =		

These two approaches are not opposites. The advantage of the second is that it can also suggest other ways of finding time – the 4 Ds:

- decommitment: identifying things that don't really need doing;
- deferment: putting things off till after the exams;
- downgrade: doing things to a less perfect standard;
- delegation: getting someone else to do things that hitherto have apparently been your responsibility.

Self-assessment texts

Self-assessment texts attempt to get students to interact with the leaflets in some way by completing a questionnaire or checking items in a chart. We have seen an example already in chapter 3 of part of a leaflet sent to new students before they start their course. It is not clear if self assessment texts are any more effective than straight text, but they do seem more appropriate for particular circumstances. And it may be that electronic versions of self-assessment texts on a Web site could be made more interactive (and attractive) by encouraging students to check items before passing on to the next part of the text, and giving them feedback. For example the leaflet above could be made interactive by providing a facility that allows students to fill in a 'time-finding' chart which then automatically calculates their available study time.

Experiential texts

An experiential text is one that offers a student or potential student a brief experience of a particular kind. Such texts are fairly rare – one example is the *Taster Packs* used in my own organization that are designed to offer prospective students a brief taste of particular courses and (as importantly) a short experience of what it might be like to be a student. As well as an excerpt from the course, they contain an assignment question and a typical answer with a tutor's comments and grade. Thus, someone reading the pack may experience something of the challenge that a student on that course has taken on (see Adams, Rand and Simpson, 1989).

It seems unlikely that this principle can be extended very far, but it may not be impossible to write texts that (for example) deal with exam stress by attempting to get a student to experience that stress in a safe situation and then try different methods of overcoming it.

Writing leaflets

Writing leaflets is not a simple task. There is always the difficulty of the balance between warmth, approachability, informality or readability and being patronizing. Apart from that, the same considerations apply as to writing letters. A good leaflet should:

- clarify and check the issue – perhaps by using rhetorical questions or carefully organized sub-sections;
- conceptualize and contextualize the issue – contextualizing an issue, for example, making it clear to students who have failed an exam that they are far from being unusual, is quite important;
- consequent action – by ending the leaflet with 'what to do now' and 'what the organization can do now' sections.

In addition, there are other simple characteristics of a good leaflet. It should:

- Be short – anything longer than one sheet of A4 may be too long. There is little point, for example, in giving students worried about their lack of time a book on time management – a leaflet might at least have a chance of being read.
- Be typographically friendly – the font and layout of a leaflet can be important. Some fonts – Comic, Arial or Helvetica – may be friendlier than Times New Roman or Courier. A two- or three-column format with simple illustrations will also be more approachable and easy to read than a single page-wide format. There are many excellent examples from medical, social and other agencies.
- Use appropriate illustrations or cartoons to break up text and illustrate points.
- Avoid the temptation to 'gravitas': often a particular issue in university level distance education where there is a tendency to see an informal style as lacking the authority and dignity appropriate to the institution. This criticism will often be phrased as 'patronizing students'. That's a danger but it arises from lack of empathy with the reader rather than a particular use of vocabulary. There are simple measures of readability that come with most word-processing programs, such as the Flesch Reading Ease score which rates text on a 100-point scale; the higher the score the easier it is to understand the document. The rating depends on factors such as sentence length. For most users it is recommended that the writer aims for a score of approximately 60 to 70. To give a feel for this in practice, the score for this chapter is 54.

Using leaflets

Writing a leaflet is only the start. There is also the issue of getting them to students at an appropriate time. There are various ways:

- on demand from a published list by post or fax back – automatic faxing from a particular number;
- blanket mailings to all students at a particular time of year – for example, a leaflet on exam stress to all students before their exams;
- specific mail to individual students or groups of students in particular circumstances – for example, a leaflet on what to do after failing an exam to all students who have just failed an exam;
- via a Web site or FirstClass conferencing system;

- via local staff who can have a resource pack of such leaflets – for example, the leaflet *Failed Your Assignment* mentioned in chapter 4 enclosed with a failed assignment by the tutor.

We shall see later that appropriate and timely response may be important to a student retention scheme.

Effectiveness of student support leaflets

It is difficult to measure the effectiveness of leaflets in comparative or statistical terms. Feedback tends to be subjective and selective. Moreover, if students do not find a leaflet useful they probably tend to ignore it rather than take time to comment on it. Nevertheless, here is an example of part of an evaluation carried out on a simple leaflet called *Helping Your Student* that appears in chapter 10:

> *Please comment on the 'style' of the leaflet.*
> 'Well set out and easy to read.'
> 'Clear and attractive – something that can be read immediately, rather than put aside until time is available and consequently never read.'
> 'I thought the style was about right: my husband thought it rather patronizing.'
>
> *Please comment on the content and length of the leaflet.*
> 'I liked the 'bite-sized' paragraphs.'
> 'You could spread it a bit to folded A3. But not more than that.'
> '. . . my wife is now a little more understanding since reading your leaflet although she's still not happy at the neglect caused by my studying.'

Student support on the phone

Of all the different media used in student support, the phone may be taken for granted. There does not appear to be much in UK literature since the article by Robinson (1984). Being an 'old' technology it does not attract the same attention and input as new, more glamorous technologies involving computers. Yet phone technology has not stood still; as well as improvements in the quality of transmission and conferencing there are developments such as voicemail that offer interesting possibilities for student support.

Advantages and disadvantages of phone support

The advantages of the phone for student support are often obvious:

- Immediacy – although this can be overestimated if several calls have to be made because someone is out.

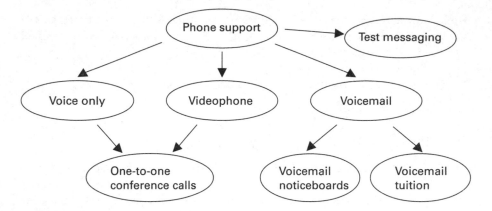

Figure 5.1 *Phone support possibilities*

- Availability – for students in remote locations or housebound, the phone offers the most practical support where there is no access to good transport. Even for students with impaired hearing there are text-phone services that may be easier than attending a face-to-face tutorial.
- Cost – the cost of a one-to-one call can be less than the postage on a letter (in the UK in 2001 a three-minute long-distance call at peak rate costs the same as a first class stamp, leaving aside the cost of writing a letter).

The principal disadvantage of course is the absence of visual cues both of the person – their expression and body language – and of their background – you may be sitting in a quiet office with no distractions, they may be trying to keep an eye on a baby while cooking a meal. We shall see some of the consequences of this lack of cues when looking at one-to-one and conference calling. A less obvious disadvantage is the invasive nature of the phone; it is clear that students are often reluctant to phone part-time tutors at work or home for fear of choosing an inconvenient moment. The indication of particular times at which to call may be helpful but we are moving towards longer availability from call-centre type arrangements – see chapter 17.

One-to-one calling

Experience suggests that the visual channel is particularly important at conveying affective information – uncertainty, stress and anxiety – but less important for cognitive transmission. If that is the case then phone contact should be more useful for academic support than non-academic. That may well be so, but it seems that in practice the distinction is not particularly helpful, as the choice may well be between a phone contact and no contact at all. There are problems in using one-to-one phone contact: it can take several calls to establish contact, it may involve out-of-office hours' work, and both students and tutors can be reluctant to initiate calls on the grounds of intrusion.

Nevertheless the phone is indispensable in ODL, and the techniques for its one-to-one use are covered in some detail later in this chapter.

Conferencing calling

Conference calls involve more than two people linked by phone (sometimes known as audio conferencing or teleconferencing). In theory, any number can be so linked; in practice, the process becomes very cumbersome with more than six people linked. The most common arrangement is having a tutor or adviser linked to students separately at different locations. This type of arrangement is shown in Figure 5.2.

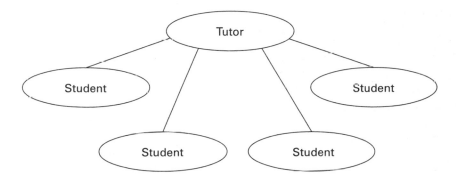

Figure 5.2   *Conference call: tutor and single remote students*

However, a conference call can be linked to a telephone loudspeaker in various different arrangements – for example, a tutor with a group of remote students at a distant centre as shown in Figure 5.3.

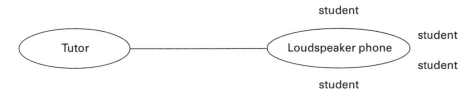

Figure 5.3   *Conference call: tutor and group of students using a loudspeaker phone*

Conference calling appeared very early in distance education and was pioneered in places dealing with large distances such as Canada and Australia. The comparative novelty attracted a lot of attention that tended to decline as the early technology was not up to the demands placed on it (a scenario not unlike the introduction of computing into ODL perhaps). Calls had to be booked well in advance (very early arrangements actually involved an engineer making connections at an exchange with a soldering iron) and the quality was poor, with connections being lost and voices being clipped if two people tried to speak at once.

Now the technology is far superior (although usually calls still need to be set up in advance). The need for preparation remains, and for a call to work well the structure needs to be very well defined. Typically, a tutor will introduce an agenda item and call for comments from participants by name in turn. Although two people speaking at once does not render both unintelligible, in practice because of the lack of visual clues it becomes very difficult to distinguish what is being said unless short turns are taken. Therefore, a typical conference call dialogue may run along these lines:

Tutor: Right, so those are the main differences between waves and particles. Is that clear to everyone? Sue, is that OK with you now?
Sue: Yes, that's fine thanks.
Tutor: Good. Jim, how about you?
Jim: Yes, OK by me.
Tutor: Liz?
Liz: I'm still not quite clear about the boundary changes, Angela.
Tutor: OK – let's just clarify that. Look at the diagram on page 16 – have you got that, Liz? [and so on]

As can be seen, the process is far more structured than a face-to-face tutorial. Note that the tutor does not address questions to the whole group, as this will create confusion as several people try to talk at once. It is important to page each participant in turn at regular intervals, so each can raise issues and queries. It requires far greater concentration, especially on the part of the tutor, but also by the students, and generally an hour is as much as anyone can usefully manage.

The point was made earlier that the phone is more suited to academic support than non-academic support because of the relative absence of emotional clues which are more often available visually. This seems to apply particularly to conference calling, and such calls seem to be used almost exclusively for tuition, although some workers have found conference calling helpful for the organizational aspects of learning such as time management (Henderson and Putt, 1999).

The costs of a conventional conference call set-up are not negligible. Currently (2002) in the UK the cost of a 30-minute call between six people over ordinary lines is about £80 (US$120: 130 euros) so it is not an obviously cheaper option than face-to-face provision.

Chat lines

One unexplored possibility is the use of chat lines. These are open-faced running conferences that can be joined at any time by anyone. These achieved some notoriety a few years ago when it was discovered that teenagers were running up huge bills phoning party lines without their parents' consent. Existing chat lines are commercial and sexual in nature and use premium rates. It can be seen that there is the possibility of setting up educational chat lines so that students could phone a particular number between certain hours and be automatically connected to other students who have phoned as well, the conference being moderated by a tutor or student support adviser.

A very modest experiment in London a number of years ago failed because of technical problems, but perhaps the area should be looked at again.

Three-way calling

A recent innovation (in the UK) has been the introduction of three-way calling. These are calls where a person can link with two others by simply dialling them both in turn. No booking or other formality is needed and the costs are little more than the joint call charges.

The ease and informality of this set-up are very attractive and look very appropriate to ODL. Currently, we are conducting some experiments in my own institution with both tutor-led and student self-help three-way calls.

Videophone calling

Videophones have been around in one form or another for a number of years but it is only relatively recently that costs and quality improvements have made them of interest in ODL – see Dallat *et al.* (1992). There are similar possibilities to conference calls.

First, large-screen units in specific locations that can link individuals or groups to individuals or groups in one or more other specific locations similar to the illustration in Figure 5.3.

Second, small home units that can link one to one with other units via domestic television receivers.

Third, computer based units that can be linked simultaneously with other networked computers.

The picture quality in all of these arrangements is still much poorer than that of ordinary television; pictures are jerky and indistinct and the effect is rather distancing at first experience, although participants clearly get accustomed to it after a while.

The main use of videoconferencing in ODL so far has been the first type where, for example, a group of students at a remote videophone location have been working with a tutor from a base location. A recent example was a group of isolated students who were linked to their tutor about 100 miles away via a videophone set up in their local college. This was clearly valued by the students who would otherwise have had a long journey to meet their tutor.

Home units of the second type are still rather expensive and have not been much used, although there may be possibilities for supporting remote or housebound students, and it is not yet clear how far computer linked units of the third type will add to the richness of computer based student support.

The pros and cons of videophone calling

While there are many sceptics, it is beginning to look as though videophones are a useful enhancement to existing technology for support in ODL. It may be that the addition of the visual channel – even if of poor quality – does ameliorate considerably the problems of stress and fatigue experienced by participants, and that videoconferences can usefully last longer than audio conferences. The visual channel does not add much to the ability of the tutor to use visual aids – picture quality is often too poor to transmit pictures, diagrams or experiments with any real value. But the mere presence of pictures of the participants clearly engenders a different and more positive feeling in the group. It may be that such groups will be more open to non-academic support activities as well as academic support use.

Of course, the extra costs of videoconferencing – particularly of equipment – will critically affect its development.

Voicemail systems

The telephone answering machine has been with us for many years. Recently the combination of computers and phone technology has allowed such answering systems to become much more sophisticated. A pre-recorded voice will offer a caller a range of options obtainable by pressing phone keys, which in turn may lead to another range of options. Recently, I had to report a phone fault to the phone company and encountered a voicemail system that took me through three layers of options before I was allowed to talk to a human being and explain my problem.

Experiences like these have given voicemail systems a bad reputation, and many people find them intensely irritating. However, most technologies can be misused, and voicemail might offer a partial solution to the issue of out-of-hours service and some students' disinclination to initiate phone calls. There are two interesting possibilities, audiotext and voicemail tuition.

Audiotext services

An audiotext service can offer a range of short messages (three to six minutes) on topics of interest to students at any time out of office hours. A simple system is currently operating in my own office. Incoming callers out of hours are offered the choice of leaving a message or the audiotext service. If they opt for the audiotext service they are offered a further choice of listening to one of six messages on topics like:

- choosing a course;
- thinking of withdrawing?
- getting behind with study?
- going to a residential school?

- course results;
- assignment queries.

Most of the messages are modified versions of existing leaflets and are about three to four minutes long. This compares interestingly with audiotext services like the UK *Which* Health Call which has more than 150 messages on various medical topics, some up to 13 minutes long. And, unlike the Health Call which uses a premium rate number, this service uses ordinary call rates so that a student can listen to a complete message, even long distance, for about half the cost of a first class stamp.

There may well be surprise that students patronize this service on any scale. Although fairly primitive it has one unique advantage: it is available at any time out of office hours. A student panicking about an exam at midnight the night before can at least receive some reassurance and useful information. A student who has a networked PC could access similar information, but it is still simpler and quicker to pick up a phone and dial a couple of numbers than to log onto a network, wait for a connection and then navigate to the right Web site.

A variation on this approach is SpeecHTML, which uses speech text recognition software to enable users to navigate and interact with a Web site using only a phone. Thus once there is a Web site for student support it is not too difficult to make it accessible to students without access to a computer. However, currently this is still at pilot stage.

Voicemail tuition (VMT)

Another system using voicemail was described by Carmichael (1995) in Australia: the voicemail noticeboard. This was designed to overcome the problem of maintaining contact with a group of distance students as an alternative to e-mail. The tutor recorded weekly bulletins on his voicemail which students could access at times convenient to them. A bulletin might cover things like where students should have reached in their studies, particularly difficult points to watch out for in current study topics, how to tackle a forthcoming assignment, reminders of forthcoming tutorials and so on.

This has recently been developed in the UK OU into an interactive 'voice-mail tuition system'. This gives students in a group the option to leave messages for their tutor and the rest of the group. It works very much like an audio analogue of a computer conference. Students can record messages and listen to them before sending them. All messages to the system go to a student's individual mailbox where he or she can listen to them, fast forward through them, skip them and delete them. A 'conversation' might then go along lines like:

Mike: Hi, it's Mike your tutor here. This is just to remind you that your assignments are due in two weeks. If you're having difficulty getting started do re-read pages 10 to 20 of the unit. By the way I'll be a little late for the tutorial next week but don't go away! – I'll be there.

Jean: Hello everyone, it's Jean here. I'm having some difficulty understanding the concept of 'syncretic formalism' on page 5. Has anyone got a handle on that?

Tom: Hi Jean, it's Tom. I'm finding that difficult too. Help anyone please!

Mike: Hi Jean and Tom, Mike here. Try thinking about the concept in concrete terms. For example . . .

VMT has some of the characteristics of computer conferencing in its availability at any time out of ordinary hours, cheaply from students' homes. It even has some advantages over computer conferencing. It does not require expensive technology, any ordinary touch-tone phone will do, and it is quicker and more reliable to log on. And speech is faster than text – although of course slower than reading.

The UK OU system is currently a pilot serving about 10 tutors and 180 students. It remains to be seen how useful it will be to students and where it will appear on the 'accessibility versus study value' chart (chapter 9).

Text messaging (SMS)

Text messaging or SMS (Short Message Service) from mobile (cell) phones was invented in about 1995. It has grown enormously, particularly in Europe, with increasingly easy compatibility between phones, and several million text messages are now sent every day.

Users enter their messages into their phone's display via their alphanumeric keypad – pressing 2 once for 'a', twice for 'b', three times for 'c', pressing 3 once for 'd' and so on. The process is quite laborious even with 'predictive text' systems. Once the message is ready (up to a limit of 160 characters) it can be sent to another mobile phone where it is displayed as an envelope icon until the user wants to read it. The system is particularly popular with teenagers as it is cheap, unobtrusive and private. Although inputting is quite slow (a new language has grown up to speed the process 'R U OK 4 2 NITE?', 'C U @ 8' and so on), there are a number of computer Web sites from which messages can be sent (often for free) using a standard keyboard. Some sites allow messages to be sent to a group of users and set up a distribution list. So inevitably there are investigations into how text messaging might be used to support students in some way.

One interesting attempt is run by a group of educators in the UK for Year 10 and 11 students (the age group 15 to 16 who are the most common users of text messaging). The aim was to motivate and reward students by playing on themes of CITV – 'Connecting into their values' – and WIIFM – 'What's in it for me'. Students subscribe by sending a simple text message to an advertised number (the only cost to them). They then receive a series of texts – three a day – which are purportedly text messages between a group of students – a text message soap opera. The messages themselves try to relate to the demands in the lives of such students and direct them towards a generic revision Web site ww.knowitall.org.uk for support. A typical exchange of messages might read:

Jez here . . . got 2 get rvsion tmetble in soon! Pain in nek!! Spose w shld do it tho. Rthr b at film 2nite cul8r j

chck this out! www.knowitall.org.uk – rlly usefl 2day cos I flt rlly stck rvsing. Lds of gd tips n stuff xabi

At the time of writing the project is in evaluation.

In student support in ODL it is possible to see applications in student progress. A tutor could text his students as a group (assuming they have mobile phones and are willing to release their numbers to him) with reminders about deadlines, hints on assignment questions, even short questions to consider. It's surprising what can be got into 160 characters: 'RU UP2 Q3? RMEMBR P & S WAVES TRAVEL AT DIFF SPEEDS! RMEMBR ONLY 1 MORE TEST AFTER THIS! PHONE US SOONEST IF PROBLEMS. BEST WISHES MIKE [143 characters]. Such a message will take less than a minute to type on a PC and will reach the students even if they're away from their PCs.

Training staff and students for phone support

Because phone support may be an unfamiliar medium for advisers, tutors and students it can be helpful to provide some kind of introduction for them.

Training tutors in academic support

This for instance is an edited excerpt from a pack *Along These Lines* (Gaskell and Spirit, 2000) which is used in my own institution for tutors who are going to use telephone tuition.

BEGINNING TELEPHONE CONTACT

There is no doubt that students benefit hugely from the opportunity of telephone contact with their tutors. Of course, that contact encompasses everything from a brief call to clarify the time of the next tutorial to a pre-arranged discussion of the current module with a student who can't get to tutorials. For tutors too the phone can be a useful and perhaps less formal way of passing on information or extra encouragement as well as a teaching aid.

As with other forms of tutoring, establishing clear expectations from the start will allow both student and tutor to make the best use of their time and protect both from undue intrusion.

An **introductory letter** to new students is a good place to clarify your expectations. You could, for example, say that you welcome contact from students by phone. State clearly any times which are off limits and suggest good times for them to call. It may be useful to ask students to reciprocate via a return sheet telling you when are their good and bad times to receive calls.

Once you are on the phone to a student there are further agenda setting issues to bear in mind. Many of these relate to the increased likelihood of mismatching perceptions between tutors and students when there is an inevitable lack of visual feedback. These mismatches may concern general matters such as expectations of the tutor–student role, or more specific difficulties, for example with interpreting pauses and estimating thinking time. Problems may also be course related, perhaps to do with the ambiguity of the relevant academic language.

The following are some suggestions for good practice, which will help to minimize such mismatches:

- **As always, establish boundaries.** A tutorial by telephone will be much more productive if the tutor and the student both know in advance what is to be discussed.
- **Make sure that you know what the student's difficulty really is.**
- **Make sure that the student does most of the work!** Avoid falling into the trap of just telling a student how to solve a problem. Even if you ask the student 'Do you understand?', they are likely to say yes to please you – and even if they understand at the time, they are more likely to be able to solve a similar problem later if they have worked through the problem for themselves. As with any sort of telephone tuition, make sure that you have a *conversation* with the student.

  If possible, get them to participate actively by writing down points. It can also be helpful for you, the tutor, to write points down as you go along so that you and the student are working together in much the same way as you would if the discussion was taking place face to face.
- **Refer to written material whenever possible.** Very often a student will ring with a very specific query from the course material. Unless you are extremely familiar with this part of the course, or have answered the same query many times before, it is probably best to have the same material open in front of you so that you can check the context of the student's query. When the student has rung with a less specific problem, or in the case of a telephone tutorial set up to help a student with a previously identified difficulty, it is still helpful if both parties can have some appropriate written material to refer to.

  It is important that you and the student are both looking at copies of exactly the same thing, otherwise confusion can easily creep in.
- **Keep it as short as possible.** Be aware that doing academic work on the telephone is demanding and both tutor and student will tire more quickly than in a face-to-face session. Be realistic about how much you can cover and take a break if either you or the student needs it.
- **Be comfortable with pauses.** Tutors sometimes feel concerned if there is silence on the other end of the telephone, but remember that pauses give useful time to think so long as both parties are aware of what is going on.
- **Encourage feedback throughout the session** to compensate for the lack of visual cues. Encourage students to tell you when there is something they do not understand and to tell you when they have understood or when something is helpful.
- **Offer some review of learning.** You and the student will find it helpful to end with some kind of summary of the ground covered. You may find that this review of points raised leads naturally into setting an agenda for subsequent tutorials.

Dealing with surprise calls

Calls initiated by the tutor. Unscheduled calls are best made with a clear purpose in mind, so simply wanting to start a dialogue with a student, however well intentioned, may not be a sufficient reason for phoning.

Starting with 'Hi there. I just thought I'd phone to see how you're getting on' is friendly, but could prove too vague. It should be more helpful to begin by referring directly to your objectives in making the call. Always check that you've called at a convenient moment.

'Cold calling' carries risks for the tutor: anything from a brush off from the student to finding yourself in the midst of family tragedy. If you sense that the call is not appropriate it may be best to put this to the student and tell them that you will write to them about the issue or allow them to contact you if and when they are ready to do so.

Receiving an unexpected call: hidden agenda. One difficulty here is that you may have to make quick decisions about the student's motivation for contacting you. It is a very common experience to find that whilst a student has ostensibly called with one query, this is in fact a preliminary to raising a much more difficult issue with you, the tutor. Once you have become aware of this, unless you feel confident about dealing with the problem there and then, you may want to arrange to call the student back to give yourself time to think and to consult if necessary.

Some of the most difficult calls to respond to are those where the student does not know or cannot articulate what their problem is. They might start by saying:' I just don't know where to start with this assignment/section/ module/ course.'

One response might be to summarize for the student what the key points are, and this 'rescue' may be just what is needed to begin with. It is still useful, however, to involve the student actively, for example by asking them to identify/remember one detail from the relevant course book which you can then ask them to link to other examples or aspects of the study material.

Some subjects seem harder to teach over the phone and it may be useful to provide some extra advice to tutors in these areas. Here is another edited excerpt from the document above for tutors teaching maths and science.

TALKING MATHS

Queries involving equations, calculations, graphs or other mathematical notation can be particularly difficult to deal with on the telephone. On the other hand, telephone tuition in this area can be very rewarding since many students (from all faculties) suffer from considerable lack of mathematical confidence. One-to-one help, often most easily provided by telephone, can provide them with a much-needed boost.

Why is it that queries involving mathematical notation can be so difficult to deal with by phone? Perhaps the most obvious difficulty is that neither party can see the other's calculations or graphs. However, this is exacerbated by the fact that students are frequently naive users of the mathematical notation involved whereas tutors tend to be 'experts'. Distance students frequently comment that they are not taught how to pronounce unfamiliar words. Similarly, they often do not know the conventions for 'pronouncing maths'. For example, they may not equate the written '10^5' with the spoken 'ten to the five' or the written $\frac{d^2y}{dx^2}$ with the spoken 'd two y by d x squared'. Even if a student understands the notation, confusion can arise: for example, does 'two plus three squared' mean $2 + 3^2$ or $(2 + 3)^2$?

Training advisers in non-academic support

The issues surrounding the development of phone skills for staff working in non-academic support are very much the same as those outlined in chapter 3. Advisers will need to cover the same spectrum of informing, commending and exploring activities, express the same qualities of warmth, empathy, acceptance and openness, and structure their dialogues through clarifying, checking, contextualizing, conceptualizing, challenging and consequent action. But all that will need to occur in the absence of a visual channel to communicate these qualities and skills and any visual clues as to the caller's state of mind.

For example, expressing warmth over the phone may perhaps involve a slight exaggeration in the tone and informality of voice. It is noticeable that call centres in the UK tend to employ staff with regional accents which are thought to convey greater warmth than the traditional 'BBC English accent' which is perceived as formal and rather distant.

The absence of the visual channel may have advantages: body language, facial expressions and appearance can all engender inappropriate and probably inaccurate prejudices. Certainly organizations like the Samaritans who run phone counselling services have demonstrated that it is possible to support people very effectively solely over the phone.

Written materials for training

It is certainly possible to produce written guidelines to help staff working in phone support. For example one of the most difficult situations is dealing with students who are distressed or angry. My own office has used a simple sheet of points to help its staff which can be pinned up beside the phone.

Some strategies for phone calls with distressed/anxious/angry students:

1. Work out your favourite starting phrase.
2. Listen carefully. As far as possible make notes. If the student is so upset or cross they're incoherent, don't try to 'calm them down'. Kind phrases or sympathetic grunts should be enough at this stage . . .

3. Let the student let off steam. Don't block weeping or grumbles. You're not paid to defend your institution against every whisper of criticism. The reason for letting the student keep talking is to find out. Something else may be really wrong in their lives and the problem with the institution may be just the last straw.

4. Let inconsistencies or irrationalities pass. Upset people say odd things . . .

5. Keep your temper. You're involved in this as a professional. It's not your personal problem. If you think you might lose it, suggest that you or the student calls back. Fix a time.

6. Remember distressed people easily become over-sensitive. So avoid saying anything that could seem negative. Try explaining how you can help, what could be done – look for positive responses.

7. Never refuse a request because of the way it is made. Consider first if the request is, in itself, reasonable. 'I want someone senior brought in on this' is a put-down but if it's an issue which may justify referral, refer and forget the put-down. (You are just as good at your job as you were before they put you down!)

8. Try not to show your anxiety. It is normal to be distressed if someone else is weeping or angry but best not to show it. Some voices waver, go shrill or strident with stressful encounter. This can make the caller more upset. Use whatever stress reduction activity usually works for you – breathe, try to drop your voice to a lower pitch, say as little as possible until you can sound more normal.

9. Beware of sounding patronizing. You have power in what some students perceive as a power relationship. If you act like the parent, it tends to make people angry or humiliated and the phone 'exaggerates' everything you say.

10. Do not be impressed by threats. If the student says s/he'll contact his/her lawyer, make sure you've offered the possibility of help from a senior person but otherwise don't discourage people. (Usually they think again.)

11. Keep on trying to bring the dialogue back to the main issue and ignore the irrelevancies.

12. If the going gets tough, offer to refer the problem to someone else. Remember that your contract has limits!

13. Do not let the conversation drag on. Think of useful ending phrases.

Role plays for training

One of the most effective training methods, however, is to use role plays to explore and reflect on the issues raised in phone support. A simple option is to sit two people back to back to simulate the absence of visual clues, give each one a separate brief (which the other does not see), and let it run. If there is a third person available as an observer, perhaps working from a simple checklist, then so much the better.

Using such role playing will need to be approached sensitively. Staff involved will need to feel unthreatened and supported in the process – see chapter 16. But used well, such role playing can be an immensely powerful way of approaching the development of appropriate skills and qualities. Here for example is a typical checklist with a pair of role-playing briefs.

OBSERVER'S CHECKLIST

1. Was the student made to feel comfortable right at the start?
2. Was the adviser's manner warm and welcoming throughout?
3. Was the student enabled to speak freely without undue interruption?
4. Was the student's concern clearly outlined?
5. Were there areas that the adviser did not follow up adequately or missed altogether?
6. If any suggestions were made or advice given by the adviser, were they appropriate and likely to be useful to the student?
7. Was the student left feeling that the interview was a useful experience?
8. Any special comments?

Role play: student brief

Your name is Keith or Kathy Cameron, an ex-teacher. You are in your sixties and are not in very good health. You do distance study 'because it makes me forget all my other worries'. A young new tutor has just failed you on your first assignment. You have never failed an assignment before, and don't like the tone of the tutor's comments. Although this discipline is new to you, you feel your essay deserved to pass. You are therefore ringing up to appeal against the grade and request a change of tutor.

Role play: student adviser

Your name is Samir or Salima Singh, Student Adviser at Erudition College. The phone rings and the telephonist says there's a Mr Cannon (she thinks) on the line – a student wanting a change of tutor. You take the call.

Briefing students

Many new students in ODL will be new to the idea of phone tuition and support. It does make sense to brief them on how to handle their end of it. This is an edited example.

A STUDENT GUIDE TO TELEPHONE TUITION (FROM JUDITH GEORGE AND JOHN COWAN, *TUTORING BY PHONE*, ROBERT GORDON UNIVERSITY, 1998)

Before you're tutored by phone please read and plan around the following eight points:

1. **Working conditions matter a great deal.** If you're juggling a book, a notepad and a telephone receiver while you're sitting on the bottom step of the hall stairs, in a freezing draught and poor lighting, you're not going to get the best out of your telephone tutorial. Work out the most comfortable and quiet place you can manage, with something to rest your materials on. Warn family and friends about your call, in the hope that interruptions are kept to a minimum.
   So get yourself settled as comfortably as possible for the call.
2. **Timing should be suitable for both student and tutor.** If you, as well as your tutor, get into the habit of checking that an unexpected call is convenient, no-one will be embarrassed when a particular call comes at a bad moment.
   Check with your tutor that your call is convenient.
   Arrange a convenient time for the call beforehand, if possible.
3. **Telephone tutorials benefit from businesslike, if brief, preparation.** If your agenda is simply the work you are currently doing, then it's worth your while thinking carefully beforehand about the questions you would like to have answers to. If your tutor has given you some questions to think about, then you will get far more out of the tutorial if you do that work.
   Do all the necessary preparation for the call.
4. **Have all the necessary study materials to hand.** You should have everything you may need – course material, writing paper, pens and so on – to hand before the call begins. If your question calls on the tutor to consult books or course material, it will be helpful if you tell him or her what you are likely to need, and then ring off for a few minutes, to allow time to assemble what is needed.
   Have all the relevant materials to hand, and let the tutor know what he or she will need.
5. **Make sure your tutor knows how you are getting on.** The more you are explicit and frank about any doubts, hesitations or difficulties you have, the better the tutor can respond to your needs and support your learning. Your tutor will find it difficult to appreciate what your reactions are in the absence of visual signals; do everything you can to put into words what you would normally, in a face-to-face situation, convey by body language or expression, smiles, nods, a frown of puzzlement, and so on.
   Tell your tutor when there is something you do not understand.
   Tell your tutor when you have understood, or when an explanation has been helpful.
6. **Be prepared to summarize.** Your tutor will probably encourage you to play back, in your own words, what you understand by key issues or important summary statements in particular. This will help consolidate your learning, and also help the tutor – and you – check that you really understand what has been said.
   Play back to the tutor in your own words summaries of your discussion.

7. **Do not let silence embarrass you: make good use of it.** It is helpful to you, you will find, if your tutor explains why he or she is pausing ('That was a really interesting question. I need a moment to think about it'). In the same way, it is helpful to the tutor if you explain similarly, or ask for a pause if you need time to think or to look back through notes.
   Let your tutor know if you would like a pause to think.
8. **Build in breaks.** Telephone learning is tiring, and you may well lose concentration through weariness. Or you may need more that a brief pause in the tutorial to think things through properly. Let your tutor know if you need a break; tutors too may welcome the chance to have a quick coffee, or to stretch their legs.
   Tell your tutor if you could do with a break.

Effectiveness of the phone in student support

As noted earlier, there does not appear to be much recent work on the use of the phone in student support. What follows therefore is a rather impressionist view drawn from my own experience and that of staff with whom I work.

There are two particular perspectives, from the student and from the institution.

How students see the phone

By and large it seems that students prefer face-to-face contact but are happy to accept phone contact if it is clearly the only feasible possibility. They are quite reluctant to initiate phone contact with individuals at home such as part-time tutors ('I didn't want to bother you . . .') but have less hesitation in phoning an organization, although that is not always simple during the day as not all students have easy daytime access to the phone.

Phoning an individual or another student appears to be much easier if there has been one prior face-to-face contact, and largely students welcome phone contact initiated by tutors and other students.

Ultimately though, despite students' reservations, research shows that phone support is probably as effective as face-to-face support, particularly in the cognitive or academic field. Phone support is certainly more stressful but the environment also often imposes a businesslike structure, a sense of purpose and progress that can be missing from face-to-face support.

Issues for institutions

There is a range of important issues for institutions to consider:

- **Out-of-hours phone access.** In distance learning, it seems likely that most students study out of conventional hours (there is evidence from computer conferencing records that suggests the peak time for study is 9.00–11.00 pm). Thus, out-of-hours access to student support may well be an issue. If an institution has a student support system that relies on part-time staff working from home, there will be some availability despite students' reluctance to initiate contact. However, the institution may still need to consider the cost-benefits of an evening service.

- **Handling calls within the institution.** It is clear that students experience considerable stress phoning an institution and being referred from one person to another to deal with their queries. Some referrals may be inevitable, but institutions need to organize their staffing and information services to minimize it. That inevitably raises the issue of how far they go down the route of becoming call centres – see chapter 17.

- **Keeping up with technical developments.** New initiatives such as audiotext and three-way calling are probably not important in themselves, but examples of how technological developments are not restricted to computing, of how even a technology as old as the phone is changing the possibilities for student support.

Audiovisual media for student support

Both open circuit broadcasting and audiotapes and videotapes have been used for student support purposes in ODL.

Videotapes

Videotapes are relatively expensive to produce and their use in student support is restricted. This is despite earlier hopes that videotapes might be used with text, with students moving from one medium to the other – watching an experiment, stopping the videotape and completing an observational chart, for example. In practice, this seems to leave students confused and has not proved a popular way of studying. It is possible that the introduction of digital video cameras linked with computer networks may change this: perhaps we shall see students down-loading video clips of their tutors from the Internet but at the moment this seems somewhat in the future.

Audiotapes

Audiotapes were one of the first extensions to text in ODL and have remained enduringly popular with both institutions and students. It is not hard to see why:

- They are cheap to produce: the cost of professionally editing a 45 minute tape (2001) is about £350 (US$500, 550 euros) compared with possibly £6,000 (US$9,000, 10,000 euros) for a 30 minute videotape.
- They are cheap to duplicate and despatch (a long run of duplications can cost as little at 25p (US 40c, 0.5 euros each, in 2001) and postage costs are little more than a first class letter).

- They can be listened to in many different locations whilst the student is doing other things – washing up, driving a car and sitting on a train – as audiotape players are cheap, easily portable and can be used with earphones for privacy.
- They are particularly good at conveying the student experience: the voices of real students talking about their concerns seem more authentic on tape than in print. This is a transcript of part of an audiotape aimed at new students in a distance learning institution. Madge is a new student studying poetry.

Interviewer:	Madge, what were the sorts of things that most worried you when starting the course?
Madge:	I think the main one was that I wasn't sure I could actually achieve the right level from where I was going on. It had been some years since I studied and I really felt 'Could I do this?', so that was my main and first anxiety. Apart from that I knew I had difficulty with things like writing essays. I was worried that I might have extreme difficulty with things like that.
Interviewer:	I also wanted to ask you about something that many students raise, which is the whole issue of time and finding the time. Was that a problem for you?
Madge:	Yes it was. I mean, I had this handbook to help you see whether taking the course was a good idea or not – it had questions and one of these was, you know, did you have the time, and it asked you to make your own timetable up to discover whether you had time during your week to actually study. I thought about it and I tried to be realistic and I thought yes I could manage the studying time that was there, but in actuality it was much more difficult. I think one of the main reasons why is that studying distance education means that you're studying on your own and that means that you have to find the commitment, you have to get yourself down to the work. And if you're surrounded by other commitments, family commitments, or the need to relax in other ways, then it's very difficult to work very hard at something else unless you're being driven by a great power behind you – I must actually attain this to get a job of some sort . . .
Interviewer:	Was the tutor helpful in that way?
Madge:	Yes, she gave me a great deal of support in that way too – she gave me confidence to go on because she had such a practical down-to-earth attitude to things. This was a high level course to go into after a gap and she made me feel I could cope with it from my own level – I didn't have to reach up to anything that was beyond me.

(continued: the tape is about 30 minutes long)

Another particularly appropriate use of audiotape is for stress management. There are a number of tapes that are aimed at helping students with exam anxiety through simple stress relief exercises. There is an exotic area of commercial self-hypnosis audiotapes available, with titles like *Improving Memory, Develop Good Study Habits, Faster Reading, Concentration* and *Taking Examinations*. How far such tapes might be effective is open to question – perhaps they might have some effect on a student's self-confidence.

Open circuit broadcasting for student support

The UK Open University (OU) still uses open circuit television broadcasting for both academic support (programmes associated with courses) and non-academic support (*Introduction to Study* programmes and programmes on particular aspects of the student experience such as residential schools). There are also examples from the developing world of using radio broadcasts in particular to support distance learning. However, broadcasting suffers a number of inherent disadvantages against taped materials.

Thus, now it seems unlikely that broadcasting will play a large part in student support. However, the proliferation of channels that will become available through digital broadcasting may have its uses at some point in the future. It will also be difficult to forecast how interactive television will develop and have an effect on open and distance learning.

I recently had the privilege of talking to a most resourceful and energetic woman from Mongolia who was charged with developing a distance education system there. The difficulties she faces are immense, not least the fact that Mongolians only have one name each. You have to hope that it's not the Mongolian equivalent of Smith. But faced with the problem of a student population living in tents and never in one spot for more than a couple of weeks, she is enthusiastic about radio broadcasting as the main – possibly only – source of support for students. So circumstances will always be important in deciding on your support media. (For a survey of the particular difficulties for support in nomadic education see the article by Pennels (2000).)

Chapter 6

Student support face to face

There is probably more effort and resource going into organizing face-to-face student support in ODL than any other area of support. And there are obvious reasons why this should be so:

- cost: face-to-face support is usually the most expensive single area in student support in terms of institutional and student time and funding;
- visibility: it is also the most visible area and often it is the area that offers support staff most job satisfaction;
- versatility: it can cover both academic and non-academic support equally well;
- richness: face-to-face support offers a richer environment with more opportunities for dialogue than any other medium.

It is also a natural recourse for mixed mode institutions such as networked on-campus situations where face-to-face meeting will be easier and cheaper and probably much more frequent. Curiously, it is not necessarily the support most highly valued by students, as we shall see at the end of this chapter, and perhaps the emphasis placed on it in ODL should be questioned from time to time.

There is of course a massive amount written about face-to-face teaching in all kinds of contexts, and it would be impossible to do more than touch on a topic that can be the subject of a year's course. Therefore, in this chapter I shall concentrate on how the use of the face-to-face mode in ODL might differ from that of other educational situations, and try to give a flavour of that difference by looking at some examples and techniques.

Face-to-face support in ODL

There are a number of differences between the face-to-face environments in ODL and other educational settings. Among these are:

- In distance and networked learning, the course material may be given and separate from the face-to-face support.
- There may be isolation of the students from each other and the institution.
- In both modes of learning, face-to-face contact is likely to be rarer and distant from the students and will therefore need more organization to ensure that the time is used to best advantage.

There are many other differences but these particular elements suggest that:

- The separation of material from support means that student support is likely to be more facilitative than in other settings.
- The isolation of the student means that support will need to pay more attention to the affective and organizational modes of support, as students will not easily be able to support each other in those ways or easily get support from the institution.
- Students who are making considerable efforts to attend rare and distant tutorials may expect a higher quality of support than students at conventional institutions who can shrug off the occasional system failure or poor tutorial.

Bearing these differences in mind, we can look at the basic ways face-to-face support can be delivered: one to one or in groups, and in both academic and non-academic modes.

One-to-one, face-to-face support

Academic

One-to-one, face-to-face tutorial support is of course the most expensive form of student support ever devised. Yet, there are situations where it may be nearly the only or appropriate form of support available: in prisons, for housebound students and for students with particular problems or needs.

Whether the skills needed for one-to-one support are very different from the skills needed for group support or even phone and computer support seems unlikely. What seems to be true is that one-to-one sessions are best run under facilitation; and they tend to be rather more stressful for both tutor and student than group sessions because of the level of concentration required. They are therefore best kept short or punctuated with breaks.

Non-academic

By contrast with academic one-to-one support, there is a long tradition of one-to-one, face-to-face, non-academic support. Such a tradition was largely inherited from the idea of counselling as an intimate and personal process. As suggested below, in the ODL environment group support may often be as effective. Nevertheless, there will always be one-to-one support, expensive as it is for both institution and students. However, support will inevitably be targeted or restricted to particular occasions, places and students (and there may be security issues):

- Occasions: such as open days, guidance sessions, promotion events, general study support events and induction sessions.
- Places: for personal callers to the institution or its branches.
- Students: those with special needs, institutionalized, housebound or deemed to be particularly at risk in some way. Identifying such students and prioritizing between them will be an issue for institutional policy: how do you prioritize between requests from students who have been doing well but are nevertheless anxious about forthcoming assignments, and students who have not asked for help but whose tutors are concerned about their progress? Alternatively, between a third visit to a housebound student who is doing well but who has no other contact and a visit to a new student who has no record of accomplishment but who has asked for a face-to-face session?
- Security issues. There will always be safety issues involved in arranging one-to-one, face-to-face sessions outside the institution. Even where group sessions are involved there can be problems. I recently dealt with a student who always stayed behind after a group tutorial at the end of the evening in an otherwise deserted college. His female tutor, although very experienced, felt distinctly unnerved by his manner. A strategy was developed for her support involving a personal alarm and support from other students, and there were no untoward outcomes subsequently.

Face-to-face support in practice

Face-to-face sessions generally follow the pattern outlined in chapter 3, using the adviser's qualities of warmth and acceptance and empathy in a framework of clarification, checking, challenging as appropriate and consequent action. This may be best illustrated by a transcript of such a session that I recorded after a tutorial (transcribed and edited down – my comments in italics).

Student: Hi Sheila, I just wanted to ask if I could have an extra few days to complete this assignment.
Tutor: I'm sure that will be OK, Peter. What's happening?
Student: I've just been getting a little behind recently with one thing and another.
Tutor: Mmm?
A simple acknowledgement

Student:	To tell you the truth the course is harder than I thought it was going to be.
Tutor:	Is there anything in particular?

Clarifying

Student:	Well – it's just that when I'm reading it doesn't seem to stick somehow. I don't seem to be able to remember what I read at all.
Tutor:	You find it difficult to recall what you're studying?

Clarifying

Student:	Well yes. When I get to the end of my work I close the book and think to myself, 'Well, whatever was that all about?' And I don't seem to be able to understand what it all meant.
Tutor:	You feel you don't get an overall grasp of what the book is trying to tell you?

Checking

Student:	That's exactly right.
Tutor:	Could you give me a clearer idea of what happens when you sit down to study. What do you do exactly?

Starting a second cycle of clarifying

Student:	Well, I sit down with the book and I read straight through a chapter making notes and underlining as I go through. Then I close the book and try to remember what it was about. And then I re-read it to see if I've got it right. But usually I don't seem to be able to remember. What am I doing wrong? You see I was never much of a student at school. I never really got a chance to find out how good I could be.

This looks like something of a diversion

Tutor:	You felt you didn't get a fair chance to prove yourself at school?

But the tutor risks exploring it anyway

Student:	Yes that's right. I mean, it may be that I'm really not very bright but I thought perhaps I could find some way of studying better. Is there a way, do you think?
Tutor:	Yes but actually your method of study sounds fairly reasonable to me.

Contextualizing

Student:	Really?
Tutor:	Yes – but perhaps I could make one or two suggestions that might help you.
Student:	Yes, please do.
Tutor:	Well, could I suggest for instance that instead of plunging straight in to the book you 'survey' it first. Just skim it – look at the chapter headings and try and get an idea of what it's about.

Continues for a little while

Student:	But you think that my basic method is sound if I just change it that way?
Tutor:	Yes I do – but try that change and see if it helps.
Student:	That's very reassuring. Thanks very much – I will try that.

Consequent action

Tutor: Let me know how you get on.
Consequent action

This dialogue is not meant to represent a particularly good example of advising, but to convey something of the flavour of one-to-one dialogue in non-academic student support.

Group face-to-face support: academic

Most face-to-face support is organized in groups for obvious cost-effective reasons. But aside from simple economic reasons, there is the enormous resource that bringing students together can offer for mutual support and overcoming isolation.

Such mutual support can really only happen if the tutor uses an eclectic mix of facilitative and didactic methods which allow students to interact with one another, share issues and problems, as well as exploit the tutor's knowledge. To give an example of what I mean, here are the notes that I made when observing a tutorial recently for appraisal purposes. The 'comments' were copied subsequently to the tutor.

Observation notes on tutor X

Room layout
My comments on the process are in italics

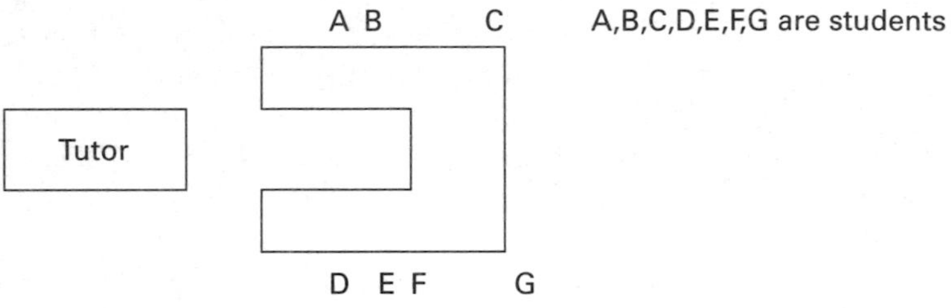

A B   C   A,B,C,D,E,F,G are students

Tutor

D E F   G

Figure 6.1   *Room layout for a tutorial*

7.00 pm   Formal tutorial start time – tutor and five students are present. Tutorials in ODL can seldom start on time as students may come directly from work.
Students are talking about where they've got to in the course. It is quite useful to have an informal activity for them while waiting to start.
7.10 pm   Two more students arrive and are greeted by name by the tutor.
You have obviously taken trouble to learn their names already – well done.

7.12 pm   The tutor announces that she is going to start and gives a brief tutorial overview of what she's hoping to cover. She asks a couple of questions to clarify the group's general understanding, to which only students A and F reply.

A clear start and signpost to the tutorial.

7.16 pm   The tutor gives out some work sheets and asks the students to work through them in pairs, telling them that they've got about 10 minutes. She leaves it up to the students to pair off, which they do as ABC/DE/FG, and start work.

This works well with AB, DE and FG working well together but because of the seating student C is rather isolated from A and B. I wonder if you could be a little more directive about moving students and furniture around!

7.25 pm   The students are still working on the sheet. The tutor is working on the sheet herself.

I wonder if you shouldn't be going round the pairs. Group FG in particular seem to be rather stuck. This is always a difficult one to call: too much interference and they never get a real chance to tackle the problem and use each other. Too little interference and they get unnecessarily stuck.

7.30 pm   The tutor calls the group back together and goes over the answers to the work sheet by a process of question and answer to each group.

You get a much better response to your questions this time – questions directed to a pair are much more likely to get an answer.

7.40 pm   The tutor gives a short presentation and a simple demonstration. There are some questions from the students.

Student B is looking anxious and seems to be having difficulties with these concepts.

7.55 pm   The tutor gives out a second work sheet and asks them to work again in pairs.

Student B is still concerned. Perhaps you should have used this opportunity to talk with her individually to see if you can help. Or alternatively match her with a student who seems to be well ahead and maybe getting rather bored with this topic. Perhaps your work sheet should have 'extension tasks' on it for students who are further ahead.

8.15 pm   The tutor runs over the work sheet in a similar way to before. She ends by asking for any general questions and then gives a brief outline of what she'll be covering next week.

8.30 pm   Although the tutorial has formally ended, students are still staying on talking informally about personal matters.

A good sign that the group is supportive to each other.

8.40 pm   One student wants to talk to the tutor about an individual matter.

Several issues may be worth noting from this observation:

Students come and go at different times in the tutorial and that can make life difficult for the tutor. On the other hand, the time could be used for individual consultations about progress.

Students can be at very different stages in their course. Students who are well ahead can be unintentionally intimidating for students who are behind. Such advanced students should be catered for – occasionally, of course, they can be used to help other students.

Tutor activities. If we look at the list of tutor activities from chapter 4 we can see that the tutor has only undertaken some of these:

- Explaining the course: she undertook some limited but useful didactic activity including demonstrations.
- Assessment: she gave the students some feedback on the work sheets, although not individually.
- Progress chasing: she did not do any realistic progress chasing. She might have used the time at the beginning of the tutorial to check with individual students where they had got to.
- Learning skills development: this was not addressed specifically except through the work sheets, and then not systematically.
- Exploring and enriching: not addressed at all, although this was perhaps rather early in the course anyway.

Of course, not all activities have to occur in every tutorial. However, given that this was an early tutorial it was a little disappointing that learning skills development was not more specifically featured. We shall have a look at ways the tutor might have done this in the next section.

Nevertheless, despite my reservations the tutor was clearly using a useful mix of didactic and facilitative methods, even if she could have been more actively facilitative than she was. While she encouraged small group activity between pairs of students, the rest of her work was very much tutor-focused – there was little interaction between the groups. On a science topic perhaps this is not so important, but if the topic had been in humanities or social science there would have been some cause for concern if she had not managed to widen the activity so that there was more student–student discussion.

Structure of the tutorial. The plan of this tutorial was quite straightforward:

- introduction in plenary session by tutor (5 minutes);
- cognitive activity in small groups (15 minutes);
- summation of activity by tutor in plenary (10 minutes);
- introduction to next activity by tutor in plenary (10 minutes);
- cognitive activity in small groups (20 minutes);

- summation and ending of tutorial by tutor (15 minutes);
- individual consultations (15 minutes).

Such a structure can be very flexible and easily adapted to students' needs as they emerge. It also conforms to the widely held view that the natural concentration span on any task is about 20 minutes, so it provides refreshing changes of pace.

Tutorial evaluation. My impression of this tutorial was that overall it was a success. The students appeared to gain an understanding from it. They had reasonable opportunity for interaction with one another in an appropriate framework, and several chances to clear up problems and queries both in groups and on a one-to-one basis. However, at this (early) stage of the course there should perhaps also have been an opportunity to address affective and organizational development as well as cognitive development – see the next section and chapter 11.

Group face-to-face support: non-academic

There are immense advantages in using face-to-face groups to address non-academic issues in student support. Face-to-face interaction offers the easiest interchange between students. It enables them to contextualize their queries and problems by sharing them and to explore methods of overcoming problems. Feelings can be more clearly expressed and received, as all the usual visual and aural cues are present.

Nevertheless, such interchange is not always straightforward. Sharing of feelings and opinions can threaten less assertive or self-confident students, and tutors will need some skill to ensure that activities go well. They will need to use advising skills as outlined in chapter 3 – warmth, empathy, acceptance and listening skills rather than the tutor skills of explication and presentation – and it may need a conscious effort to switch between those styles.

A tutor will also need skills in encouraging and developing group discussion and dealing with the problems that can arise in discussion. The kinds of topics that are appropriate in non-academic discussion will be how students feel about starting study, how they organize their time, and developing exam stress management ideas. We shall look at a more detailed programme of activities in chapter 11. In the meantime, there are some general issues about group discussion that are relevant to face-to-face support for both academic and non-academic groups.

Group face-to face support: methods and problems

Methods

Many tutors will have had the dispiriting experience of trying to get a discussion going in a group. Simply addressing a question to the group often leaves it hanging in the air, with only sporadic and individual attempts to respond from students, and usually directly to the tutor.

There are various simple ways of getting discussion started, however:

Snowballing or pyramiding

Set students a task of some kind, either on their own or in groups of two, and allow them two or three minutes to work on the task. Then ask them to get together with another person or pair to discuss the results of their task for another five minutes or so. Then after a few more minutes combine the twos or fours into fours or into the plenary group to report back, taking as long as seems useful.

This is possibly the most useful group method. It is easily adaptable for practically any topic and size of group. It encourages even the most reluctant students to participate as they do not have to face the whole group until they have had experience of expressing themselves to one or two others. It can, however, easily be overused and become a little predictable.

To snowball well the tutor should be able to:

- choose suitable topics and ensure that students have a clear idea of what they are trying to do;
- be sensitive to the level of noise so that he or she knows when to move on to the next level of discussion;
- use the plenary session to bring out general lessons, focus discussion on relevant topics, give appropriate information and advice, and explore further – and know when to stop!

Brainstorming

Set the group a problem and ask them to suggest solutions, but do not allow any discussion of the solutions until they seem to have run out of further ideas. Then group the ideas if possible and discuss them in the plenary session.

Brainstorming can be a useful change from snowballing, and be a quick and light-hearted method of introducing a change of pace into a session. However, the range of problems that can be tackled this way is limited, it only works with a well-established group, and it is not usually an effective way of generating discussion that is more prolonged.

Concept cards or hot-seating

Individual volunteers talk for a few minutes to the whole group about particular concepts or topics, possibly drawn from a selection generated by students and placed as slips in a hat.

Games

Games can be a very powerful method for group work but can require much preparation. Possibly the simplest examples are best – straightforward quizzes run between teams are a good example.

Role plays or simulations

These are a useful variation on the games theme, where students are invited to play appropriate roles: for example, to be a tutor marking an assignment and giving feedback.

Of all these methods, snowballing is the simplest to use and most adaptable. We shall see it in action in chapter 11 on learning skills development.

Problems

Although group support is a powerful weapon in the student support arsenal, it is not without its problems:

1. The domineering or over-participative student: if someone is talking too much to the detriment of group dynamics then the tutor will need to take charge gently but firmly. They will need to say something like, 'That's very interesting – can we hear from someone else on this topic?'
2. The silent or non-participating student: such students can often be encouraged to speak by catching their eye and smiling encouragement. Another way is to go round the group asking each person for a short contribution on the topic. Nevertheless, tutors should avoid picking on individuals for non-participation: their right to silence must be respected if they are happy with it.
3. Silences: periods of silence may be indications that people have run out of things to say, or indications that they are silently formulating their next response. Experienced group leaders will have a feel for which is which and will let silences last appropriately.
4. Irrelevancies: opinions will differ on what is relevant to the discussion. However, students who have invested time and energy in coming to sessions will not thank tutors for allowing the focus to go too fuzzy too often.
5. Directing everything to the tutor: this is a particularly common problem, putting the tutor in the role of having to respond to each student in turn. If students insist on addressing themselves to the tutor exclusively, then one method that usually seems to work is for the tutor to look round at other people in the group instead of at the speaker. The speaker's eyes will tend to follow the tutor's, and he or she will end up addressing the other students directly, who will probably respond directly in turn.

Chapter 7

Delivering student support by computer

The advent of relatively cheap desktop computers has revolutionized ODL in much the same way as the 'Penny Post' made correspondence education a reality. Education programs are now available internationally on the Internet, so ODL institutions can compete across the world and indeed with other organizations such as commercial entities who are well placed to offer courses. It is expected that the prices of equipment and Internet access will fall, that faster and easier broadband connections will become available so that the growth in computer access and use in ODL will continue at an ever-increasing rate.

However, the parallels with early correspondence education are still close. Just as early correspondence courses made no allowance for student support and assumed that supplying materials to students was enough to generate learning, so early attempts at education on the Internet assumed that it was enough to set up an attractive Web site for learning to take place. 'In the corporate training world at least e-learning was originally conceived as a cost saver; a way of substantially reducing delivery costs. Learners saved on travel time and expenses and employers could cut back on training centres and trainers' (Shepherd, 2001). Costs indeed could be reduced – depending on student numbers, a typical e-learning package might cost as little as about £2 (US$3, 3.5 euros) per person compared with a cost of anything up to £500 (US$750, 800 euros) for a day of face-to-face training.

But it soon became clear that e-students need support just as much as conventional students, both from tutors and other students. 'Without the purposeful formation of an online learning community in distance learning, we are doing nothing new and different' (Palloff and Pratt, 1999).

Finally it appears that even in a training context learners and their managers prefer e-courses with support. In a relatively recent survey nearly 90 per cent of learners and managers wanted a tutor assigned to their course, and more than 60 per cent were more likely to select a course with a tutor involved (Masie Center, 2000).

Other trends are becoming visible: the decision by the Massachusetts Institute of Technology to place its course materials on open access online may mean that the emphasis in e-learning will move from materials to student support, assessment and accreditation.

Issues

However, there are a umber of important issues connected with the use of computers in ODL such as access, quality and effectiveness.

Access

The issue of access is a particularly important one in open and distance learning. The current (2001) cost of a networked PC in the UK can be up to £1200 (US$1800, 1900 euros). People who are thinking of study are having to invest a considerable capital sum before they are fully committed to their course. Neither are online costs negligible: a student online for only five hours a week for a 30-week course will still be spending (in the UK) up to £150 (US$220, 250 euros) in call charges. Clearly, this militates against educationally disadvantaged students being able to enter ODL systems even if there are loan systems. This is a particular problem for open learning institutions: currently (2001) in the UK the percentage of potential students in the lowest socio-economic groups who have never used the Internet is 83 per cent. There are counters to this problem, none entirely satisfactory:

Falling costs

Some of the arguments for introducing computing into ODL have centred on the promise of falling costs. In fact, although the cost of individual elements of the hardware has fallen, computers have been produced to ever-higher specifications and ODL providers have been unable to resist raising the specification that is required of students to join. Therefore, costs to the student have not fallen greatly yet. Further falls are predicted but they may remain elusive.

Access via institutions and other providers

There is certainly far wider access now, both in ODL institutions themselves and other providers such as libraries. Such access is always time-limited and can be unsatisfactory. It seems that in order to take full advantage of computers they need to be available for longer than most schemes permit, and students need to be even better organized than their counterparts with direct access. Some institutions have loan schemes particularly for financially disadvantaged, remote or housebound students. However, these schemes are expensive as computers do not have a long life or high resale value and must be written off quite early in the loan cycle.

Alternatives to computers

Investigation is continuing on the use of much cheaper alternatives to fully networked computers. There are experiments on sending the Internet into homes via new transmission lines direct to television sets, and experiments are underway with interactive television, although it is hard to see that it will be easy to study this way without the addition of some kind of keyboard, printer and other facilities.

Quality

There has been criticism of purely Web-based delivery systems that have sometimes been of poor quality, since anyone can set up a site with no quality control mechanisms. In the United States where online technology is most widespread, the first wave of enthusiasm for online teaching may already have crested and there are calls for institutions to retain a mixture of delivery systems (Daniel, 1999).

Effectiveness

There are still queries hanging over the use of computers, particularly for non-academic support, in much the same way as there are reservations about the use of the phone. It is suggested that certain types of computer support – for example diagnostic activities such as computer assisted vocational guidance – may not need face-to-face mediation in order to be effective, but research needs to be undertaken to establish how far this is true (Tait, 1999).

We shall come back to these issues when we look at how students use computing in practice.

E-learning

It is characteristic of e-learning courses that they are often mixed mode. For example, the course material may be entirely online but equally may be in the form of some online material together with a CD ROM, a correspondence package or a book. This is because reading off a screen is tiring and inflexible and download-ing and printing material is costly. Sending students a correspondence package or a book saves them time and money. And a book is still a cheaper and more flexible medium for study than any computer. A CD ROM can be a useful compromise as it is cheap, interactive and avoids the cost of having to be online for long periods.

Similarly the support element of an online course may be a mix of media – Web based, phone, correspondence, CD ROM, even a face-to-face meeting, especially at initial stages, as well as e-mail and conferencing. For example, in the early stages of a course a student might phone a tutor to be talked through some particular problem; a student might need a correspondence package or CD ROM to describe how to get started on computer conferencing; and some high population courses might justify a face-to-face meeting – they are certainly very popular if feasible.

In addition, there are ways of using computers in student support, although the distinctions between them are sometimes blurred. Essentially these are e-mail, the Internet and CD ROM. See Computer conferencing in student support (chapter 8).

One-to-one e-mail in student support

E-mails are electronic messages that can be sent from one networked computer to another networked computer. Messages can carry attachments that may be electronic documents, clips of videotape and audiotape and Web pages. Although there are a number of different e-mail systems, they are now mostly compatible although attachments may not be.

In some ways, one-to-one e-mail correspondence rather resembles the one-to-one written correspondence referred to in chapter 5. However, closer examination suggests some differences.

First, e-mail can be much quicker. However, although transmission can be within minutes, even from one computer to another, the messages do not effectively arrive until they are read. Dialogues are therefore asynchronous and can be quite slow. There is a considerable difference here between people working on a full-time basis with computers who leave their machines permanently networked and can exchange messages within minutes and those (typically students and part-time tutors) who are working from home, have to pay for connections and therefore only log on occasionally, perhaps only two or three times a week. There is the facility for chat: when two people are logged on simultaneously they can choose a synchronous dialogue where messages are exchanged as though notes were being passed across a room.

Second, the communication conventions of e-mail are different. Whether it is the speed of communication or the ease with which e-mail can be sent by one click of a mouse button, it seems to attract a different choice of language. The vocabulary of e-mail tends to be brief and informal. People seldom re-read or spell-check it and it is very easy to reply to messages without taking the longer consideration needed for a letter. Exchanges can become quite rude and result in 'flamers' – particularly hostile comments sent without prior thought. In particularly bad cases, this can lead to an increasingly abusive dialogue – the 'flaming spiral'. This is presumably because although e-mail appears to mimic phone conversation in some ways, even the voice cues of phone conversations are missing as well as the body language cues.

Third, 'netiquette'. A whole range of conventions has grown up to overcome the problems of communicating electronically – 'netiquette'. Typical conventions are: 1) using acknowledgements – since there is no visible evidence such as a smile or nod of a head that particular contributions have been read it is important not to ignore contributions – 'thanks for your comment Sue' and 'I agree with Bob's contribution'; 2) not being dogmatic but expressing views as personal – the abbreviation IMHO, 'In My Humble Opinion', is sometimes used to indicate this; 3) not using all upper case letters WHICH CAN FEEL LIKE BEING SHOUTED AT; 4) making it clear when you are joking or being ironic: 'smileys' or 'emoticons' are sometimes used for this purpose :-) or 8-) or :-((view them from the side) or simply interpolating (!) or <g> for grin or <joke>.

Fourth, e-mail can be sent to a group of people as easily as to one person. Once one has a list of e-mail addresses, it takes no longer to send an e-mail to everyone on that list than it does to one person. This has substantial implications: tutors can communicate with all their students as easily as with one. On the other hand it also means that it is possible to be on the receiving end of large quantities of mail that are irrelevant to the reader: 'junk e-mail' or 'spam'.

Using one-to-one e-mail

An analysis of one-to-one e-mail suggests that it is used in different ways. For academic support, most traffic is addressed to the tutor rather than to other students. However, there seems to be a tendency once some kind of rapport has been established for students to use the phone as more immediate – particularly where tutors are offline and only log on every two or three days.

For non-academic support, a high proportion of traffic is between students and appears to be to do with reassurance – where students have reached in a course and stress management – and sharing of experiences. Thus, e-mail is used very much to break down the isolation of the distance learners rather than for academic discourse (Blanchfield, Patrick and Simpson, 1999).

Student support and e-mail: group e-mails

The impact of e-mail on the student support sections of an ODL institution will be considerable.

Receiving e-mail. Institutions will need to ensure that they have systems in place to deal with incoming e-mail quickly, re-routing it as necessary. The nature of the medium is that students will expect speedy answers even if they themselves only log on infrequently. It may well be worthwhile having an automatic reply system which acknowledges receipt of e-mail, giving some idea of how long it might take to give a reply. Replies themselves will not be so very different from the ways that ordinary correspondence is used (chapter 5): e-mails will need to acknowledge and clarify the issue, unpacking more complex queries carefully. One helpful aspect of e-mail is the way that a reply can easily include the original e-mail text broken up into its different sections, each section followed by a separate response.

Institutions will need to be careful about the size of their replies, as large messages can overwhelm a student's mailbox and cause it to crash or load up very slowly. So it will be important to avoid the temptation to use an institutional logo in the reply or attach large documents (which the student's system may not be able to read anyway). If attachments are needed then they could be in the form of Web site addresses (URLs) which can be checked to bring up the text from the institution's Web site. For example, a reply to a student who has fallen behind might contain a URL which takes him or her to a site with a text on strategic learning and catching up (chapter 5).

Using e-mail proactively: group e-mails

From the institution's point of view e-mail is a very cheap communication method with groups of students. Write the text, paste a list of students' e-mail addresses into the 'To' box, press 'Send' and away it goes. Nothing is quite that easy of course: unless the e-mail addresses are largely correct error messages may bounce back swamping the system, too many e-mails may be viewed as 'spam' or rubbish by students, and there's no guarantee that e-mails will be picked up within a given time scale or at all.

Nevertheless, there are distinct possibilities for using e-mail for a proactive support system of 'motivational communication' (Visser, 1998). This relies on the thesis that short, relevant, and above all timely messages sent to students can have an effect on their progress.

For example, as an experiment in the UK OU in 2000 a short text was e-mailed to several hundred new students about 10 days before their first assignment was due. The text was a simple series of points:

Dear Student
　Your first assignment!
　Your first assignment is due shortly – if you've already sent it please ignore this e-mail.
　If you're still working on it we hope it's going well. Here are a few points that we hope will be helpful.

- Are you stuck and not sure how to start? The most difficult part of writing an assignment is that first sentence – get that down and the rest will follow. But if stuck contact us – we'll be pleased to help.
- Are you unsure what the question is asking for? Contact us and we'll be happy to clarify it for you.
- Are you running out of time? It'll be OK if you need a few more days but let us know if you're going to be late.
- Are you not going to be able to complete it fully? Send it in just the same – a part assignment is much better than none and will still help you towards passing the course.
- Any other questions or problems? Get in touch with us.

From OU Study Support

The submission rate among students who were contacted was 3 per cent better than non-contacted students, a small but significantly cost-effective improvement from the institution's perspective.

Internet support

Clearly there is a great deal of interest and effort going into the provision of student support on the Internet. As ever, the attractions of the Internet for the institution are obvious; the cheapness, immediacy and the attractions to students may be less so. The requirement of logging on, paying a phone connection, navigating to a site and printing out study support materials at your own expense compared with the same materials arriving neatly bound through your letterbox make the attractions of the Internet not so obvious.

Nevertheless, every ODL institution will need to supply its wares via the Internet if it is to compete in the international marketplace. There seem to be two particular uses for the Internet in student support: supplying information of various kinds, and offering interactive and diagnostic programs.

Designing a student support Web site

The design of a student support Web site could be a costly and complex affair, but probably starts with two central questions: what is the Web good at, and what is the student's perspective?

What the Web does best

It can provide up-to-date specific information, the possibility of interactivity and a way of connecting people. It can offer ways of developing relatively self-contained specific skills such as (say) writing references for a report. What it is not so good at is providing more discursive, less well-defined and complex responses to students' needs or ways of developing more generic skills such as writing the academic report in the first place.

The student's perspective

My guess is that students approach the Web most often with a problem-centred perspective rather than a developmental one. In other words they are more likely to enter a Web site with the query, 'Why didn't I do very well on that last assign-ment'? than the presumption, 'I need help on academic report-writing skills', even if the latter is in reality the answer to the former. A student-centred Web site would take the student from the question as simply as possible to what we hope is the right response. But at the same time the site will allow the student to interact in some way, such as doing a diagnostic activity in order to clarify the issue, connect to the institution itself with clear links to other sources of help, and finally to other students with similar issues. This is a tall order, and an ideal student support Web site of this kind may be a distant prospect.

A simple Web site for student support

This is the draft structure for a simple Web site for student support in a distance education institution. It is certainly not an example of best practice, but an example of an institution that is trying to start from the students' perspectives.

The home page is largely free of pictures or 'shock-wave' animations and so on which make it slow to load over a modem. It has four main sections – too many options are confusing. The sections are:

● assessment: leading to assignments and exams;
● courses: leading to course choice materials;
● tutorials: leading to tutors and timetables;
● admin: leading to Fees and Registration.

Each sub-section opens with a list of frequently asked questions (FAQs) about the topic. In some cases the answer leads on to a slightly more detailed text which can be downloaded to read at leisure. For example on the assignment page there is an FAQ about what to do if an assignment is behind schedule. Clicking on the simple answer leads to a text which offers more detailed advice on strategic learning and time management, including an interactive time management exercise. Yet another button will take students to a more advanced series of texts on various aspects of learning skills: writing, numeracy and so on.

On every page there is a home button and a 'contact us' button which allows the user to send an e-mail to the appropriate address in the institution. There is also a 'search' button which enables the user to search on particular words or phrases. Finally there's a 'chat' button which takes users to a chatroom where they can interact with other students who have similar concerns.

Other areas on the Web site take users to their own 'home page' which contains their personal details (which they can update at any time), and an assignment management page with a simple piece of software that tells them what is due and when, and what they still have to do to pass the course.

Searching for a Web site that might fulfil some of these requirements, I could find many that gave helpful and apposite advice, but there were few that felt immediately useful. Among the more straightforward were:

- the University of Waterloo, Canada 'Study Skills package' which covers issues like time management, listening and note-taking skills (www.adm.uwaterloo.ca/infocs/study/studyindex);
- the University of St Thomas, Minnesota 'Study Guides and Strategies' site which also covers learner self-assessment tools (www.iss.sthomas.edu/studyguides/index);
- a UK site aimed at Year 11 students so it has a lot of flash animations (www.knowitall.org.uk).

More specialized learning sites which might be of interest are:

- accelerated learning (www.alite.co.uk);
- Herman Braun Dominance Profile (www.hbdi.com);
- new approaches to learning (www.newhorizons.org);
- memory maps (www.modellearning.com);
- whole-mind reading (www.learningstrategies.com).

A short search on cognitive skills such as numeracy, or organizational skills such as time management, or affective skills such as stress management, would have revealed similar sites. But these searches also indicate one of the issues about such materials, which is how searchers assess their quality and how they choose which to use.

Finally as an experiment, recently I surfed my own institution's site to see what I should do about an overdue assignment. Putting late assignment, overdue dates and several other terms into the search engine all received the same reply: 'Your search found no matches'. These must be teething difficulties . . .

This is a site aimed at new UK OU students who may need support with their writing skills. It is called *The Effective Use of English* and the home page is shown in Figure 7.1.

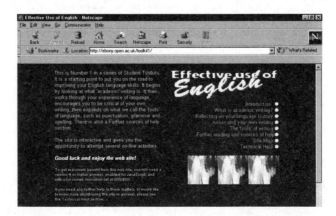

Figure 7.1 *Home page for The Effective Use of English*

Clicking on any of the buttons on the right will lead to that page. For example *Reflecting on your language history* leads eventually to the activity shown in Figure 7.2.

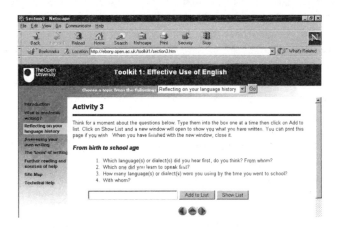

Figure 7.2 *Reflecting on your language history*

It continues through the equivalent of some 40 pages of text.

While they are attractive, it is yet to be established if such materials are effective, especially when downloaded and printed, which is how most students are likely to use them.

Student support on CD ROM and floppy disc

In theory, many things that can be done on the Net can also be done by sending CD ROMs or (unusually these days) a floppy disc to students.

CD ROMs are cheap to produce (about the same as an audiotape) and to mail. They do not require students to have Internet connections and bear the cost of those connections. They can record hypertext links to Web sites but once they are mailed they cannot be easily updated except by sending a replacement disc.

Thus, CD ROMs tend not to be used for student support information as they quickly become out of date. However, because of the ease of access they are quite often used for other purposes such as diagnostic programs. There are a number of examples.

Diagnostic computer programs for student support

A variety of diagnostic programs has been developed for various purposes, not necessarily in ODL but they may well have ODL uses. They all work in the same way: the user is presented with a series of statements or questions to compare or answer. At the end of the series the user's answers are processed and various options or analyses are fed back to the user. Here are a couple of examples.

Computer Assisted Vocational Guidance (CAVG). There have been various careers advisory programmes around for more than 20 years: CASCAID (Computer Assisted Careers Aid), Gradscope and JIIG–CAL (Job Ideas and Information Generator, Computer Assisted Learning). Taking the latter program as an example, users are taken through a series of questions which ask them to compare how much they would like various activities in a job. The activities are always in pairs; for example, 'Would you like a job where you:

1. help unemployed people find jobs or;
2. do calculations for designing bridges or;
3. produce new designs for a toy manufacturer; or
4. manage a branch of a bank.

This continues for about 60 pairs of comparisons. This produces analyses of the users' preferences for six occupational interest types, ranging from practical work, working with living things, office work, art and crafts, special needs and speaking and writing. The program then takes the user through a range of job factor questions ranging through preference for place – indoors, outdoors, in one place, in several places, abroad – through hours, activity, people and risk for some eleven questions.

At the end of this process the program will produce a series of job suggestions for the user in order. This is a typical list:

- journalist;
- air traffic controller;
- writer;
- social worker;
- careers adviser;
- lecturer;
- tour guide;
- probation officer;
- lawyer;
- minister of religion.

It gives some further information about each. (I will confess straight away that the selection above is mine and raises many doubts in my mind as to my qualifications for doing my current job . . .)

StudyScan® is another example of one of many computer-assisted diagnostic programs. This is designed principally to identify dyslexia. It comes in two forms. First, StudyScan is a full battery of tests of various skills such as memory, literary attainment, numeracy, cognitive skills, reading and writing speed that can lead to a diagnosis of dyslexia. It needs the presence of a supervisor for certain parts and can take a couple of hours. Second, Quick Scan – which is of more interest for the purpose of this book – is a short (10–20 minutes) questionnaire designed for a computer network. Its stated purpose is to help users who want to know more about how they learn, and give them an outline of their individual learning preferences and study style.

Although StudyScan was originally developed as a tool for diagnosing dyslexia it may have implications in other areas.

Advice to new students. If it can be shown that there are links between learning styles and success in studying in ODL, then it may be possible to offer new students realistic individual advice on adapting to learning in ODL.

Building self-confidence. It has already been suggested that for new students to be told that they are any kind of learner at all is a confidence-building statement. To be told that by a computer program even appears to add authority to the statement. Even CAVG appears to have a similar effect. I remember talking to an elderly lady who had taken a computer assisted careers diagnostic program. 'It was a splendid experience to know what I might have been had things been different,' she told me, clearly re-motivated by the experience.

Of course, there are several issues in using computer diagnostic programs in student support.

- *Validation.* Computer assisted vocational guidance programs have been around for a number of years and they are validated by much experience in their use. Other more recent programs, although assessed, have yet to be validated through experience in that way. For example, although StudyScan may be useful for diagnosing dyslexia it is not clear yet that the learning styles analysis is reliable and valid.
- *Mediation.* There is a substantial school of thought that insists that programs can only be a tool to assist advisers who mediate results to users, preferably in face-to-face sessions. Indeed licensing arrangements used to specify that such sessions must occur. As programs grow more sophisticated it may become more possible to see them as stand-alone tools and establish if human mediation is essential to derive any benefit from them.
- *User behaviour.* If programs are reasonably valid then the question of how they affect users' behaviour is central. Will telling users that they are 'kinaesthetic learners' or that they need to develop further kinds of learning skill actually alter their behaviour? Alternatively, does there have to be some kind of human interaction in order to make computer diagnostic activities effective?
- *Costs.* As suggested earlier, once development costs are authorized the cost of such programs to the institution is small.
- *Future developments.* If diagnostic programs are effective then there are a number of obvious important uses. Particularly in open learning, the issue of offering potential students diagnostic feedback as to their level of preparedness for a course becomes increasingly important (if only for litigation reasons). Programs can be developed for numeracy and reading skills.

Computers in student support: the future

We shall look in more detail in chapter 9 at which media students prefer for support and why. As far as computers are concerned, there has been a tendency to see the growth of networked computing as the answer to all student support problems. However, nothing is that straightforward. Even before issues of access, there are many other issues to illuminate. The difficulties that students experience in using the Web have been pointed out (Laurillard, 1993), and we shall see that computer conferencing may be among the least popular media of student support.

Ultimately it will be necessary to test all new developments in this field, as in others, against the questions, 'What will this do for students?', 'Will it help them develop useful learning skills?' and 'Will it help them overcome isolation?'

As Daniel (1998) writes:

Success rests on four pillars:

One: high quality, multiple media learning materials, preferably developed by teams of academics and experts;

Two: personal support to each student from a living, breathing human being who knows the student's name and aspirations;

Three: efficient logistics and administration. If you can't get the right material, information and people in the right place at the right time forget it, because the students will.

Four: as I've already mentioned, teaching rooted in research. It sounds like an optional extra but it's not. It makes the courses intellectually active, which is an important way to be active in a university.

In Daniel's scenario, new technology is important but needs to be treated sceptically:

Forget about the magic medium that will be the total answer to teaching and learning. If you're serious about enhancing access remember that students can't engage in advanced technology-based learning unless they have the advanced technology. Don't believe everything you read in the papers about everyone now being online and wanting to live most of their lives two feet from a computer screen.

Remember that students must want to use the technology. Does it allow them to do exciting new things or is it just a complicated and inconvenient new way of presenting the same old content?

Chapter 8

Computer conferencing in student support: online tuition and support

Computer conferencing differs from e-mail in a number of ways, but essentially an e-mail sent to a computer conference can be seen by anyone in the conference who in turn can respond with a message and so on. The analogy is of a face-to-face tutorial where individuals can contribute in turn and be heard by the whole group.

Ordinary e-mails can be used for addressing groups of people using a list of e-mail addresses in the 'To' box and with receivers using their 'Reply all' facility. The important difference is that conferences allow for the ability to 'thread' or 'string': that is, follow a particular topic through other topics. A conference can have several threads running at the same time from which participants can choose, or it can move in a more orderly way from one thread to another. This is similar to the way a face-to-face group may divide into two or three smaller groups simultaneously discussing different aspects of a topic (with people moving from one group to another) or discuss topics in plenary session one after the other.

In addition it is possible to set up sub-conferences within a conference to discuss different topics, rather as if a face-to-face group split into groups in different rooms to discuss different issues while the original discussion continued. The sub-conferences of course can divide up into threads as well.

If this begins to sound confusing then it's because it is. One of the biggest reasons for computer conferences failing is because participants get lost in a maze of threads and sub-conferences (and sometimes sub-sub-conferences). We'll come back to this when looking at how to structure conferences.

Conferencing software

Conferences can be run directly on the Net by using a Web-based system: there are many different ones available such as WebCT. Although relatively easy to access and use they can be limited in various ways, so specialized conferencing software such as FirstClass® by Software has been produced. Some of the advantages of such software might be more facilities (such as 'Chat': see later) and user-friendly graphical interfaces. The most recent edition of FirstClass offers audio facilities which can be accessed from an ordinary phone. This may allow some kind of voicemail conferencing – see chapter 5. In addition FirstClass allows students to work offline, an advantage where there are online phone costs or the family phone is tied up when online..

These facilities have to be paid for in the increased complexity of having to acquire the software either from a CD ROM or by downloading from the Internet, and the time taken to become familiar with how it works. There is a Web version of FirstClass which needs no software, but this has the disadvantage that different users are seeing different things on their PC screen, which may be very confusing when looking for items or trying to give help at a distance. To give a better idea of how different systems look and how they compare, here are two contrasting examples.

Supporting students online: a Web-based conference

This was a conference set up on this book, so it is an example of an online conference supporting a hard-copy text. (It experienced a problem typical of such conferences in that it was presented around the time the first print-run was sold out, so some participants had difficulty getting the book before the course started.) After logging on the participant is offered a series of sub-conferences on different chapters with various sub-conferences.

Clicking on one of these sub-conferences brings up the entries in the conference so far (Figure 8.2) and clicking on the entry brings it up. See the example in 'The e-tutor at work', later in this chapter (Figure 8.1).

The 'Course Choice Fair': an example of the FirstClass system

This time when a user logs on, he or she is presented with a 'desktop' containing a number of icons (Figure 8.3). Each icon leads to a conference or a set of sub-conferences.

In this case clicking on 'Course Choice Fair' brings up a set of sub-conferences which are devoted to students discussing their possible future courses (Figure 8.4). There are various topics in this conference (the codes are for different courses) and the 'threads' or 'strings' are represented by Re(2)xxx, Re(3)xxx and so on, depending on which contribution the sender last referred to.

Clicking on any name opens the message from that contributor. Here's a brief sample: some students are discussing a 'Modern Art' course.

Address	http://......				
WebCT	WEBCT I RESUME COURSE I COURSE MAP I HELP				
Hide navigation Expand content	**Delivering Student Support Online** Home I Discussion Board				
Course Menu Homepage Discussion WebCT mail Resources Participant Profiles About Sean	**Select a topic to see its messages**	Compose Message			
		Search			
		Topic	**Unread**	**Total**	**Status**
		All	1108	1243	
		1. Class Introductions	329	329	public
		2. Chapter One	198	198	public
		3. Chapter Two	88	88	public
		4. Chapter Twelve	125	138	public
		5. Chapter Thirteen	58	60	public
		6. Chapter Three	25	25	public
		7. Chapter Four	29	29	public
		8. Chapter Five	6	15	public
		9. Chapter Six	6	11	public
		10. Chapter 8	7	10	public
		11. Chapter Eight	9	9	public
		12. Chapter Nine	7	7	public
		13. Chapter Ten	7	11	public
		14. Chapter Eleven	9	9	public
		15. Chapter Fourteen	1	7	public
		Conversations with O. Simpson	3	38	public

Figure 8.1 *The home page of a Web-based conference (adapted schematic representation)*

Address	http://......	
WebCT	WEBCT I RESUME COURSE I COURSE MAP I HELP	
Hide navigation Expand content	**Delivering Student Support Online** Home I Discussion Board I Chapter 6	
Course Menu Homepage Discussion WebCT mail Resources Participant Profiles About Sean	**Discussion Messages 9 Chapter 6**	Compose Message
		Search | Mark as read | Update listing

		Electronic support
		
		☐734 Sean Chamberlin Jul 8 18.50 NEW
		 ☐970 Kay Patterson Jul 11 13.01 NEW
		  ☐1115 Andra Dorlac Jul 15 12.19
		   ☐1137 Kathie Wentworth Jul 16 07.17 NEW
		  ☐1189 Kathie Wentworth Jul 16 06.45
		   ☐1132 Maureen Connely Jul 18 11.00
		    ☐1237 Patsy KrechJul 20 12.29 NEW
		     ☐ 1242 Anita Crawley Jul 21 19.31 NEW
		    ☐1263 Sean Chamberlin Jul 25 16.42
		   ☐1301 Ormond Simpson Jul 27 14.31
		    ☐1341 Maureen Conneley Jul 29 12.01 NEW

Figure 8.2 *The next page of the conference (adapted schematic representation)*

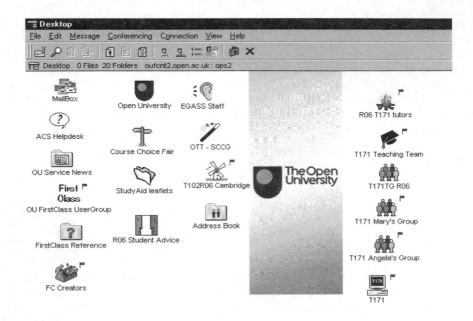

Figure 8.3   *A typical FirstClass 'desktop'*

Name	Size	Subject	Last Modified
Andrew Moran,oufcnt1.open.ac.uk	2K	Any info on A354	13/11/99 00:00
Cilla Surcouf	3K	Re(4): A425	11/11/99 04:22
Angela Harris	3K	Re(3): A425	08/11/99 20:39
Cilla Surcouf	2K	Re(5): A425	04/11/99 15:30
Stephen Neville	2K	Re(4): A425	04/11/99 11:07
Cilla Surcouf	2K	Re(3): A425	04/11/99 10:40
Jackie Doubtfire	3K	Re(3): A425	04/11/99 09:24
June Horne,oufcnt1.open.ac.uk	3K	Re(2): A425	03/11/99 20:24
Angela Harris	2K	Re(3): A425	22/09/99 20:31
Cilla Surcouf	2K	Re(2): A425	19/09/99 13:02
Angela Harris	2K	Re: A425	19/09/99 09:26
Cilla Surcouf	2K	A425	17/09/99 05:47
Justin Harris	2K	Re: A429 what's going on?	09/11/99 11:17
Esther L. Trussell	2K	A429 what's going on?	07/11/99 19:47
Clive Beasor,oufcnt1.open.ac.uk	2K	Re: A220	08/11/99 00:01
Natalie West,oufcnt1.open.ac.uk	2K	A220	14/09/99 00:00
Cilla Surcouf	2K	Re(2): A211- Philosophy	02/11/99 20:11
Mark Earls,oufcnt1.open.ac.uk	2K	Re: A211- Philosophy	02/11/99 13:16
Cilla Surcouf	2K	A211- Philosophy	02/11/99 06:47

Figure 8.4   *A typical FirstClass conference listing*

String 1: about course 'Modern Art'

Message 1
Hi,
Can anyone give me information on the length of essays required for Modern Art? I have done mostly science courses but also a couple of history courses that have required essays of up to 2000 words which I have managed with ease. I'm very interested in modern art and would like to jump straight into this higher level course. Is this wise? It would be my last course before graduating.
Thanks
Brenda

Message 2
Hi Brenda
There are eight essays of 2000 words each. Since it will be your last course, I recommend that you go for it. It's tough – I know because I have done it this year. The only preparation I had was the art bit of the Arts Foundation course. I enjoyed it so much that I have registered for two art history courses next year! It would be a good idea to try to read some Foundation material for preparation. If you do go for it, I wish you the best of luck. Feel free to pick my brains during the course, if you like.
Regards
Stephanie.

Message 3
Thanks Stephanie
I have decided to go ahead with Modern Art next year.
I tried buying the art history unit from the Foundation Course but unfortunately they are now out of production. I am reading as much as possible about Impressionism from the recommended book list. If you have any other suggestions I would be grateful.
Regards Brenda.

Message 4
Can I loan you mine for a year?
Cilla

Message 5
Hi Cilla,
It's very kind of you to offer the loan of the Art History Unit. I will email you my address, and will gladly refund postage.
Regards Brenda.

This short excerpt may give a feel for some of the characteristics of computer conferencing including its informality – these students have not met before but they have immediately adopted first names and informal modes of address ('Hi . . . !') – and the fact that messages raising particular queries tend to be picked up by one or two respondents and a brief 'string' of interchanges occurs before the topic is dropped. Other strings can proceed concurrently like conversations at a party, the difference being that all conference conversations are recorded from the start of the party and can be replayed by new arrivals.

The choice in the end between Web-based and specialized software for conferencing may depend on the size of the conference – an easily accessed Web-based system may well be preferable for short one-off courses where it is important to get up and running quickly. Where a longer course is running which might spawn many threads and sub-conferences then it will be important to have a structure that keeps things as clear as possible and a specialized conferencing software package may be important.

Different types of student support conferencing

Once a conferencing system exists, it is very easy to set up sub-conferences and they can proliferate. Within the UK OU system, for example, there are several thousand conferences although not all these will be very active. It is difficult to classify conferences, indeed the system can be quite anarchic. One tentative classification is into actively moderated conferences which are quite closely controlled by an adviser or tutor and non-moderated conferences where there is little or no institutional input. (In fact, all conferences have to have some element of survey to prevent abuse of the system.) Thus, there are four types of conference:

- non-academic support: non-moderated;
- academic support: non-moderated;
- non-academic support: moderated;
- academic support: moderated.

Non-academic support – non-moderated

In the UK OU's FirstClass set-up there is a large range of conferences that on first sight have little to do with study. They are run by the Students' Association and appear under an icon called 'Common Room'. This icon leads to yet another subset of about 20 topics: Books, Holidays, Sports and Lifestyle, each of which leads to a further 20 or so actual conferences such as (from Lifestyle) Women's Issues, Parenting, Hearing Impaired, Health, Ethics, Beliefs and Ageing Rockers. They range from the relatively serious – Parenting contains a discussion about the problems of studying whilst being a single parent – to the entirely frivolous – Beliefs (despite its name) seems to be mostly about the BBC children's television programme *Teletubbies*.

These conferences seem to be used for conversations that appear to have the primary aim of overcoming isolation. They certainly mimic the conversations one might hear in any student bar or Union and perhaps that is reason enough for having them.

Academic support: non-moderated

As well as the 'Common Room', the Students Association runs a range of specific course conferences. Here discussion is clearly much more focused, although a considerable number of contributions are still in the affective area ('Is anyone else out there as worried about the exam as I seem to be about three weeks behind! Is everyone else ahead of me?') But there is also considerable academic dialogue, particularly surrounding assignments ['I can't understand the second paragraph of Question 2 at all – can anyone give me some tips on what it means?']

The query above also illustrates one of the delicate issues that can arise in computer conferencing – that of plagiarism. Before conferencing, it was likely that students would only have contact with other students in their own tutor group. There was a reasonable chance that students over-collaborating on work would be spotted by their tutor marking both assignments. Now, depending on the structure of the organization, it is possible for students at the opposite ends of the country to collaborate and different tutors to be quite unaware of that collaboration. Alternatively, by using the Web it is possible that the era of international plagiarism is now here, with students able to purchase assignment papers with a range of titles from anywhere in the world. Such developments will test the ingenuity of both assignment setters and software writers to write programs that might identify plagiarizsed work.

Moderated conferences: academic and non-academic support

I have taken these two types together as in my experience they are hard to distinguish. Even more than in conventional media a tutor might well be operating in academic and non-academic modes in alternating inputs to a conference.

There is still a body of opinion that holds that online support, academic and non-academic, is fundamentally different from all other media. However there is also growing agreement among practitioners that the underlying pedagogy of online support is actually much the same as any other kind of tuition (Stephenson, 2001). Thus the e-tutor's role is to facilitate his or her students' learning in the same way as a face-to-face or other kind of tutor. Clearly the medium imposes very substantial constraints although it also has some advantages. These are a few examples however you may be able to think of others:

- The fact that all exchanges are typed and that students only log on at intervals means that an exchange of ideas which might take five minutes in a face-to-face session may take a week or more in a computer conference.
- On the other hand it is possible to take time to compose a response in a conference which may therefore be of higher quality than in the face-to-face equivalent. And it is perfectly possible to have several topics running simultaneously.
- Students can participate when they want and from home or possibly work.
- On the other hand contributions will be asynchronous – arriving at different times – and so may easily get out of step. Student C will comment on something that Student A wrote but the topic may have already moved on to Student B's topic.
- The online tutor cannot assume that a particular student has read a message or discover that student has become inactive, without checking back against the 'History' of a message (if there is such a facility in the conferencing software), to see if the student is listed as a reader.
- On the other hand a tutor can send a private message to a particular student or group of students without the others being aware.

Whatever the differences it seems clear that the essentially facilitative role of the tutor described in chapter 4 remains the same and the challenges and problems of the tutor are very similar.

Characteristics of conferences

Given the pedagogic similarities and practical differences of computer conferencing for student support, how might e-tutors go about their work?

Setting up the conference. The tutor may be able to choose the conferencing system, in which case there will be a basic decision about whether to use a Web-based system such as WebCT or a software system such as FirstClass. Whichever is chosen or imposed, the tutor will need to be as familiar as possible with the mechanics of the conferencing process. Even if there is a help desk, students will inevitably turn to the tutor for assistance in getting started or overcoming glitches.

Group size. Again the tutor may have a group imposed or have some control over enrolment. The best size for a group is difficult to guess, but in my own experience it is hard to get a lively conference going if the numbers are too few (say less than six) and conferences can be very confused if the numbers are too large (more than 20). But so much depends on the commitment of the participants, and the drop out rate.

Length of conference. Conference inputs take longer than their face-to-face equivalent by a factor of at least five (the ratio of typing to speech time). If conferences log on for half an hour a day then it will take up to two weeks to replicate a one hour's tutorial online. So a conference will probably need to last several weeks to allow time for a satisfactory exchange on even a relatively encompassed topic.

Course material. While there may be courses which appear entirely on the Web, most online courses will make use of other materials: texts, CD ROMs and so on. Students will need strategies for integrating this material with their online work.

Conference structure. In any conferencing system it is easily possible to set up sub-conferences on different topics so that students can choose to participate in several discussions more or less simultaneously. This is not something that could be replicated in a face-to-face situation, and it can help conferences become more challenging and lively. Or it is possible to have sub-conferences appearing at different times as the topics move forward. Students can still refer back to a previous topic at any time. Finally another model can be set up to create sub-conferences with different students on them reporting back to the main conference rather like 'snowballing' in a face-to-face situation.

Threads. Within any conference or sub-conference the tutor or students may start new topics and thus create simultaneous 'threads'. The structure and aims of the threads and sub-conferences are critical: too few and progress will be slow, too many and students will get very confused (especially late arrivals) and be unable to participate fully. The responsibility for keeping the sub-conference structure simple and keeping threads within reasonable limits is perhaps the tutor's most important and most difficult job.

The e-tutor at work

The e-tutor is now ready to start work. The conference system is chosen, the course material is available (although watch out for late delivery), and there is a list of students who are aware of the start date (although watch out for late arrivals who will need extra support).

Aims

The first task will be to set out the aims of the conference to students as clearly as possible. There might be some negotiation about these but, given the time that it takes to get responses from a number of students, it will be risky to be too flexible at the outset.

Introductions and help

There will probably need to be two sub-conferences available from the outset. One will be the introductions conference where students can place a brief biography of themselves, contact details and (possibly) a note on their particular interests. This conference also serves as a useful check for the tutor on who has actually made it onto the conference and who might still be having difficulty getting started.

The other conference will be a training and help conference where students can find out more about the conferencing system and raise queries with links to a help desk if available. It will be important not to underestimate the difficulties students may have with access to the Internet and particular Web sites or software, and other problems with hardware and software.

Structure

The e-tutor then needs to decide on the conference structure. This can be left open to some extent and determined by the e-tutor's perception of student needs, but that has to be done carefully. The structure will also depend on the course materials. If, for example, that is a book with 17 chapters then one structure might be to set up 17 sub-conferences but only direct students to them one at a time over the life of the conference.

However, given that each sub-conference will have half a dozen or more threads running, after a while there may be up to 100 different conversations going on. Or if students are slow to participate there will be insufficient input to get conversations going well. The e-tutor must be ready to adapt strategies to needs.

Getting the conference started

Experienced face-to-face tutors know that one quick way to kill a tutorial is to start it by asking 'Are there any questions?' They know that it will be important to start by asking a question on the course or by setting a task. In the same way it will be essential for the e-tutor to do the same. The actual question or task will depend on the course, the students and the stage they have reached.

Keeping the conference going

Once students have started to conference then the e-tutor's e-facilitating skills will come into play. Responses will need to be encouraging and facilitative. Inevitably at first the comments are likely to be directed to the tutor so that he or she will need to use the electronic equivalent of looking round the room and pose the question 'What do others think?', or rephrase the question to try to generate alternative views. The process will be similar to that described in chapter 3, with the tutor as facilitator, helping participants to go through cycles of clarification and conceptualization as the material develops.

A Web conference example

(I am greatly indebted to Sean Chamberlin of Fullerton College, California, for this example: interpretations are my own.) This is an example of a conference set up in July 2000 on the topic of this book. Following the headings above:

Choice of conferencing software. Sean chose WebCT which has the advantage of needing no special software and is relatively user-friendly. Needing little in the way of acclimatization it is particularly suitable for short one-off conferences such as this.

Aims. The aims were covered in the conference publicity and in this case were very open-ended: to explore some of the issues raised in the book about delivering student support online with colleagues from around the world in a structured, non-assessed, non-credit conference.

Introduction and help. The conference started with a 'Class Introductions' conference where participants gave brief introductions of themselves. Help was covered in an easily accessible area from the Toolbar at the top of the screen: see Figure 8.1.

Conference structure. The basic structure was based on the chapters of the first edition of this book moving from one conference to the next over a period of a week or so. However, once opened, conferences remained open so that discussion could continue over several weeks.

Within each conference participants could respond to Sean's initial thread or start threads of their own. As suggested before, this meant that the number of simultaneous discussions could rapidly reach up to 100 or so although of course some discussions would tail off as participants moved on. Thus clicking on (say) chapter 6 (see Figure 8.1) would take the participant to the chapter 6 conference threads (see Figure 8.2).

Getting the conference started. Sean started each sub-conference with a question or series of questions to which participants could respond. For example, Sean's first questions on chapter 6 (chapter 8 in this second edition) were:

- What issues arise in attempting to support students in the electronic environment?
- What is the most effective way to manage e-mail in a large class?
- What are the essential ingredients for an online support centre?'

The framing of such questions is fairly critical to getting a conference going. The most effective questions should be clear and open-ended, not inviting yes/no answers, be challenging but (in the initial stages) not too broad or difficult. In this example a multiple level question was posed, which on the positive side gives participants a better chance of finding something to answer but which on the negative side could invite short close-ended responses.

Keeping the conference going. In the event the opening question received a first response as follows:

- *What issues arise with attempting to support students in the electronic environment?* 'Academic integrity – how to provide the support without revealing the answer. Time frame: establishing a system of when responses will be made to student requests.'
- *What is the most effective way to manage e-mail in a large class?* 'Establish a time frame up front. Tell students to expect responses to e-mail at certain regular times.'
- *What are the essential ingredients for an online support centre?* 'Good communication skills, caring, well-trained tutors, and administrative support.'

In following up such a response the facilitator will need to wait a while. (It can be seen that responses only appear every two or three days and sometimes longer.) It will be a matter of judgement on whether to intervene if responses are slow, or hope that other participants will come in with relevant and apposite contributions. In this example the facilitator held back and other participants came in with various apposite comments.

Synchronous conferencing

The example illustrated above was of an asynchronous conference: responses are separated in time, sometimes by several days. Synchronous conferences take place in real time with participants typing in responses to messages that have just appeared using software such as NetMeeting or MSN. The process is not foolproof; it is easy to get out of step with responses to (say) message 1 appearing as message 4 after message 3 has responded to something in message 2. The effect can be a set of rather disjointed conversations being conducted simultaneously between a group of people at a party.

Nevertheless synchronous conferencing has an immediacy which is an attractive alternative to the rather ponderous nature of asynchronous conferencing. It is obviously less suitable for international conferences spanning several time zones but may be particularly appropriate for online campus situations or commercial training schemes where students can log in and out of 'chat' ad lib. It can also be very helpful in generating a sense of identity if used occasionally in otherwise asynchronous situations.

Effectiveness of computer conferencing in student support

It is not yet very clear how effective computer conferencing is as a medium for support. We shall see in chapter 9 that its popularity is limited unless it is a compulsory element of a course – or the only mode possible. Indeed perhaps the most important characteristic of computer conferencing is that it enables support to be given in situations where other media are unavailable, across time zones and international boundaries, and is the first truly globalized support system with all that that implies.

The implication of the previous discussion is that computer conferencing is a possible, indeed likely, replacement for other forms of support. A closer analysis of what is going on suggests that this may be misleading. For example, it is clear that:

- *Student use.* The proportion of regular users of the UK OU FirstClass conferences is relatively small: perhaps only 30 per cent of networked students make regular use of the system. There is some evidence that a number of students initially log on but find the system confusing and rather alienating and do not proceed. Certainly, a close inspection of individual conferences suggests that most contributions to a particular conference come from a relatively small number of students, perhaps up to a dozen.
- *Lurkers.* There is also evidence that there are many lurkers: students who join conferences, read messages and do not contribute. One study suggested that there are up to ten lurkers for every student who contributes. Presumably such students are deriving some value from their activity but this is hard to assess.
- *Activity level.* Again, a brief glance at a particular conference can suggest that there is a lively repartee under way. In fact, the average conference attracts perhaps two to three contributions per week, and students generally only log on every three to four days.
- *Personal conversations.* Finally, quite a number of conference threads can turn into effectively personal conversations between two or three students. Other students happening on such conversations can find them as off-putting and as difficult to join as overheard private conversations at a party.

Having said the above, it is not surprising that in surveys of the popularity of various media for student support, computer conferencing is actually quite low down (see chapter 9). Nevertheless, this may still represent high popularity among a small number of students. Certainly, surveys also suggest that computer conferencing is highly valued by certain groups of students:

- Disabled or housebound students for whom conferencing is a lifeline.
- Remote students who may well have no other contact. This is particularly true for students studying abroad who are not only unlikely to be near other students but who face prohibitively high international phone call charges for ordinary calls. The costs of Internet connections are small in comparison, especially if they can be made via an employer's connection.
- Students on mathematics, science and technology courses where conferencing is only a relatively modest extension of the use they would make of their computers.
- Students who, for whatever reason, find face-to-face or even phone contact uncomfortable or even threatening.

Ultimately, how far computer conferencing is an important part of student support remains an open question. Certainly much research is needed, particularly into the key question: is what happens in conferencing some kind of isolation-overcoming discourse, or is it just chat?

Student support staff conferences

Conferences can also be set up for staff and can fulfil a very useful support and staff development purpose. Groups of staff working on a particular course or topic can share problems and experiences in similar ways to students.

I came across a simple example recently of a new tutor sharing a problem with her colleagues. One of her students had sent a general message to an open conference saying that he had not been able to contact her. This left her feeling anxious and rather humiliated. One of her colleagues was able to reassure her, pointing out that confused students often sent messages to inappropriate places and that she should not take it personally but contact the student and sort it out directly with him by phone if necessary.

Chapter 9

Media for student support

In the last four chapters I have surveyed briefly the rich range of media available to deliver student support:

- at a distance, using correspondence, phone and audiovisual technology;
- face to face;
- by computer.

The choice available to the institution of which media to use can therefore be very wide, with costs and retention issues riding on the outcomes of that choice. How does an institution choose a particular media mix?

Evaluating the effectiveness of different media

Are there media which are best for particular purposes? For example, if one wants to advise intending students about to start study, there may be a choice of sending them a package of material, advising them over the phone, holding face-to-face meetings, or possibly a combination of all these. Which you choose may well have to do with where your students are and the costs of reaching them. It will be much harder to decide which is the best medium or media mix from the point of view of supporting students most effectively, and difficult to see how to gather evidence towards making that decision.

There is evidence about students' preferences for various media. This example is taken from the Student Research Centre of the UK OU's Institute of Educational Technology (IET) survey of more than 17,000 UK OU students. See Figure 9.1.

This survey does not specifically select out student support activities from course materials and will be institution-specific, so I must be careful in drawing conclusions from it. Nevertheless, there are interesting points that emerge:

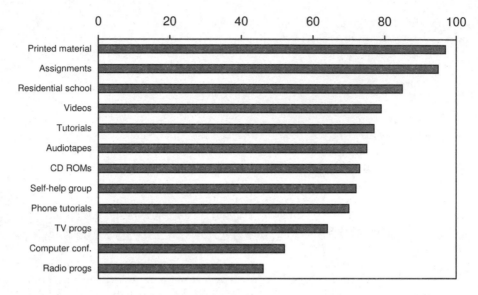

Figure 9.1 *Percentage of respondents who found the component very or fairly helpful*

- The relatively low value of face-to-face tutorials (less helpful, for example, than videos). Tutorials are only marginally more helpful than audiotapes, CD ROMs and self-help groups. Phone tutorials are not as helpful as face-to-face tutorials but only slightly less so.
- Open circuit broadcasting – both television and radio – is seen as almost the least helpful, possibly for the reasons suggested in chapter 5.
- Most interesting is the relative unpopularity of computer conferencing. Given the emphasis on it in much institutional planning, this is a worrying finding and would repay further research.

Students' media choices

It is difficult to draw clear conclusions for any particular institution about what media work best for its particular students. It will be worth bearing in mind that what may seem technically attractive to the institution may not be so to all its students, and that different students will find some media more appropriate than others. Different media may also be appropriate at different stages in a student's studies. Blanchfield, Patrick and Simpson (1999) have argued that in order for a particular medium of support to be useful to a student it must be accessible, in terms of reasonable cost and time taken, and add 'study value': students must feel that there is a clear personal pay-off in terms of how their studies have moved forward, particularly with respect to assessment.

Thus face-to-face support may well have high study value but be unpopular because it is inaccessible: costs and time of travel, for example. That may depend on the students' stage in their course: the first tutorial for a course may well have enough study value to make it worthwhile. A video may have lower study value but will be used because of its accessibility. Computer conferencing may be unpopular on both study value added and on accessibility.

Accessibility may be low on grounds of cost: online time costs can mount up, together with the inconvenience of tying up family phone lines. Keyboarding times are much slower than conversation and conferences are often asynchronous: dialogues that would only take minutes face to face can take days on a conference. And of course if the student does not have a computer but has to travel to a library or IT centre then accessibility will certainly be low even if that means online costs are zero.

Study value may be low: it can take some time to find useful conferences and then the general level of 'chat' may appear trivial and unhelpful. There is also the relative barrenness of the exchanges, especially when compared with the richness and speed of exchanges in face-to-face tuition.

Thus for any individual student there will be a 'accessibility versus study value' chart that will determine what media the student uses. For any student the points will appear in different places and students will choose their media accordingly. There may be a 'usage line' where media inside the line will be used and media outside not used.

There are other factors to take into account.

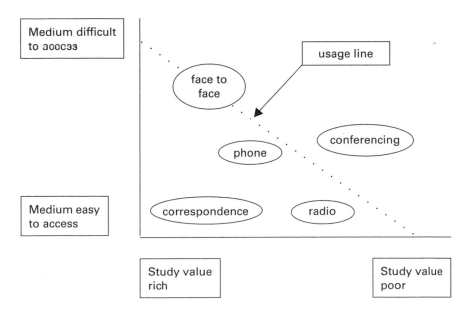

Figure 9.2 *Accessibility versus study value diagram*

Congruence

Their choice will also be influenced by a third factor: the congruence of any new medium with their familiar media. Adapting to a new medium – like using a new study method – will take some time, and learning may be more inefficient during that time. Students will therefore continue to prefer familiar media.

For example, there is evidence from elsewhere in the UK OU IET survey that, where students are required to computer conference in order to complete the assessment demands of the course, it is rather more popular. This suggests that once it is no longer so unfamiliar it becomes more acceptable.

Too many media

Finally there is some modest qualitative evidence that having too many media to choose from is confusing to students. They are faced with a problem: should they contact their tutor by e-mail, phone up another student, go to a face-to-face tutorial or leave a message on the voice mail tuition system? In providing students with a choice we may be more inclusive at the expense of more confusing.

Institutions' media choices

Any institution faced with a bewildering array of media choices will need to pick a path between cost to the institution and the effectiveness of the media with different students. It may be possible to choose on the basis of a cost-effective analysis (Hulsmann, 2000), although both effectiveness (as a learner medium) and costs are difficult to assess. There may be non-cost-effective factors involved: for example, the maintenance of very expensive TV broadcasting as a shop window for the institution, or the continuance of face-to-face tuition for the purpose of maintaining tutor morale and student confidence.

Some institutions in developing countries may appear to have little choice of media: computers may be out of reach probably for years to come. In such situations it is helpful to remember the words of Ernest Rutherford who split the atom in the 1920s, 'We haven't got the money, so we've got to think!' In other words, institutions may not have hi-tech resources but might (for example) have very highly developed family networks which can be used for support.

Finally, it is probably worth noting the first of Hulsmann's recommendations for cost-effective media choice: 'If there is a choice to be made between print and screen, go for print!'

I have just been talking with a group of students who have been taking a course that is entirely online except for one initial face-to-face meeting. All of them said how much that initial meeting had helped with the subsequent conferencing and phone contact, as well as generating a feeling of group enthusiasm and morale. 'It was brilliant,' said one, 'without that meeting everything would have been so much harder. I'd have liked to have a follow-up later in the year as well!'

So different students will choose support media according to different criteria at different times of their study lives. Getting to know these criteria for its students will be an important aim for an institution that will need to choose the particular media mix and timing for its student support delivery.

Chapter 10

Student support outside the institution

Interest in outside support

This may seem a curious byway for this book – after all, student support outside the institution can hardly be susceptible to management by the institution and so can only be of passing interest. Yet there are at least two good reasons why such support is important. First, there is evidence that students rate some kinds of outside support more highly than internal support, and second, such support can be very economical and cost effective.

Sources of support outside the institution

There are a range of sources of support outside the institution: work colleagues, staff in other agencies such as libraries and advice centres, as well as more formal arrangements such as head teachers mentoring students in teacher training schemes. There are three which seem particularly important:

- partners, family and friends of the student;
- other students of the institution;
- employers.

In a recent small-scale survey (Asbee and Simpson, 1998), UK OU students were asked to rate the relative importance of support from their partners, families, friends, tutors, other students (whether on their course or not) and from the rest of the institution. (Support from employers was not covered in this survey.) The

Table 10.1   *Percentage of students giving source as most important*

from family and friends	32 per cent
from tutors	29 per cent
from other students	21 per cent
from the institution	17 per cent

proportions which gave particular modes as the most important source of support were as shown in Table 10.1.

Support from partners and the like was more highly rated than support from tutors and other students. Nearly twice as many students rated support from partners as most important as those who rated support from the institution as first.

Support from partners, families and friends

Thus, it appears that the most important single form of support for their students is outside institutional control (and may be largely ignored by institutions). The report also raises two questions: who gives the support and what kinds are most valuable? And can the institution enhance that support in any way? Asbee and Simpson (1998) wrote:

> In the majority of cases the support was from a partner but not always so. There were cases such as a woman whose most important support was from her father, and a mother and her teenage son being mutually supportive by working together on their studies, although the son noted ruefully a negative aspect: 'lack of meals on assignment days'.

The kind of support that is most valuable varies:

> Ideal partners help most by providing time and space for their students to study by taking on child care and chores. Many partners also help more directly by proof reading assignments, providing transport and setting the video recorder.
>
> Partners also provide emotional and moral support through encouragement, showing an interest in the course and keeping students in touch with their motivation – 'He helped me to keep going even when I felt thoroughly fed up with it all.' They can also help keep studies in proportion – helping students put a low assignment grade into perspective, for example.
>
> They will also provide support by putting their own needs second from time to time over such things as holiday dates.
>
> They will even support by simply leaving alone – 'He allows me to get on. I don't get nagged about doing essays. . . . I'm allowed to do what I need when I need.'

Above all, what came through in this part of the survey was a loud and clear message – that partner's, family or friends' support is overwhelmingly important – 'It has to be a joint commitment. Involve your partner if you want to succeed.'

This was made even clearer by the minority of students who had not been helped well by their partner. 'He's not selfish particularly but I've always wanted to be there for our small son so I've had to juggle everything together'; 'To be honest my husband and family have not been much help. . . . I seem to have been doing it very much alone. They all resent my studying as a waste of time which I find quite traumatic' – this despite being the mother in a family with three graduate children.

Partners can be resentful and even obstructive. One student was studying entirely in secret using a neighbour's address. Certainly study can upset the status quo – 'He was happy with the stout floral-clad housewife he had before; he is not so keen on the woman who is not dependent on him for opinions or confidence.' And conversely, this study has again demonstrated the devastating effects of relationship breakdown on student progress: 'Since starting studying I have separated from my husband of 21 years. I don't think my studies were the cause but it may have been a small contributory factor. Studying after the breakdown of my marriage has subsequently been very difficult.'

Enhancing support from families and friends

Enhancing families' and friends' support from the institution is not easy. Nor has it necessarily been seen as important hitherto. I note that my own institution's introductory brochure makes no mention of the importance of family support or even of discussing the decision to study with the family.

Nevertheless, there may be simple ways of acknowledging its importance. One finding that emerged from this report was the need for partners and families to know more about what 'their' student had taken on, what was going to happen to them and how they as 'student supporters' might help them more. The following extract is taken from a short leaflet that I wrote for partners to give to their students, *Helping Your Student*. (I have recently received a similar leaflet *Helping a Student* from Australia, and a German example that suggests that this is becoming a more recognized need.)

HELPING YOUR STUDENT: A LEAFLET FOR PARTNERS, FAMILY OR FRIENDS OF INTENDING STUDENTS

To intending students: do please pass this leaflet on to your partner, family or friends. It's designed to help them help you in the most effective way and to tell them a little about what you will be doing as a student.

To the partner, family or friends of an intending student.

Thank you for taking a few minutes to read this little leaflet. Our research has shown that one of the most important factors in the success of our students is good support from their partners, families and friends. This leaflet is designed to tell you a little bit about what 'your' student will be doing and to help and encourage you to support them.

What will happen to 'your' student?

The start. Your student may be starting well before the formal course start. They'll get their first mailing of material up to three months before. So if there are any jobs needing to be done round the house it would be a good idea to get them done now – including bookshelves to help store all the materials you're going to have thudding through your letterbox!

Tutorials. There are regular tutorials from start to finish. Your student doesn't have to go to these but they'll find the support and contact very helpful so do encourage them to go.

Assignments. Your student will have a number of assignments to do during the year. These are usually essays or reports. Assignments are generally the focus of considerable stress, both in doing them and then getting them back with the tutor's grades and comments. So your support and encouragement is essential – especially for that vital first assignment which is the biggest hurdle for any student.

Exams. The most stressful activity of all is the final exam. Many new students won't have taken an exam for some years and may need extra support over the revision period.

And then . . . there is a short break (household jobs again?) until the whole process begins again.

So how can you help?

There are various problems that face any student but the most important are:

Time. A student on a course will be studying for X hours a week. This will be an average – some students may need more or less, and it may go up near an assignment or the exam. Some students can study an hour or so here or there, others need longer blocks of time. Some students tell us that the time should be negotiated at the outset, so partners and family know clearly what is study time and what is family time – you should decide together what is best for everyone concerned.

Stress. As suggested earlier, there are various stress points in the course such as assignments where your support and encouragement will be essential. You could offer to read an assignment (that's not cheating) or make sure the children are out of the house at critical times.

Seeking help. Some students find it particularly difficult to seek help when they're stuck. Your student may need encouragement to contact their tutor. Remind them that that is what he or she is there for!

Motivation. At some point some students begin to wonder if it's all worth it. Your job will be to talk it through with them and (hopefully) put them in touch with their motivation again – if indeed it's right for them to carry on. Sometimes the right decision will be to drop out and that's fine. We don't see dropping out as failure and students are welcome to restart whenever they are ready.

Perhaps your support is best given if you and your student are a team. Your student may be doing the reading and writing but your role in the team is just as vital to their success.

The pay-off

The final aim of course is graduation. But many students report pay-offs well before they get there in terms of their own intellectual development and satisfaction. And more than two-thirds of students who have career aspirations say that their studies have benefited them in vocational and financial terms.

However graduation is the goal for most. We hope to see you at the graduation ceremony – the applause will be as much for you as it is for them.

Questions?

If there is anything in this leaflet that raises queries in your mind, or if there are any problems that arise during your student's studies that you would like to discuss, then you are welcome to talk to us about them. Write or phone us.

And remember that we have many partners actually enrolled together: wife and husband, mother and son, even wife, husband and son. If you'd like more information on study for yourself just phone or write to us.

How far such a simple device can enhance external support remains to be seen, but generally such leaflets seem to be well received – this was the leaflet on which comments appeared in chapter 5.

Support from family and friends online

A recent survey of UK universities revealed that many of them are taking family, and of course especially parent, support very seriously and have dedicated Web pages, with electronic newsletters for parents. There is one Scottish university where the parental Web site has a link to a local food store that will take orders over the Web to deliver food direct to allegedly starving offspring.

My own institution has recently approved a Web page development for family and friends based on the text 'Helping Your Student' quoted earlier. The intention is that there will be a link from the page to a chat facility where family and friends will be encouraged to exchange experiences, moderated by a family and friends coordinator.

Support from other students

Support from other students can fall into two types: support from students on the same course or at the same level (peer support) and support from students who have completed the course in question or are on the same course but have more experience (mentoring support).

There are differences in the experience of these categories of support (peer or self-help groups have been a feature of ODL for many years; mentoring support is a relatively recent introduction), the ways they are set up (peer support can be set up relatively simply, mentoring requires much more substantial input), and the activities they undertake (peer support can be informal, mentoring requires rather more structure).

Peer support

Peer support in ODL has been around for many years and, as noted previously, is highly rated by students – often as highly as tutor support. Strictly speaking it is not external to the institution, which, although having little control over it, can do quite a lot to organize, encourage and enhance it. It is obviously especially important to particularly isolated students. Peer support groups can be of any size from two upwards, although it is unusual to find groups of more than about six.

There are several aspects to peer support: the initial setting up process, the media of contact, how peer support groups operate, and the queries and problems that can arise.

Initial setting up

Peer support groups can be set up with the encouragement of a tutor. Since the effectiveness of groups appears to be very much dependent on one initial face-to-face contact, this is often the best way to get groups going. It does mean that tutors need to have it clearly in their role specification, that the institution needs to support that role with appropriate resources – lists of students and forms for address release – and that there needs to be staff development to help tutors acquire appropriate techniques for encouraging students into peer support groups. Such techniques would certainly include small group work with students as described in chapter 11 with the aim of not only developing learning skills but allowing students to experience the value of small tutorless groups for themselves.

Apart from stimulating peer groups from face-to-face contact, tutors can also use phone contact, such as the three way call system previously described, to encourage peer groups. But this can potentially be very time consuming.

Other ways of initiating groups tend to be less successful. Institutions can offer the opportunity in a general mailing to students, collating the responses and mailing out lists by course (although this can be labour intensive). However, it is quite difficult for any student to take the initiative to 'cold call' someone else from a list, and then even more difficult in security conscious times to set up a face-to-face meeting with people who may be unknown.

Media for peer support groups

Peer groups can meet by various media. Face-to-face groups appear to be the most popular but people may experience difficulties in travel. Phone networks can work very well but their value tends to be underestimated by students. Curiously, although computer conferencing is surely the most accessible peer group, as has been seen it is the least popular.

What happens in peer support groups

What evidence there is about peer groups suggests that groups operate best if they meet relatively regularly, have a clear agenda and focus and take turns at various roles. Some sort of guidance from the institution may be helpful. This is an excerpt from a leaflet that is sent to UK OU students at the start of their course.

GETTING TOGETHER: A GUIDE TO ORGANIZING STUDY GROUPS

Why a study group?

Do you feel that you are studying in isolation? Are you having problems with a course? Is it difficult for you to get to tutorials? Would you like to try out ideas for tackling an assignment before you put pen to paper?

If the answer to any of these questions is 'yes', then a study group may help you. Informal groups of students following the same course can provide valuable support. And groups needn't be used just for study – you could also use your group for arranging lifts to tutorials and so on.

Contacting other students

There are several ways you can find other students in your area on the same course.

- We can help. Complete the attached form and return it following the instructions. You will then receive a list of other students on your course who have completed the form. The more people who do this, the better the chance of finding someone near you. So do return the form even if you are not actively contemplating becoming a member of a group – at least you will then have a list of people who you can turn to in an emergency – eg your course material failing to turn up.
- Your tutor can help you organize a study group by asking his or her students if they are willing to join.
- Group registration. A very satisfactory method of ensuring a viable group is group registration for a course. If you have been involved in a successful tutorial group one year, you could consider the possibility of moving onto the same course together the next.

Remember: Telephone networks. You don't necessarily have to meet face to face. You can just arrange to keep in touch by telephone with other students on your course – phone numbers to be obtained by methods listed above.

Organizing the first meeting

To actually get the group going, someone (perhaps you?) will need to take the initiative to contact some others and suggest a time and place. It may be that when you've contacted one or two students they'll agree to contact others themselves.

The number of people you'll want in your group will depend on how many there are in your area but successful groups have been run with numbers from 2 to 20.

Where to meet? Obviously you can meet at someone's home or any public meeting area. At the first meeting it's a good idea to decide on arrangements for the first two or three meetings – when, where, etc – and whether to appoint a convenor (or take it in turns) to act as a link.

Running the meeting

You shouldn't necessarily expect the convenor of the meeting to have the responsibility of running it – the responsibility should be shared. Equally the meeting shouldn't really be run like a tutorial with one person trying to teach the others – unless of course you have someone in the group who happens to be an expert on a particular topic. Nor should the session be like a business meeting with a chair trying to reach the most efficient decision.

The aim is that group members should share their understanding and problems in the course. By talking things over in a group you can extend your knowledge and increase your awareness of the range of opinions, values, experiences and techniques. Here are some ideas for getting the discussion going.

Breaking the ice

The first meeting can be awkward because members don't know where to begin. Try going round the room with members introducing themselves, saying why they're doing the course and what they hope to get out of the study group. For a larger group (more than eight or so) use a 'snowballing session' (see below) to share experiences and expectations.

When the group has warmed up the discussion may follow naturally. Or you may want to structure it in some way in which case try the following.

Discussing the next assignment

Remember it's not cheating to discuss assignments as long as the assignment you finally submit is your own work. You could discuss:

● the meaning of the question;
● the approach to answering it;
● the background.

Just chatting?

Sometimes people complain that their study groups spend their time 'just chatting'. In fact 'chatting' can be very useful – sharing experiences and getting reinforcement – more valuable perhaps than an intellectual discussion that doesn't touch anyone personally. However, 'chatting' can mean that the group doesn't know where to start, is bored or doesn't feel at ease.

The group doesn't know where to start? It's important to discuss and agree on what the group is going to do in any session.

The group is bored? Perhaps everyone has said all they have to say on the topic or is simply not interested. Don't be afraid to suggest moving on to something else.

On the other hand you may be quite happy about the way the discussion is going. However, if a group does want to adjust its level of talk here are two practical suggestions.

If the discussion is dominated by a few people and others are having difficulty getting a word in, then agree to give everyone (say) two minutes of the group's time to say what they like about the topic.

If the discussion is slow and people are reluctant to contribute then split into pairs and share ideas on the discussion topic with one other person for ten minutes (it's normally easier to talk to one person than several). Then report back to the full group.

Videotapes

If your course uses videotapes and you have access to a video then agree to watch a programme together and discuss it.

Leading on a particular topic

If there is an individual in the group who has special knowledge of a particular topic he or she might be willing to lead the group on that topic.

Snares and pitfalls

(Ignore this section if your group is running well)

- *Talking too much or too little.* People vary enormously in the amount they contribute in discussion. That doesn't matter as long as everyone feels happy.
- *Uneasy?* Sometimes groups develop a critical, judging atmosphere which makes people anxious about talking openly. Try and ensure that the group can accept all the opinions offered without putting people down or insisting on simple answers.
- *Conflicting goals?* An underlying reason for difficulties in a group can be that not all members are agreed on their goals. They may have different values and expectations.
  - *Different values?* Conflict can arise when members interpret issues solely in terms of their own outlook on life and don't accept that other people may have different values.
  - *Different expectations?* Group members must feel free to say what they would like the group to be doing. Tolerance and frankness are the most important qualities in running groups.

This leaflet

We hope you've found this leaflet useful. Do follow it up and organize yourself a group if you can – even if it's only two of you. Time and again we find students saying how helpful they had found their groups and how they wished they'd made contact earlier. Give it a try!

Peer support online

In developing peer support one of the principal difficulties is the actual linking of students. For security reasons it's often not possible to simply issue an address list of students on a course. In a distance system it's usually necessary to contact them individually and ask for permission to release their address. You then have to list the address-release-agreed students and send it to them again. In a system with face-to-face sessions it's easier but even so there is a risk of missing non-attending students who are thereby even more excluded than before.

Using the Web can make linking students much easier. If there are computer conferences then linking students may be as simple as directing them to their tutor's conference or a non-moderated conference for their course. But not all students want to link into a large group any more than all students want to participate in a face-to-face tutorial. For them it would be simple to set up a 'Find a Study Friend' Web site where students can register their name, course and whatever contact details they are happy to give. Then anyone logging on has some kind of choice of how they would like to network, on a one-to-one or small group basis if they wish.

Mentoring support

Mentoring support – student support from students more senior in the system – has a long history reaching back to the Greeks. It was used by Joseph Lancaster in England in the 19th century but became discredited as merely a way of saving money on teachers. It was rediscovered in a full-time education context in North America in the 1960s and supplemental instruction (SI), as it is called, is now used in up to 300 US higher education institutions. It has spread to the UK and elsewhere and involves student leaders, often second year students, helping new undergraduates.

Given the particular characteristics of ODL – the isolation and lack of confidence, particularly of new students – the characteristics of mentoring might make it particularly appropriate. Mentoring in full-time education is seen as informal, supportive, empowering and confidence building and a 'bridge between the teacher who has forgotten what ignorance was like, and the new learner who has not yet reached knowledge and understanding' (Wallace, 1998).

However, while it is relatively easy to set up mentoring schemes in face-to-face education, it becomes much harder in ODL.

Organizing a mentoring scheme

In a very small-scale pilot in 1998 (Asbee, Simpson and Woodall, 1999), a colleague and I set up a mentoring programme in our own institution. The individual stages in such a scheme are:

- Finding volunteer mentees and mentors from new and existing students.
- 'Vetting' volunteers for possible problems.
- Matching and linking them.
- Briefing them.
- Monitoring and evaluation.

There are issues at each stage. Will enough mentors and mentees come forward? What kind of briefing would be appropriate? How can you vet mentors and mentees in ODL when all you know of them is an application form? For example, just on the last issue, to interview every volunteer would be a mammoth task and not necessarily reliable. On the other hand the very isolation of students makes the vetting processes less critical, as it is possible to release only phone numbers not addresses for safety reasons. And the situation and possibilities for harassment are no worse than in any other student–student contact.

Briefing mentors and mentees
It is also very important that mentors and mentees know what to expect of each other, particularly the boundaries of the roles. This is an excerpt from a short briefing document which we sent to both mentors and mentees after they had volunteered and been matched.

After an introduction on various ways of linking up the leaflet goes on.

What kind of advice can mentors expect to give?

The most valuable asset that mentors have is their experience of a course. That means they are very well placed to give you the student's perspective on:

- finding your way around the course materials;
- getting started on the course: what works best?
- time – how much do you need to spend?
- going to the first tutorial: what happens?
- tackling the first assignment and getting it back;
- falling behind and catching up;
- preparing for the exam (if there is one);
- surviving the exam.

What issues are outside the mentor/mentee relationship?

Mentors are not experts on the university's administrative, or academic systems, and mentors should refer their mentee to his or her tutor or Study Support as appropriate.

Mentors should not try to 'teach' the course in any way and should always refer mentees with academic queries or any other concerns affecting their ability to study to their tutor. A tutor cannot help if s/he does not know there is a problem! Mentors are there to lend a sympathetic ear and to offer encouragement on general study-related issues. Some examples of issues which should be referred:

To the tutor

- content of assignment;
- extension for assignment;
- difficulty with assignment;

- any domestic/health/personal difficulties affecting the mentee's ability to study or tutorial attendance.

To Study Support

- exam arrangements;
- financial difficulties;
- disability/special needs;
- withdrawal;
- exam counselling.

What happens if after the course has started, I find I don't really need my mentor? I don't want to cause any offence!

Not a problem. Your mentor is there to offer an additional point of contact and support, but if you find you don't need that support, all well and good! Just contact your mentor to thank him/her for the support, but saying you're now launched and can cope unsupported. Alternatively, contact our mentoring coordinator and she will get in touch with your mentor on your behalf.

And if it doesn't work?

Obviously we can't guarantee that the relationship will be a positive and productive one for everyone every time. Everyone who takes part agrees that the relationship can be ended by either side at any time. If you're finding that the relationship isn't working, you can simply inform your mentor/mentee in a friendly and polite way, or contact our mentoring coordinator and she will inform your mentor/mentee on your behalf. Either way s/he needs to know if you are no longer working together.

We hope this mentoring partnership will prove valuable and rewarding, but do remember: mentors' advice is unofficial and informal. They are not in any way responsible for their mentee's academic progress. Finally it is the responsibility of the mentee to approach the Centre to check details and current information or advice/action on any of the points listed above. If you are unsure whom you should approach, contact our mentoring coordinator who will refer you to the right section.

Good luck and enjoy working together!

Mentoring outcomes

In the event, in this project there were considerably more volunteer mentors than mentees, and the linking and briefing processes were carried out simultaneously by phone by the pilot project worker. Such a labour-intensive approach would not easily work if the project was scaled up. Yet the results were very positive. Mentees reported that in some cases support from their mentor made all the difference between withdrawal and keeping going. 'I got a very low grade on my first assignment and I was on the brink of withdrawing. I just didn't feel I could contact the tutor and if I hadn't spoken to my mentor I would certainly have withdrawn.' 'My mentor had only just completed the course so it was very fresh in his mind and he could really relate to my difficulties. I don't know if my tutor ever studied this course but it must have been a long time ago!'

It was not too difficult to see what mentees got out of the scheme, but interestingly mentors valued it very highly. It values and broadens their experience and there might even be a qualification outcome for some students. 'It was an extraordinarily rewarding experience,' wrote one mentor, 'the improvement in her scores and general level of confidence during the year was really dramatic!'

Mentoring support online

Again the Web offers a variety of possibilities for linking students on a mentoring basis. If there is a large enough group of volunteer mentors it's possible to set up a system where mentees can 'select' a mentor who looks as though they might be in tune with them.

Possible future for mentoring support

While mentoring on a small scale is clearly successful, there are certainly problems in scaling it up to be an effective element in an institution's student support armoury. And it is by no means low cost. Yet the essential rapport between mentoring and the general methodology of ODL seems very close. If I had to put money on a significant development in ODL in the next few years, it might well be on mentoring.

Costs of student–student support

Student–student support does not come for free. There can be quite high administrative costs in canvassing for volunteers, vetting them, linking them and monitoring the scheme. In mentoring schemes there is an issue of possible payment to mentors and the question of how high to set the payment – too low will seem derisory rather than an incentive and too high will render schemes unaffordable. It may be helpful to know that in a recent informal comparison of two schemes in my own institution, there was very little difference in volunteer rates between a scheme that offered £40 (US$60, 70 euros), a book token and a purely unpaid scheme.

Support from employers

Student support from employers is usually of a fairly straightforward organizational kind: payment of fees for particular courses, sometimes conditionally on passing, time off for study and exams and promotion possibilities. I do not know of any research that has assessed the affective or cognitive support from employers, but it would be reasonable to assume that there are workplaces where such support exists either formally or – more likely – informally. With ODL now so wide-spread it is very likely that there will be management and co-workers who have had some experience of ODL and act as mentors if not peer supporters.

It certainly seems worthwhile to supply students with an employee version of *Helping Your Student* for them to pass on to their employers, but I have not seen anything from any institution along these lines. My own institution is currently producing a leaflet.

Other support outside the institution: referral agencies

It is important to remember that there are many possible support organizations outside the institution to which students can be referred when circumstances dictate. There need be no formal referral mechanism and probably should not be a recommendation – simply the suggestion, 'You could try . . .'

For example, students who suffer severe exam stress may be surprised at the suggestion that they should see their doctor, but there are certainly doctors who are sympathetic to stress problems and able to offer useful help. I have had occasional success by suggesting students could try hypnotherapy for similar problems.

At any rate a referral list is like a lifejacket under your plane seat – you hope you will never use it but it is nice to have it there. It is also a help in setting boundaries to your support. My current 'suggestions' list contains the following (these are UK terms but similar organizations exist worldwide):

- student's doctor;
- Citizens' Advice Bureaux – useful as a starting point for many things;
- law surgeries;
- Relate (a relationship counselling organization);
- disability resource centres;
- Samaritans;
- volunteer centres;
- careers guidance offices;
- educational guidance offices;
- housing advice centres;
- Age Concern.

Above all, remember as a student adviser or tutor that there are other resources for students to turn to which may be more effective sometimes even than you!

Chapter 11

Learning skills development and student support

What is meant by learning skills

It has been argued that the principal aim of student support is to produce students who no longer need that support: students who are independent learners or have good 'studentship' qualities. These are students who can embark on any particular course of study with a reasonable anticipation of success because they have acquired high quality learning skills. In fact the term 'studentship' is in many ways a better one for the purpose of student support, as it covers a wider range of skills and qualities than is implied by the term 'learning skill'. However, the latter term is in such wide use that I shall use it with the proviso that, in ODL at least, it covers far more than reading, writing and numeracy.

However, there is not necessarily a great deal of agreement on what good learning skills are. Students appear to be able to study in an extraordinary range of different ways and achieve good results. I remember a student who described her approach to study to me: 'I spread all my books out on the floor in front of the television. Then I turn on the television and if what's on it is more interesting than what's on the floor I watch it: if it's the other way round I read my books.' Since this particular student achieved a first class honours degree I had to assume that either her method was particularly suitable to her or she had achieved her results despite her methods.

In addition, there do not seem to be many research findings that clearly support particular skills as being essential to learning. For example, the skill of taking notes would seem to be a vital element of any student's learning skills, yet studies have consistently failed to show that note taking produces a better outcome than not taking notes. Some research has even shown a negative association (Gibbs, 1981). The same appears to be true of writing an essay, for example. Students are often advised to plan their essays in considerable detail by academic staff who, if asked to write an essay themselves, would possibly write it straight off the top of their heads.

Indeed, there is some evidence that giving students prescriptive advice on study skills may even be counter-productive: either they try to take the advice and struggle with methods that are not actually helpful to them or they ignore the advice but lose confidence in methods that have suited them reasonably well (Gibbs, 1981).

Therefore, I have taken five principles to underlie this chapter:

1. There is no absolute set of learning skills that are totally appropriate for all ODL students at every stage.
2. Most students tend to use the study methods that they have always used, possibly acquired at school. These may or may not be appropriate methods for them in an ODL environment.
3. Changing a student's methods of study is a difficult and challenging experience that is unlikely to be achieved by just giving advice to that student.
4. Changing a study method may well result in less efficient study until the new method is sufficiently practised.
5. The function of student support in developing learning skills is to encourage students to reflect on their methods and experiment with them.

In writing these phrases, I realize that quite unconsciously I have been experimenting while writing this book. I have tried writing in different locations at different times of day for short and long periods. I have tried writing off the top of my head, planning in some detail or composing directly on to a computer. So far the best way seems to be to hand-write it from sketches whilst travelling on a train – alas, too expensive a method to adopt more than occasionally....

Categorizing learning skills

Learning skills cover a far wider range of skills than note-taking, essay writing and so on. It's convenient (if rather arbitrary) to break them down into two broad categories: *course specific skills*, applicable to a particular course, such as scientific report writing, experimental design or literature searching, and *generic skills*, applicable to a range of courses, such as literacy and numeracy skills.

Generic learning skills can be further broken down into the 'phrenological' categories mentioned in chapter 2: for example:

● cognitive skills: numeracy, reading and writing skills;
● affective skills: stress management, assertiveness, self-esteem development, motivation building skills;

- organizational skills: time management, priority setting and material navigation skills.

It is now acknowledged that generic skills are important to the development of course specific skills but that they are nevertheless best developed in the context of a course. In other words it is better to develop time management skills within a particular course's demands rather than in abstract.

Proactive student support for learning skills development

If proactive support for learning skills is to be effective it will have to be targeted at students at the times when it is most appropriate. There are a number of times in a student's progress when critical issues have to be dealt with, new challenges have to be faced, fresh experiences assimilated or decisions taken. This is a typical list of such critical issues although the stages and timings will be different for each institution.

Table 11.1 *Critical issues*

Stage of course	Critical issues
1. Early pre-course start	Decisions about starting study
	Feelings about becoming a student
	Motivations for learning
2. Later pre-course start	Finding the time
	Getting support from family and friends
	Getting support from other students
3. Course start	Tackling course materials
	Planning study
	Numeracy/reading skills
4. Before the first assignment	Tackling the assignment
	Feelings about being assessed
	Stress management
	Writing skills
5. After the first assignment	Learning from assessment
	Dealing with failure
6. Mid-course	Reflecting on progress
	Going on or dropping out
7. Pre-exam period	Revision
	Exam stress
	Exam skills
8. Result	Dealing with failure
	Preparing for the next course

It can be seen that this list is a mixture of cognitive, affective and organizational skills. Running through every stage will be course specific skills, such as problem solving, experimental design and literature searching. It is impossible to illustrate an example of learning skills development at every stage and in every medium so I will give some examples of face-to-face group activities and suggest how they might be extended into other media.

Examples of learning skills development in face-to-face groups

Pre-course start

Several issues could usefully be explored in a group activity, especially at the induction.

EXAMPLE: CLARIFYING MOTIVES
(TOTAL TIME 25 MINUTES)

Suggestions to the tutor:

1. Introduce yourself (2–3 minutes). Give some personal details about yourself and tell them about your role. Try to avoid giving a long introductory speech. It is more important to give your students a chance to feel at home. So,
2. Run a short introductory 'snowballing' session (10 minutes).
   - Get the students into pairs and say, 'I want you to introduce yourselves to each other and say briefly why you are taking the course' (3 minutes).
   - Depending on how big your group is, get them into fours and say, 'Now I want you to share your introductions and motives.'
   - In a plenary session go round and get everyone to introduce himself or herself (there is a version of this exercise in which students introduce each other; this can be quite threatening and is not recommended) and say why they are taking the course (7 minutes).
3. General session (10 minutes). Give the students a chance to ask any general questions, then wind up the session with an invitation to anyone with an individual query to take it up with you.

The assumption behind this activity is that in sharing their thoughts students will clarify their own motives and discover that they share them with others. A student who is clear about the 'why' of study will be well on the way to developing one critical learning skill.

Course start

'Not enough time' is the single most important reason that students give for dropping out. That may be a post hoc rationalization in some cases but it also suggests that spending a little tutorial time helping students organize their time would be valuable.

EXAMPLE: TIME MANAGEMENT (20 MINUTES)

Sketch a chart of common time-consuming activities on the board (or use the chart from chapter 5). Say to the students, 'Here's a list of things that might currently take up your time. See if you can estimate how much time you are currently spending on them each week and how you might reduce it' (5 minutes). 'See how you're going to find the X hours we think you'll need.'

When students have completed their charts you say, 'OK, now share it with a partner and answer the following question together: "So how am I going to reorganize my life to find this time?" You have ten minutes.'

You can then take five minutes at the end to draw out ideas about:

● organizing and prioritizing time;
● concentrating activities;
● getting other people to take on work.

Before the first assignment

This is likely to be a testing time for students so a short exercise on stress might be helpful.

EXAMPLE: STRESS MANAGEMENT (15 MINUTES)

This activity is designed to help students analyse sources of stress in their lives and, if not eliminate them, at least keep them under control. This session uses a slightly different format for variety's sake – too much snowballing can be too predictable!

1. Say, 'In groups of three, think of current sources of stress in your life. These "stresses" might arise from your job, your family, the institution, your environment and so on. Go round the group and let each person take two minutes to talk about these stresses in their lives and how they deal with them. One of the other two people should take notes as the first person talks.' Go round the group in turn (6 minutes).

2. 'Then the note takers should feed back into the group what they have picked up, drawing together particular strands. Draw up a list of stress management strategies/ideas/resources/activities.' (5 minutes.)
3. In a plenary session you can draw together some of the ideas that people have found effective in controlling their levels of stress.

Mid-course

The mid-course period can be a low point for students: the end is some way off and there seems a long way to go. This is a good time to review progress.

EXAMPLE: HOW DO YOU FEEL ABOUT THIS SO FAR? (40 MINUTES)

1. Duplicate the sheet below, write it on the board or simply call out each item in turn.
2. Say, 'Give yourself a quick grade A to E on the following study skills. Do it quickly and trust your first response. It's not a test, just a way of finding out where you feel you have got to.'
   A = very competent.
   B = reasonably competent.
   C = not sure whether I have mastered this.
   D = some problems with this.
   E = definite problems with this.
3. Then say, 'Now go back through the list and highlight those study skills you feel you need to improve (if any!) and ask yourself how you might improve them, for example by asking for help.'
4. You could then snowball at this point to draw up a list of the most common concerns and how to overcome them. This list could be very helpful in deciding if you should run follow-up sessions on particularly popular problems.
5. You might find it helpful to tell the students that similar but longer checklists completed by full-time students reveal that 80 per cent felt that they were only moderately competent (Gibbs, 1981). Full-time students felt inadequate in handling worries about their courses, at skim reading, at exams, revision planning and organizing study time. Their chief fear was whether they were working hard enough. A similar checklist with part-time students revealed similar concerns. But it was also found that completing the checklist improved the students' perceptions of their efficiency. It seemed to help them focus on areas of work needing improvement.

Table 11.2 *How do you feel about it so far?*

Topic	Statement	Grade
Studying	1. Being able to concentrate well	
	2. Being able to skim read and select out important points	
	3. Keeping reasonably up to date	
Assignments	1. Finding out what is wanted in an assignment	
	2. Planning an assignment	
	3. Producing an assignment of a quality that satisfies me	
Tutorials	1. Getting the most out of them	
	2. Getting help from my tutor when I need it	
	3. Getting help from my fellow students	
Organization	1. Keeping up with family commitments	
	2. Keeping on top of my job and domestic duties	
	3. Not getting too worried about it all!	

Cognitive skills development

In the sections above I concentrated on the affective and organizational aspects of learning skills development. Developing general cognitive skills – reading effectively, writing essays and reports, numeracy, and perhaps IT skills – is too vast a subject to be tackled here in depth. But I would suggest that the same assumptions apply to both individual and group skills development: that is, establishing that there is an issue, looking at what a student is doing, clarifying, conceptualizing, contextualizing and challenging the student's responses. This is rather more complex than simply demonstrating the right methods to students and hoping they will copy them.

For example, students who are having consistent difficulties with algebra manipulation may need rather more than just being shown how to solve a problem; they may need to be taken back a little way in their understanding to see where their difficulties are arising.

Similarly, group methods for developing cognitive learning skills will need to encourage students to reflect on their cognitive learning in a similar way to their affective and organizational learning. Here are examples of such activities.

Course start

This will be a good time to help students experiment with different ways of tackling course materials and developing strategic learning methods.

EXAMPLE: TACKLING COURSE MATERIALS (BOOKS, TEXTS, ETC) (20 MINUTES)

1. Ask the students to bring in some course materials.
2. Ask the students to make some notes about the following questions on their own (5 minutes):
   - How are you going to tackle this text?
   - Are you going to read it, skim read it several times, or what?
   - Are you going to take notes? If so, how?
   - When will you look at the assignment?
   - What are you going to want from tutorials on the text?
3. Then snowball as far as appropriate, asking the students to draw up a list of possible strategies for tackling the text (10 minutes or more).
4. In plenary session, lead the discussion picking out the useful ideas for examination.

EXAMPLE: SKIMMING AND SUMMARIZING (40 MINUTES)

Two of the most useful study skills that hopefully will emerge from the discussion are skimming and summarizing material.

1. Ask the students to bring in a particular text, preferably one well ahead, in the course.
2. Tell them, 'Imagine you have got to tell the group in three minutes' time what this text is about – what its central messages are. Jot down some notes so you can do that.' (3 minutes)
3. In pairs, 'Compare what you have written down and how you found it. Do you think you have got to the heart of it?' (5 minutes)
4. (Optional) 'You have now got another ten minutes to summarize the text, but before you start decide with your neighbour just how you are going to go about it.' (10 minutes)
5. In plenary, 'Right, what have you got and how did you get there?' (20 minutes)

Before the first assignment

This is often a critical point in a student's progress. For some students this may be the first time in years that they have submitted work for assessment, so it will be a formidable hurdle.

EXAMPLE: TACKLING THE ASSIGNMENT (20 MINUTES)

Run a short simple snowball along the lines of the 'Tackling course materials' activity on how each student is going to tackle the assignment. Snowball to a plenary and draw out some of the most useful ideas.

Another possibility is to put students into the tutor's shoes.

EXAMPLE: ASSIGNMENT WRITING SKILLS

Find a couple of short reports or essays – one to two pages each – and duplicate them. Try to make one of the essays 'good' and the other 'poor'.

1. Ask the students in pairs to go through the essays and mark them, giving a grade and comments to justify the grade.
2. Share the grades and comments in plenary sessions, bringing out what elements seem to make an essay good or poor.

Revision and the exams

You will not need convincing of the general anxiety that surrounds the exams. These activities are not meant to replace advice to students on revision, exam techniques and tackling specific exam questions. They are intended to get students thinking purposefully about the way they tackle such things so that they are more likely to change their behaviour as a result.

EXAMPLE: REVISION (35 MINUTES)

1. Ask the students on their own to note down the revision techniques they have found most helpful in the past or are intending to use this time (3 minutes).
2. Share these techniques in pairs (10 minutes).
3. If appropriate, pool the best techniques in fours (10 minutes) or go straight to:
4. A plenary session where students can explore the most promising techniques with your help (20 minutes).

EXAMPLE: TACKLING THE EXAM (35 MINUTES)

1. Ask the students on their own to note the techniques they are going to use for tackling the exam paper (3 minutes).
2. Share the techniques in pairs (10 minutes).
3. If appropriate, pool the best techniques in fours (10 minutes) or go straight to:
4. A plenary session where students can explore the most promising techniques with your help (20 minutes).

Many other activities can be devised around these themes according to the tutor's tastes and skills. But they should all have the same characteristics: brevity, student interaction and reflection.

Scheduling learning skills development activities

Development activities for group learning need to be scheduled both within a tutorial and within a tutorial programme.

Within a face-to-face session

Group learning skills activities seem to work best when embedded within the course as far as possible. Students need to feel that any activities clearly relate to the overall goals of the course. Activities should be relatively brief and with clear outcomes, and be a welcome change of style and content.

Taking the tutorial I observed in chapter 6 as an example, I would have suggested to the tutor that she should have placed a short learning skills activity at some middle point in the tutorial – perhaps on an affective topic as a contrast to the cognitive work in the rest of the tutorial. A good activity at this early stage of the course, as the pace quickens, might be on stress management. Thus her tutorial plan might have been:

- introduction (5 minutes);
- cognitive activity in groups (15 minutes);
- summation of activity by tutor (5 minutes);
- affective activity in groups: stress management (15 minutes);
- introduction to next cognitive activity (5 minutes);
- cognitive activity in groups (20 minutes);
- summation and ending of tutorial by tutor (10 minutes);
- individual consultations (15 minutes).

Total: 1 hour 30 minutes.

Such an affective activity would provide a welcome change of pace and style within a tutorial that was otherwise rather pedestrian.

Within a tutorial programme

Group learning skills activities are clearly best concentrated at the front end of a course. Indeed for any new student there is a race between acquiring the skills to deal with challenges and the oncoming tide of such challenges. Students who are overwhelmed by those challenges may be likely to drop out. Thus a typical tutorial programme will look very similar to the structure outline in 'Proactive student support for learning skills development' earlier. The actual number of activities and the proportion of time that is taken will obviously depend on the incoming students' entry backgrounds and qualifications and the institution's structure and policies.

Students and learning skills development

How do students respond to programmes like these? There is evidence that students do value affective and organizational support as highly as purely cognitive and course specific support. See, for example, Entwistle and Ramsden (1983) in commenting on a survey: 'The inseparability of cognitive and emotional components of understanding was very clear in the comments made by students.' There are some caveats:

- The purpose of such activities must be clear.
- They must relate as far as possible to the course content – for example, pieces of text used for reading analysis work far better if taken from the course.
- The activities must relate to the course structure. This probably means again that most are best placed very early in the course. As the course moves on, cognitive and course-related skills activities will come to predominate.

Helping students overcome learning problems: 'study counselling'

Over the years I have worked with a number of individual students who have run into study difficulties. It has often struck me that while some of their difficulties are obviously cognitive (simply not possessing the appropriate knowledge background for a particular course), many if not most are affective and organizational. In particular there is a problem of 'study stress'. Obviously study is always stressful to some level, particularly for part-time students with all the other commitments they have, but sometimes there is a circle of stress which creates problems. Anxiety about study leads to:

- setting unrealistically high goals, which in turn leads to:
- failure to meet those goals, which causes:
- more anxiety, which in serious cases can grow into:
- depression about study and loss of motivation.

'Study counselling' is often a process of evaluating the student's current study methods, helping them move towards modifying these methods where that is appropriate and dealing with the symptoms of the stress. The process can be as follows:

1. First establish if there is a learning skills issue and what kind of issue it is. Is it cognitive, such as learning to tackle new material, or affective, such as dealing with the stress of assessment, or organizational, such as finding the time to study? Of course, establishing the issue may take a while and indeed there may be more than one problem: problems of finding the time may be connected with issues of self-confidence and lack of (say) numeracy skills.
2. If there are reasonably clear issues then look at what the student is doing. Use open-ended questions such as, 'How do you go about reading a new book?'; 'What happens when you start to write an essay?'; 'Tell me how you start to solve a maths problem?'; 'How do you organize your time'; 'What do you feel when you're writing up an assignment?'
3. Clarify, conceptualize, contextualize and challenge students' responses in such a way as to get them to reflect on their methods.
4. Where there are clear inadequacies in the skills, encourage the student to experiment with different methods. For example, students who merely read a book without interacting with it in any way or asking questions on what it is about may need encouragement and advice to experiment with scanning techniques, using notes or highlighting text to see which method might work better for them.

Here for example is an excerpt from a leaflet which I use as a prompt when working with students.

ARE YOU FINDING IT HARD TO CONCENTRATE OR GET DOWN TO STUDY? MANY PEOPLE DO – HERE ARE SOME IDEAS TO HELP

1.   Look at your study methods

First of all think about how you're studying now. Start by asking yourself some of the questions below [tick the boxes]:

When you start to read a course do you:

- [ ] get stuck straight in?
- [ ] skim read it and then get stuck in?
- [ ] look at the assignment for that Unit and see if you spot any points that might be relevant?
- [ ] ask yourself what the course is about and see if you can get an overview?
- [ ] go through it highlighting things?
- [ ] take notes on a separate sheet of paper or scribble in the Unit or not take notes at all?
- [ ] none of the above?

When tackling an assignment do you:

- [ ] sketch out some rough ideas that seem to be relevant and then get down to work?
- [ ] start writing straightaway to get something on paper?
- [ ] carefully plan out your essay in entirety before you start to write it up in detail?
- [ ] none of the above?

How did you start reading this leaflet? Did you:

- [ ] read it from start to finish?
- [ ] glance at the headings to see if it covered the sort of ground that might be useful to you?
- [ ] neither of the above?

Now the importance of doing this exercise is not that one of these methods is correct and the others incorrect; it's that the important thing is to experiment with different methods to see if one or other of them makes you feel better about studying than you do now.

So next time you are studying try using a method you haven't ticked, even if it's difficult to start with; it may be your first step on the way to dealing with the symptoms of study stress.

2.   Deal with the stress: the 'stop' method'

Loss of concentration and the feeling of not being able to cope are the main symptoms of study stress so it may be helpful to find ways of managing that stress by responding to the symptoms. This idea is very simple but students have told me that it works. When you're studying and begin to feel loss of concentration or feelings of anxiety just:

- lean back in your chair;
- say to yourself (out loud if possible) 'STOP';
- dangle your arms down by your sides;
- breathe in deeply and blow out gently two or three times;
- and start again, repeating as often as necessary.

3.   Contradict 'negative thoughts'

Another symptom of stress is the intrusion of constant repetitive 'negative thoughts' whilst studying. Typically these are thoughts like:

- I'm not understanding this at all.
- I haven't done enough.
- This isn't going to be good enough.
- I'm going to let myself/family/colleagues down.

Do you get anything like this? What's your commonest 'negative thought'?

Identifying negative thoughts is the first step on the way to coping with them. The next step is to find some 'coping thought' that will help you to terminate them. For me the coping thought is a brief expletive followed by the thought that 'I'll show them . . .' You may find something more subtle according to your tastes – what might be your coping thought?

Finding a coping thought may not be easy. Remind yourself of all the things you're good at and can manage outside study. Perhaps an answer may be in past experiences at school where you were 'put down' for being seemingly slow or something like that. Whatever it was, it doesn't have to apply now, does it?

4. Lower your sights

Finally I have spoken to many students who are finding study difficult because they are setting themselves impossibly high standards to start with. Sometimes they actually are unable to submit an assignment because they don't feel it's good enough. In this situation perfectionism is the enemy of success. If you are like this then it will be important to allow yourself to set more modest goals to begin with. You will achieve these more easily and this in itself will reduce your stress and enable you to gradually increase your standards. Remember your tutor would far rather have a modestly attempted assignment than none at all so 'get the thing in!'

5. Manage the external stress

Study isn't the only source of stress in your life. Family, job and money worries all create stress that spreads over into your study. You have to find ways of managing these 'stressors' at some reasonable level. What works for you? One of the simplest and best 'de-stressors' is gentle exercise – simply stretching for a few minutes or better still taking a brisk walk.

6. Talking to someone

Another good way of helping yourself is to talk to someone. Best of all talk to:

- Your co-students. You will discover that you're not alone. Nearly 80 per cent of students say that they worry that they're not studying as effectively as they might. Someone among your colleagues might have some useful ideas about how to study more effectively that might work for you.
- Your tutor. He or she has had lots of experience and will be able to help and advise you.
- Contact a study counsellor at your institution.

Your tutor or your study counsellor may be able to suggest particular workshops or readings that may help. They may even spot that your problems are more serious – you may have dyslexic tendencies for example – and be able to offer specialist help.

This leaflet was based partly on an article by Watts and a book by Main (see References). There is an example of a simple learning skills development dialogue in chapter 6, under 'Face-to-face support in practice'. Such an approach raises several issues:

- How far can student support for learning skills be proactive, reaching out to students who may not be asking for help but just quietly floundering?
- If such support can be made proactive, how can it be organized?
- What media can be used?

Learning skills development in other media

Everything that has been written here about learning skills development refers either to one-to-one or group face-to-face activities. If such development is important is it possible to carry it out in other media?

Computer conferencing for learning skills development

It is certainly possible to set up the computer conferencing equivalent of group activities for learning skills. For example, tutors can post a learning skills activity in a conference and get students to respond to it in a way similar to how face-to-face groups might respond. Here is an example from a course conference for a course that runs entirely on the Internet. The paper on *Clear Thinking* to which it refers is part of the study skills section of the course material which is posted on the Internet.

From Kathy (tutor)
I'd like each of you to post one message here, based on your reading of the paper on *Clear Thinking*. Find one point in it which you would like to highlight. Tell us why you think it is important and give an example of how it could affect your own studies.

Once these messages have been posted I will make a collective list of the main points which you have identified from the paper.

Hi Kathy
I believe most people start with their own theories on a subject and for some it is difficult to accept that they may be wrong. *Clear Thinking* highlights this and to me it's saying don't believe all you read at first but look deeper into it and read or listen to other people's points of view on a subject or activity then evaluate everything before making a decision.
Sue

Kathy
I was particularly attracted by the point of thinking about the people who had written the piece and how their experiences might have affected their writing. Earlier in the week I had read an article in the newspaper and knew both the journalist and the person interviewed. Therefore I possessed background information and was actually cross that people would take the piece at face value. A point that should be remembered with the wide-ranging material available on the Internet.
Beth

(I'm responding to Beth's point) This is the stuff that journalism and the media are made of and realization is only the first step. The difficulties often really start when one tries to clear the fog of bias to find a basis on which to form a valid opinion of the reality.
Brian

Web and CD ROM for learning skills development

There are certainly learning skills materials available on the Web or via CD ROM and we have seen examples of Web pages devoted to specific skills in writing in chapter 7.

Correspondence for learning skills development

Obviously learning skills can be addressed by correspondence. Looking into my local bookstore recently I counted at least a score of 'teach yourself to learn' books on the shelves, many of them aimed at the ODL market. A closer examination suggested that many of these books dealt largely with cognitive and course specific learning skills and were quite prescriptive.

As I suggested earlier, the field of learning skills is wider than the purely cognitive and simply giving advice does not in general alter students' behaviour. In addition it also struck me that some of the texts were surprisingly densely written – to the extent that anyone starting to read them would need to have reasonably well-developed learning skills to get beyond the first few pages. I found myself wondering if there was any evidence that such books really worked and whether such materials could take more account of the affective and reflective nature of learning skills.

A related idea is to embed learning skills into course material, and an increasing number of courses are doing just that using a qualification framework as an incentive. Students can choose to demonstrate core skills that are similar to some of the learning skills discussed in this chapter. It is not yet clear how popular this approach is with students.

Chapter 12

Student support for different students

Introduction

One of the most obvious (and attractive) features of open and distance learning is that it brings in students from a wider range of backgrounds than conventional education. For many of these students ODL is a second chance; for some whose previous educational experience was very poor it is almost a first chance.

Whoever they are, their support needs may be particularly marked. They may at the same time find it hard to identify and express those needs, and the needs may be different for a variety of reasons: previous educational disadvantage, physical and mental disability, institutionalization and language problems, for example.

Support for educationally disadvantaged students

Educational disadvantage can arise in a number of ways through both previous educational experience and current circumstances.

Previous educational experience

Students' previous educational experience may have been disrupted through illness, family breakdown or in other ways. They may have had a poor educational experience at school or become part of a peer group that did not value education. Whatever their experience it has probably alienated them from ideas of study and learning. They will be characterized by extreme lack of self-confidence, motivational concerns, poor learning skills (see Datta, 1998) and a considerable fear of further failure.

Certainly previous educational qualification is the principal predictor of progress in ODL. Again in my organization there is a clear decline in retention rates from 80 per cent for students with existing degree level qualifications to 50 per cent for students with no previous educational qualifications.

Current circumstances

Circumstances that appear to disadvantage students are being a shift worker, unemployed, isolated in some way, being a man, and studying maths, science and technology-based courses (McGivney, 1996). Unfortunately it is difficult to disentangle all of these characteristics. Is shift workers' higher tendency to withdraw a reflection of their socio-economic class, sex and educational level? The same applies to the unemployed, and more men than women tend to study maths, science and technology courses which have higher drop out rates.

Clearly more sophisticated research is needed in this complex area. I have always been fascinated, for example, by the number of low qualified students who succeed. What is the difference between them and their failing co students?

Targeting support for educationally disadvantaged students

There are clearly issues about targeting support on students who are educationally disadvantaged.

Identify educationally disadvantaged students

Such a process will need some kind of algorithm that identifies students most at risk. The algorithm will depend on student progress data collated by the institution as to the particular characteristics of its failing students, and emphasize the importance of collecting and evaluating such data. Combinations of factors such as low educational qualifications together with unemployment and apparently inappropriate course choices may be used. However, such algorithms are never particularly accurate.

The medium of support that is appropriate

It seems very likely that the only kind of suitable support will be on a one-to-one basis. Calling together a group of educationally disadvantaged students hardly seems a positive way forward. Being identified as being at risk in such a way might well be more demoralizing and all too reminiscent of being 'picked on' at school. Offering general induction workshops on learning skills to all new students may well be a useful solution, but may be found threatening by the very students one is trying to reach. All too often in my experience the majority of students who come to such workshops are those who do not really need them and who are already reasonably well prepared. A colleague of mine sometimes refers to what she calls the 'dreaming syndrome' – would-be students who, having nerved themselves up to apply, are unable to deal with the consequences of that decision and go forward hoping that somehow it will be all right on the night. Such students are particularly hard to reach in general ways.

There is one particular exception to the problem of using groups. Where a group already exists then the group itself can be an extraordinarily powerful support medium. Young mothers on an estate who have come together as a child care group who go on to study together, a group of workmates following a particular interest, a pair of friends who decide to learn together, have all been successful against the odds in the past. Building on the work of such informal and more formal access groups can be the most effective way of overcoming educational disadvantage. But finding or setting up such groups is certainly not an easy task.

The kind of support that is appropriate

If support is to be offered largely on a one-to-one basis then there are two key areas. The first is pre-course start. Support in this period may well centre particularly on enhancing the potential students' self-confidence to the point where they are able to help themselves, undertaking preparatory and learning skills development work.

The second is at the pre-assignment point. For many educationally disadvantaged students this may be the first time they have undertaken any assessed work since the last time they failed an exam at school. Sensitive encouragement to submit will be critical. It may be worth building some formative assignment into the course programme, that is, work that is not counted towards the course grade but is assessed by the tutor and feedback given to the student. But the effectiveness of such assignments is hard to assess even if the approach seems very logical.

How effective and ethical targeting is

As so often with student support activities it is hard to assess how effective targeting support on at-risk students is. There is some evidence (Thorpe, 1988) from the UK OU on a project that required tutors to target and report on educationally disadvantaged students. The project appeared to enhance the progress of such students and indeed to bring their pass rates to somewhere near those for better qualified students. Nevertheless, there are still problems. The cost of such an individual approach is very high and must be at the expense of support that is more general. What are the ethics and equal opportunity implications of the diversion of such resources?

Support for students with physical disabilities

Students with disabilities are particularly drawn to open and distance learning. For many, ODL may well be the only form of education open to them, their disabilities making it impossible for them to study in full-time or face-to-face settings. There are an increasing number of technical aids to assist such students but the most important source of support will be the awareness and sensitivity of the institution's staff. Such staff will need well-developed equal opportunities skills.

Disability awareness

It may be easiest to illustrate the issues around disability awareness through a couple of brief case histories.

Case study 1

A tutor is holding a session with a group of new students. He notices that one student doesn't seem to be paying much attention and isn't responding to the questions that he is putting on the board. He gets the impression that she is bored, and he is mildly irritated. However, he makes a point of talking to her afterwards and she explains that she is visually handicapped but didn't declare it beforehand. She can't actually see the board clearly. The tutor arranges for her to receive enlarged material and ensures that he writes larger figures on the board.

Case study 2

I have arranged a workshop for new students in a local college. The main rooms all have wheelchair access but as numbers increase at the last minute I have to book a temporary classroom as well. I know that a wheelchair user is coming but fail to check the room out, and sure enough when he turns up (a little late due to parking difficulties) he has been allocated that room which turns out to have steps. He refuses the indignity of being carried up the steps and refuses to have the groups switched round to accommodate him. He leaves in an unhappy frame of mind.

These studies illustrate how being aware of the possibility of disability can allow simple but effective action, but also how it must be a factor in everyday planning.

They also illustrate that students with disabilities can be both very non-assertive and not want to cause any bother like the visually handicapped student or, alternatively, angry when their needs are not met and sometimes perhaps over-react like the student with impaired mobility. Above all, students with disabilities generally want to be as independent as possible but have their needs met when they want.

Diagnosing disability needs

Students' needs can vary very widely even with the same disability and the simplest method of diagnosis is to ask students what they believe their disability is and what help might best compensate. They may need to be reassured of the flexibility of the institution in meeting their needs since their previous experience may not have been particularly good in that respect. Help can be offered mainly in two ways: technical and organizational.

Meeting specific disability needs

It is impossible to list the full range of disabilities or the corresponding help that can be provided. This is a very brief list:

- *Visual handicap.* Technical aids can be enlarged print or Braille materials, magnifiers including CCTV scanning systems, audiotapes, text–voice converters or simply readers. Organizational help will include setting up a well-lit, quiet environment (some visually handicapped students rely particularly on their hearing) and allowing extra time to complete assignments and exams.
- *Hearing impairment.* Technical aids can be using hearing loops, text phones, transcripts and (in some cases) interpreters or lip-speakers. Organizational help will particularly involve briefing tutors on the practical considerations and best environment for lip reading using handouts.
- *Mobility impairment.* Mobility impairment can affect either people's ability to move around or their ability to hold and move objects such as books or pens. Technical aids can include specially adapted typewriters or computers and comb-bound materials. Organizational help could include the availability of parking or transport arrangements and wheelchair access and special arrangements for assignments and exams.
- *Learning difficulties.* The most common learning difficulty is dyslexia. Indeed dyslexia students seem particularly drawn to ODL, perhaps because of previous unsatisfactory educational experience and consequent comparative lack of educational qualifications. Their dyslexia may well not have been diagnosed, and one organizational aid is to brief tutors and advisers to be aware of symptoms of dyslexia such as poor spelling, expression and organization of work, especially when oral work suggests evident abilities. It may then be possible to suggest assessment. Although that has to be carried out by educational psychologists and is costly, it can be very helpful to students both in terms of their confidence and in suggesting different learning strategies. Technical help can include computers and possibly using tape recorders to record notes and tutorials.

Support for students with mental health problems

In a similar way to dyslexia, students with mental health difficulties can be drawn to open and distance learning. There are indeed students for whom learning can be therapeutic and offer validation that is hard to find in the rest of their lives. But students with mental health difficulties can be significant because of not only their support needs but also the occasionally very difficult demands they can make on institutional staff.

Mental health awareness

These demands arise because such students seldom identify themselves (although with the de-stigmatization of mental health difficulties it is thankfully becoming easier for them to do so). Thus the first evidence that there may be a problem can come as a surprise to staff and not be easy to understand or handle. Therefore staff need to be aware of the symptoms of illnesses like schizophrenia, depression, anxiety and autism. They should also be aware of the boundaries of their roles, and what support is possible and what is not. They must be prepared to take action where necessary to protect the interests of other students who may become involved.

Case study 3

Recently I was contacted by a tutor who was concerned about a student's strange behaviour in a tutorial. The student was attempting to dominate the discussion with personal references and introducing irrelevancies. The behaviour was not in itself unusual but (and this is typical) it was the degree and persistence that worried the tutor. His efforts to modify the student's behaviour proved unfruitful and some of the other students approached him with concerns.

On checking our records I discovered that the student had identified herself to us several years previously as having a 'psychotic condition' following a mental breakdown. In a not unparalleled administrative breakdown, this information had not been passed on to the tutor. It was also apparent from the records that sadly the student had not made any progress in her studies since her breakdown.

The tutor found this news very reassuring: after some discussion he decided to persist with his efforts to modify the student's behaviour. On my part, I agreed that if he found he was unsuccessful and the student became unreasonably disruptive, we would take steps to exclude the student from the tutorial and offer some phone support instead. In the event he was able to contain the situation.

Such a case is typical of the way that staff can blame themselves for not being able to contain a situation and are subsequently relieved to find that it is not their fault. It is also typical of the way that the institution may need to step in to protect the interests of its staff and students as a last resort, whilst remembering equal opportunities requirements.

Support for specific mental health difficulties

Again it is impossible to describe the full range of possible mental health difficulties that staff may come across. Four conditions crop up more frequently than others.

Anxiety or phobia

This is excessive fear in ordinary situations such as being in a crowd or even in a public place (agoraphobia). Phobics are particularly drawn to distance learning and in fact can do quite well. A small-scale study of self-declared phobics suggested that they made better than average progress in their studies (Palmer, 1984).

For example, 'Jenny' is a relatively mildly agoraphobic student. She can drive and can even attend face-to-face tutorials as long as the groups are less than five or she can sit near the door (her 'escape route' as she puts it). The only specific support she needs is to be allowed to sit her exam at home since the combination of exam stress and agoraphobia is intolerable for her.

Depression

This is characterized by feelings of deep sadness that do not seem to arise out of the person's situation. Depression sometimes alternates with short periods of over-excitement and inflated self-esteem (manic depression). Depressed students can sometimes be recognized by their irregular production of assignments and their inability to respond to contact and great reluctance to express any optimism or sense of self-worth about their studies.

Depressives are not as successful as agoraphobic students but some can make progress, particularly in periods when the depression is under control. They can be helped by being given encouragement and maximum flexibility in their studies. They do not usually present problems to staff or students although depressive students can be difficult to support and do not have a very good track record of progress. Manic states can very occasionally cause problems and recently I have been trying to support a tutor who received a threatening phone call from a student in a manic state. However, this is only the third time in 20 years that I have had to deal with such a difficult situation.

For example, 'Alan' is a depressive. At first his tutor did not realize that there was a problem, but on trying to contact him she realized that he was often not responding. She was worried about this and tried offering more and more support to which again he did not respond. She began to feel rejected and inadequate. Finally with some help she set herself realistic boundaries, giving him praise and encouragement when she could and not hassling him about assignments. Alan has made erratic progress but has had some success.

Schizophrenia

This term is used to cover a variety of symptoms which generally relate to people's inability to distinguish between their own and other people's realities. Paranoid schizophrenics will have experiences of imagined plots against themselves.

Schizophrenics are very seldom able to study effectively, as it is hard for them to keep to a rational train of thought and concentration. They are easily distracted and will introduce irrelevancies, and a tutor may have difficulty controlling them in a tutorial.

Support is very difficult and must be within agreed boundaries. These boundaries will need to be carefully defined once schizophrenia is a possible diagnosis.

For example, his tutor noticed that 'David' behaved in a very odd manner in tutorials. He would sit out of the circle of students and would refuse to participate although continuing to attend. The other students found this disturbing and eventually asked that he be excluded. This was done to the distress of the tutor who felt that she had failed him in some way. Eventually it was discovered that David was a paranoid schizophrenic and the tutor was reassured by this. She continued to offer him one-to-one support and he made some progress.

Autism

People diagnosed as autistic tend to have difficulties developing social relationships and are unable to understand emotional expressions such as voice tone and body language. They appear uncommunicative and obsessive. Sadly they are unlikely to be able to study effectively in any way.

For example, 'Bill' is autistic. He is quite disruptive in tutorials, interrupting, being irrelevant, wandering around the room. His tutor found him threatening and came close to resignation. Eventually he was excluded from tutorials. He subsequently dropped out.

Implications of support for students with mental health difficulties

The case studies suggest that there are two particular implications of trying to support students with mental health difficulties.

Protecting staff

Unanticipated contact with such students can be very upsetting for staff who may become too involved, not realizing what the underlying problems are. The institution will need to have clear policies about setting boundaries for staff, supporting them and taking action to protect them when necessary.

Not prejudging issues

It is important to remember that many students with mental health difficulties will be able to progress their studies with sensitive and appropriate support. Staff may well need help in deciding what is appropriate and in overcoming their own prejudices.

Support for students in institutions

This is likely to be a minority interest but there has been a growth in recent years in the number of institutionalized students – students in prisons, secure mental health units or long-term nursing care – for whom open and distance learning is one of the few possibilities available. The comments below apply particularly to the prison situation.

Issues for students in prison

Many of the problems that students in prison encounter are similar to those encountered outside but greatly magnified.

Isolation. Students in prison may not be allowed the use of the phone or e-mail. There may not be other students in the prison and there may be an anti-educational culture. As a prisoner said to me: 'There's an anti-intellectual environment here – people can harass someone who's trying to study because they resent it!' Visits from tutors will be very restricted and contact with other students almost zero (although at some lower security prisons I have had some success in getting small groups of outside students to go in with the tutor for a tutorial with an inmate. They all emerge saying that it had been an important experience for them).

Disruption. Students' prison lives are very fragmented. They can be moved to other prisons at very short notice; security alerts can put them in cells for days without their course materials. The physical environment is very unhelpful: constant noise and interruption from other prisoners, television and radio are fatiguing and badly affect concentration. 'Prison is rarely quiet. It's hard to concentrate with the noise – particularly as the television always seems to be on' (prison student).

Time. Contrary to received opinion, prisoners do not usually have much free time. They may have to work and may have very little effective free time and privacy in which to study.

Stress. Prisons are very stressful places. To add the stress of study on top can be overwhelming: 'At times the thought of studying starts me into a real panic – I just feel that I've made a big mistake taking this on' (prison student). That stress can ultimately be overwhelming. Only a few days before writing this I took a call from a high security prison. One of our students had just transferred in from another prison which had failed to pass on his course materials. In such a position of total disempowerment he had slit his wrists. How serious his suicide attempt was I cannot say, but it was enough for the prison to put him on a 15-minute 'suicide watch'. We were able to find a tutor willing to go into the prison and talk to him and I am hoping for the best.

Issues for tutorial staff

If being in prison is a stressful experience for students then going into prison can also be very stressful for tutors.

Security. Particularly at a high security prison the procedures to get in are formidable. There are previous security checks, 'rub-down' searches and emptying pockets and bags for X-ray. Then being led through the prison passed endless locked doors hearing keys jangling and dogs barking can reduce even the calmest of people to a state of dependent anxiety.

One-to-one support. In normal circumstances one-to-one support can require considerable concentration and be very draining. In the prison environment the stress of such support is increased: 'You do sit there occasionally wondering what the man on the other side of the table did to get 15 years' (tutor at a high security prison).

Yet, despite these difficulties for tutors and students, there are very special rewards: 'I really didn't know what to expect but my student was very pleasant and intelligent. I enjoyed tutoring him.' Students can study in prison successfully and achieve quite extraordinary results. Last year I was in a high security prison at a 'graduation ceremony' for a student nearing the end of a 15-year sentence. He had previously been a lorry driver but had ended up successfully studying high level mathematics and could now discourse on advanced vector algebra. His parents had come in for the ceremony and at the end he stood up and said that this was the first time in his life that he felt he'd been a credit to them. He then burst into tears – and he wasn't the only one.

Support for older students

Clearly older students (aged 50 and up) can find open and distance learning very much suited to their needs. The flexibility of ODL, the way the study can be introduced into a routine without the complete upheaval involved in full-time study, and the wide range of courses available can make ODL attractive to such learners. Since the older age groups are growing in the population at large and more people are retiring early, the numbers are likely to increase substantially in the next few years.

That being the case, do we need to offer them special support? Do they have particular difficulties because of their age and experience? The answers appear very largely to be 'no' on both counts. What research that has been done suggests that older students differ relatively little in their needs from younger ones (Clennell, 1987). It may take them a little longer to adapt to learning but they often bring a wealth of previous experience to their studies. We should nevertheless be sensitive to needs that, while not unique to older students, are perhaps particularly pronounced among them. They may, for example, suffer more frequently from fatigue or mobility problems. They may feel inhibited among younger people in a face-to-face environment and need more encouragement to contribute without being obviously singled out.

Support for students abroad

Competitive pressures have meant that many ODL institutions now actively recruit outside their country's borders. In addition, of course, one of the great advantages of ODL – its portability – means that ODL students who are posted abroad will want to take their studies with them.

The problems such students face are predominantly those of isolation: not just from the institution and its tutors, but isolated from other students.

Isolation can be ameliorated in the usual ways but only at greater expense or inconvenience: phone calls cost much more and may be difficult to make because of time differences, mail costs more and can be subject to delays that can be considerable. Assignment feedback is delayed and the possibility of a dialogue by correspondence is even more unlikely.

The one form of communication that does not cost more and is as quick as ever is electronic, and there seems little doubt of its popularity with students. They tend to be enthusiastic users of e-mail and to feel that they have some personal links with other students as a result.

Even those students who do not use e-mail want as personal a contact with their tutors as possible. As I write these paragraphs I am fresh from a lunch given for students from Hong Kong, Greece and Ireland who told me that even trivial details such as getting a photograph of their tutor would help them feel less isolated.

Second language students

If students are recruited abroad then inevitably some will be attracted for whom the language of instruction is their second language. The issue of support to such students in terms of diagnosing their skills and providing appropriate help is too big for this book. However, anyone providing support should be aware that such students might well be more at risk in situations where their language skills are under stress.

At the lunch I attended, I complimented a German on his excellent English. 'I still have a problem,' he told me. 'When I have time to write I do very well. But when I am under pressure my language skills tend to desert me. So I never do very well in exams.' Thus support to such a student may well need quite sensitive and empathic understanding of how his language skills may be affected by the different stresses of learning.

In the long term, overseas students may have unexpected effects on ODL institutions. As such institutions grow to become global providers they will attract substantial numbers of students who may not share the common cultural background of the institution. Their demands may well affect what the institution does in terms of both its course and its student support.

Support for students from different cultures

Even if an ODL institution does not recruit students from overseas it will certainly have many students from various ethnic and cultural backgrounds in its home population. Such students may have different educational and social values which may make supporting them a more subtly different process. Again support staff will need to have an acute awareness of equal opportunity issues. For example, in some cultures the influence and authority of the family may well be more than others. This can be both positive (the high value placed on education by many Asian families is thought to be a factor in the relative success of their children) and negative.

A student of Vietnamese extraction talked with me about family support for his studies. His problem curiously was too much support: his mother took a highly developed interest in his studies and put him under tremendous pressure. I hope that talking to me was a little help at least in managing the stress of the situation.

A female student from a very strict religion also wished to study with us. However, her family and husband held very firm views as to what was allowed to a woman in their culture and refused to let her enrol. She was quite determined, however, and used a neighbour's address for post and studied while her husband was out at work. We arranged for a tutor to visit her at her neighbour's occasionally to support her. This in itself raised some ethical issues: how far were we encouraging her in what could possibly be a dangerous course of action? At any rate she passed her courses with ease and graduated.

Other examples of cross–cultural issues can arise from (for example) the use of cultural references which may be unfamiliar. In the first edition of this book I received a number of comments from readers about references which I should have recognized would not be understood outside a British context.

There are also subtler cross–cultural issues of style and approach. I have had the privilege of having some of my materials adapted to other cultures. In front of me as I write I have a version of a leaflet I wrote from Botswana. I note that the writer has produced a much firmer, less tentative document, which I imagine is more appropriate for his students than the original.

Support for the different sexes

Finally it seems clear that support is received and used differently by the different sexes. Research (Kirkup and Von Prummer, 1990) conducted in the UK and Germany suggests that men and women make different demands on student support services. Women tend to be more regular attenders at face-to-face sessions and appear to value interaction with other students more than men.

It is certainly a matter of frequent observation in student support that women appear to seek advice and help more often than men in face-to-face situations. It is possible that men may make more use of 'neutral' media such as e-mail. Thus the gender balance in an institution may be a factor in deciding on the design of a student support service. It is certainly again an issue for an equal opportunities analysis.

Chapter 13

Student support for access, acquisition, retention and retrieval

Support for student retention

I argued right at the beginning of this book that one of the justifications for student support was student retention. This was because retention was likely to become an even more important issue in ODL in the future due to issues of quality assessment, student assertiveness and institutional funding.

Of course retention is not solely a function of student support. Retention depends also on course structure and content and institutional policies. Indeed it could be argued that retention is much more influenced by courses and policy; no amount of quality support can outweigh the problems caused by a badly written or inappropriate course or a particularly student-unfriendly policy.

In addition, it could be argued that the overriding aim of student support may actually be to assist students towards their personal goals. Clearly, students' goals in studying do not always coincide with the goals the institution might have for them. Students who withdraw can nevertheless be perfectly satisfied with their experience but will count as failures from the institution's perspective.

Nevertheless student support and retention are closely enough linked to take a 'retention perspective' on issues of student support.

General principles of student retention

Until now in this book the 'student as customer' analogy has been resisted. Students invest a great deal more emotion and effort in their studies than in (say) the purchase of a washing machine, and have a correspondingly close relationship with the institution. Nor do the manufacturers of washing machines test their customers to see if they are fit to go on owning a machine, and finally if machines go wrong customers tend to blame the manufacturer, not themselves, a contrast to the way that students usually blame their own inadequacies for failure.

There are other problems with the analogy. Tett (1993) argues that the 'market-place' model of education disadvantages both participants and providers and is flawed (for example) from the point of view of individuals who are not able to make 'actual choices'.

Nevertheless, I think there are occasionally useful analogies. Clutterbuck (1995) identified a number of steps towards managing 'customer defection', some of which I have adapted:

1. Ensure that customer defection is the responsibility of specific people or teams within the organization.
2. Identify the customers you wish to attract and keep.
3. Identify those most at risk of defection.
4. Identify the dynamics of their go/stay decision.
5. Identify the points at which they go or stay.
6. Develop and implement a retention programme.
7. Benchmark and refine the programme.

Translated into student support terms these become as follows.

Responsibility for student retention management

This can be surprisingly diffuse in many educational institutions. There will be staff responsible for tuition, for advisory services and for quality but there may well be no 'Student Progress Manager' or equivalent who is responsible specifically for student progress monitoring, intervention, data evaluation and policy changes as a result. Even if individual staff or teams of staff are responsible for some aspects of retention they may not be responsible for others. For example, you may find that responsibility for progress within a particular course or module is the responsibility of the course or module tutor. They may well be the best-equipped people to deal with what I think of as 'micro-progress' issues of monitoring students' progress through a particular course.

That will still leave issues to do with retention across an entire programme of courses or modules such as might make up a qualification – the 'macro-progress' issue. Once students have moved on from a module, is there a gap into which they can fall before moving into the care of the next module tutor?

Which students to attract and retain

Which students to attract

There are difficult issues, particularly for open entry institutions which rightfully wish to become more accessible to educationally disadvantaged students. Since such students are more likely to drop out, there is a danger that widening access offers such students not an open door but a revolving door which sweeps them out of the institution as fast as they enter. Widening access will therefore imply a consequent enhancement and focusing of support for such students.

Institutions with entry qualifications obviously use a 'customer selection' process but do not entirely avoid the problem. For example, in the UK the main school leaving qualification, A level, is thought to be a bad predictor of final degree performance and it seems likely that the selection process is actually weeding out potential students who could be as successful as the students selected.

Which students to retain

Almost anyone working in student support will wish to retain as many students as possible. And yet a kind of 'triage' operates (triage is the process by which military surgeons decide who is worth treating on the battlefield).

Recently I spoke to a tutor about one of her students who had persistently promised to submit an assignment for several weeks. She had chased him on nearly half a-dozen occasions but nothing had materialized. As quite often, I found myself suggesting that she had done all she could and that we should now leave it up to the student to deliver or not. Any more time spent on him would inevitably be taken out of the time spent with other students who might respond positively. In addition, I was concerned that her morale and commitment might be affected by an almost certainly unsuccessful outcome of her efforts.

It is conceivable that with mounting pressure on staff such boundary setting to support will become the norm.

Which students are most likely to drop out

We have noted previously in chapter 12 that there are a number of predictors of student drop out of which previous educational level is probably the most important. An example taken from the UK Open University suggests a clear relationship between drop out and previous educational level.

It is interesting that even those students with the highest level of previous education still have a residual drop out rate of about 20 per cent. This suggests perhaps that there is an irreducible minimum in drop out; that these are the students who would have dropped out for reasons beyond our control.

Chapter 12 again suggests that other predictors are work and economic circumstances, sex, location and course. Take two extreme examples from my own institution. A white middle-class woman at home with children living in the town

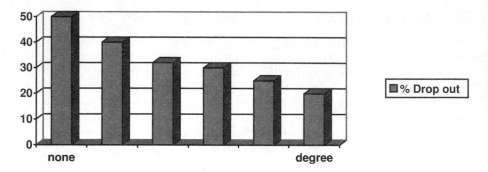

Figure 13.1 *Drop out rates versus increasing level of previous educational qualifications*

of Cambridge and studying arts courses has more than an 85 per cent chance of passing her course, as against a black working-class unemployed man living in London studying maths who has only a 16 per cent chance of passing.

These factors cannot be the only ones operating and must in any case be interrelated. And even if we could identify other factors, or even find tests that could identify students particularly at risk, a number of issues would remain such as targeting support and getting support accepted.

Targeting support

I have already discussed (chapter 12) the ethics of targeting support and suggested that targeting can be effective if the ethical problems can be overcome. However, there are also issues about students being offered support who do not accept it. Clearly students cannot be forced to accept help, and students who can accept help may be among the 50 per cent who would succeed anyway.

It is often noticeable that there are students who, while apparently good candidates for targeted support, do not take up offers of help. This is particularly true of students who before courses start – I have already referred to them as 'dreamers' – do not take up offers of support, ignore advice about course choice and take on levels of study that are inappropriate for them. It is as though for them study is a gamble: something to have a flutter on with a modest chance that it might work this time. If this simple analysis is true, it is hard to see how such students might be reached.

The dynamics of students' go/no go decision

There are two aspects to this issue: post hoc rationalizations of why students drop out and the actual dynamics of the drop out action.

Why students drop out: post hoc rationalizations

This question always has the virtues of apparent simplicity. If we knew why students dropped out then we could do something about it. However, as ever with student support nothing is that simple. If students are asked why they have dropped out in ODL then their answers will differ in detail from one institution to another, but there will be broad agreement on the main answers and the order in which they appear:

- lack of time;
- change of family or employment circumstances;
- illness;
- bereavement;
- inappropriate course choice;
- poor support;
- a host of miscellaneous issues.

Overwhelmingly, the institution can do very little about these issues. But it is important to ask if the answers are reliable. It is not that students are consciously hiding the truth but clearly 'lack of time' may be a symptom of an underlying cause such as:

- intellectual difficulties with the course;
- inadequate skills;
- inadequate preparation.

Indeed, when tutors are asked the reasons why particular students on their course dropped out, they are much more likely to identify such issues as being the 'real' causes of withdrawal. Whether they are right or not is not quite material; the point is that the question 'why do students drop out?' is not susceptible to simple answers. As McGivney (1996) says, 'there is a chronic lack of reliable data on the extent and nature of student withdrawals'.

Dynamics of the drop out decision

Another aspect of 'the drop out question' is that the answer is invariably a post hoc rationalization – it is an answer derived from an examination of the pieces of wreckage after the crash. But we could do with the 'black box' of withdrawal: we need to know more about the events leading up to the crash. Why in particular might two students experience apparently similar events – illness and bereavement – and yet one be able to continue whilst the other withdraws?

Clearly, personal qualities over which we have little control will be important factors in deciding who does and does not withdraw. But some unpublished research in my own institution suggests that there is one particularly important factor that distinguishes successful and unsuccessful students, particularly in the early stages of their courses. We have mentioned it much earlier in another context – it is the factor of isolation. The difference between successful and unsuccessful students is that the former have more and more effective support networks. Such support networks can be both informal – from family, friends, mentors, fellow students – and formal – from tutors and the institution. The more networks a student can tap into and the more effective they are, the better that student's chances.

It will therefore be important for the institution to maximize the student's networks and help enhance their efficiency. This will certainly require proactive contacts especially at the earliest stages.

The points at which students can drop out

Students can drop out at several points in their progress, from initial enquiry as potential students through to the successful completion of their studies (a drop out point at which support may still be important if students are to be good ambassadors for the institution).

The number of ways in which students can leave may be surprising. My own institution provides a wide range of drop out opportunities and others may do the same:

- enquirers who do not register for a course;
- students who become dormant – they do not withdraw but do not submit assignments;
- students who 'actively' withdraw;
- students who submit assignments but do not take the exam;
- students who fail the exam outright;
- students who fail for administrative reasons – not paying fees, etc;
- students who fail, are granted re-sits and fail them;
- students who fail, are granted re-sits but do not take them;
- students who pass one course or module but do not reserve or register for another.

Thus there are nine 'holes' through which students may 'leak'. Many of these holes will generate no response from my institution. If other organizations are the same then it will clearly be important to set out a retention strategy that ensures that students cannot leak away without some kind of attempt to keep them in by the institution. It is also important to be aware of the scale of student loss at these various exit points. For example I found that a 'river' diagram helps me understand how students exit in my own institution: the width of the river at any time is proportional to the number of students active at that time.

This (much simplified) diagram illustrates that student drop out is very heavily front-loaded: nearly 30 per cent of the students on this course do not get as far as the first assignment. This has important implications for the timing of student support activities.

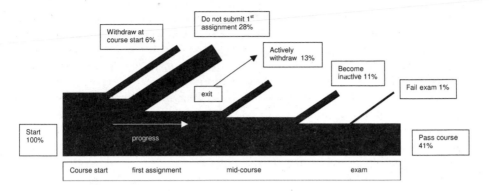

Figure 13.2   *A 'river' diagram of withdrawal from the UK OU*

Developing retention strategies

There will be different retention strategies at different stages.

- Access and acquisition: recruiting new students (access) and ensuring that they are properly engaged with their studies and the institution (acquisition).
- Retention on course: keeping students going on the course.
- Retrieval: getting withdrawn or failed students back to study.

Access, acquisition and student support

Access

Access is of course a fundamental characteristic of open learning schemes but is too large a topic to cover in this book. However, it may be helpful to look at a model of access in order to discuss the framework of support for access. One model (Darkenwald and Merriam, 1982) suggests that the barriers to participation in education may be as follows:

- *Informational:* it may be difficult to supply or get adequate and appropriate information about (say) course content and availability, or brochures may be dense and inaccessible, or promotion and marketing inadequate.
- *Institutional:* an institution may have unfriendly systems, difficult enrolment procedures, hard to contact advisory processes and so on.
- *Situational:* the possible student's personal situation may be a barrier: travelling to face-to-face tuition or getting computing facilities may be difficult or impossible.
- *Psychosocial:* the possible student may hold beliefs or attitudes which are likely to inhibit their progress – 'I couldn't possibly do that', 'I'm too young/old/unskilled for that' – the lack of self-esteem of the learner.

Thus student support for access must take into account these barriers and how they apply to students.

Acquisition

Assuming that the institution has developed systems for overcoming informational, institutional, situational and psychosocial barriers as far as possible, there is still the process of ensuring that new students become fully engaged with their studies; that is they become properly 'acquired' by the institution and feel a real part of it. As can be seen from Figure 13.2, in the UK OU, as in many similar institutions, up to 40 per cent of students effectively withdraw without engaging with their courses.

There are three particular aspects of acquisition support (often referred to in the UK under the blanket term 'guidance'). These are:

● course choice: getting students on to the right course for them;
● preparatory support;
● induction support.

The 'right' course choice

The 'right' course may of course be a different course from the one initially chosen, or it might be fewer courses or no course at all. Recruiting students is a delicate balance. There will be tensions between the institution's marketing aim desire to 'sell' courses and the support section's wish to recruit only students with a reasonable chance of success. If the institution is committed to an access policy there will be another delicate balance between the gentle encouragement needed to build up the confidence of students from educationally disadvantaged backgrounds and the truth of the difficulty of what they are taking on. There will be two aspects to consider.

The first aspect is materials for course choice. Institutions will rely heavily for recruitment on the descriptions of study and courses in the institution's brochure. These may be inadequate in several ways: course descriptions can be optimistic and one-sided, for example. To give students a fair picture of a course it may be necessary to offer them sets of 'competing perspectives' such as those discussed below.

Taster or sampler packs

These are short extracts of the course material, together possibly with sample assignment and tutor assessments for that course. Such taster packs can be designed to give students not just a taste of the level of the course, but if selected to be a certain length of work they can give some sense of the time needed for a course.

Students' comments on courses

The views of students on courses they have taken can be particularly illuminating for intending students as long as it is clear that they are individuals' idiosyncratic perspectives. One simple way of providing a variety of perspectives is to collate the views of a number of students who have taken that course. This is an example of different views on one particular UK OU course which is part of a set of comments on all UK OU courses. These comments are available to intending students via a Web site.

> Course: 'Approaching Literature'
> 'A highly rewarding and stimulating course, but demanding in its reading requirement. An open mind is needed to make the most of the course. Those who resist the course's call to explore literature in a variety of ways will waste energy and miss out on some of its riches. Those who tackle the course in a positive way will find much that is both challenging and enjoyable, and have their literary horizons permanently widened.'
>
> 'Extremely "gendered" throughout the course – not just in the Literature and Gender block – at times aggressively so. The course is very fractured and made an overall picture difficult to form. Also it was never made clear why the traditional six Romantic poets were considered to be so good, or why others were excluded. . .'
>
> 'I have really enjoyed this course. It is a well-structured and balanced course and the texts were interesting and well chosen. Of course, there were parts which I enjoyed more than others, but having said that, none of it seemed fruitless.'

It is interesting to note that the UK government is now discussing following the Australian practice of allowing students to comment on their courses on Web sites specifically for the information of potential new students.

Tutors' comments on courses

Where courses are taught by different tutors, their views on the courses are also valuable and can be offered in the same way.

> Course: 'Approaching Literature' (each comment is by a different tutor)
> 'This course will give you an excellent grounding in literary studies, providing highly interesting texts to study, and investigating why some of them have become part of the course and others not. It challenges you to investigate the relationship between society and literature using a variety of texts. The reading load is heavy but supplemented by specially commissioned and contemporary production of the play text on video. This course is for students who want to be abreast of, and engaged in, all that excites us about literature today.'
>
> 'Recommended to all those who enjoy literature but also feel they'd like to know a bit more about current critical method and theory. The course

offers a variety of different approaches to literature, each of which is in its own way illuminating, instructive and challenging. It is not always easy. The rewards are not only greater understanding but also increased confidence in your own ability to formulate and express critical opinion.'

Diagnostic materials

Quizzes which relate to the background knowledge and the skills needed to undertake a course can be useful to intending students. There can be two kinds: those which can be self-assessed by the student and those assessed by the institution. While the first is non-threatening there may be little incentive to the student to undertake the activity. And while it is relatively easy to write self-assessed diagnostic materials for maths, science and technology subjects with clear right and wrong answers, it is less easy for arts and social science subjects where answers are less easily self-assessed. The second possibility can be expensive for the institution and in an open-entry arrangement appears very much like an entrance exam.

There will also be a need to contact individual students, particularly those identified as being at risk, and advise them probably by phone or occasionally face to face. Such advice will be based on knowledge of their previous education and exploration of their motivation and experience. Advisory activities can also tailor preparatory advice to particular students' needs.

Nevertheless, it is not clear that advisory contact always has the institutionally desired outcome. There is evidence that such contact can persuade students to reduce their workload but is less successful in changing course choice or preparatory behaviour (Johnson, Mayes and Doolittle, 1999). It seems that once intending students have taken a particular choice they become quite committed to that choice and can be hard to shift. It may be that the most effective recruitment tactics are to combine materials and activities together so that spoken advice is reinforced by materials for reflection.

Preparatory and induction activities

I have suggested a distinction here between induction and preparation.

Induction is engaging students with the ethos, procedures and processes of the institution and encouraging them to see themselves as effective learners.

Preparation is the process of helping students develop the supporting knowledge needed for a course and the generic and specific skills needed for studying that course.

Induction

Starting or restarting study is about fresh beginnings, and the importance of those beginnings to the student can seldom be underestimated. Induction is important because any new beginning is difficult and because institutions can be forbidding and impenetrable. Open and distance learning institutions are often good at the organizational aspect of induction – telling new students about systems, rules and regulations – but less certain on the affective nature of the induction process.

I have no prescriptive answers to that conundrum here except that it is important to put oneself in the position of new students and ask how they might be feeling at this stage. If, for example, there is some kind of face-to-face gathering for new students, how does that work? Are students greeted properly as they arrive? Are they made to feel welcome and valued? If they are late is that taken care of? What feelings will they take away? If there is no face-to-face induction, how does the distance induction work? Is it just a package of administrative material or is there some kind of attempt to make the new student feel like a valued member of the institution?

Preparation

To some extent we have covered preparation in chapter 11 on learning skills development. Any preparatory programme for new students will need to take on board two particular aspects: the generic versus course specific study skills issue, and the supporting knowledge for a course.

First, generic versus course specific skills. I suggested previously that generic skills are best taught within a specific context: for example, historical essay writing skills using historical texts within the course itself. Thus the preparatory skills become part of the course rather than an add-on. But this formulation ignores the fact that institutions may have little choice. If, for example, there is a wide range of students on different courses within an area, then any group face-to-face skills development is very likely to have to be generic.

Second, supporting knowledge for a course. Clearly it will not be possible to help students acquire substantial background knowledge for a particular course. They would be better advised to start on a different course. But it is possible to envisage advising students to undertake particular items of reading or to acquire particular areas of knowledge through preparatory courses or literacy and numeracy workshops, particularly if there is a long lead-on time to course start.

Case study

Chris is a 27-year-old plasterer. He left school at 16 because he was fed up with it. Since then he has bummed around, doing short-term building jobs, drinking, going to discos and generally leading the life of a 21st-century 'lad'. He comes from a single-parent home and recently his mother, increasingly fed up with him, told him to leave home. He is hard up and cannot afford a car or computer or even a video.

But he does have a feeling that he doesn't want to go on for ever like this. He has a girl friend who has just gone to university, and although the relationship is not easy it's survived so far and she's an example to him. He would like to work with animals in some way and realizes that even at school he was always interested in science, so he has registered for an ODL science course. From the access model perspective Chris has already done quite well. He has overcome most of the informational barriers, although he may not be quite clear what he's taking on in the course he has chosen. He has dealt with the institutional barriers so far, but there are situational barriers to come: face-to-face tutorials are not held in his town, the closest are in a town difficult to reach by public transport. And without a fixed address at the moment he does not have a phone.

But Chris's biggest problem may be the psychosocial barriers: he is more than intelligent enough for the course but doesn't believe it. He certainly lacks any confidence in his learning skills, although they are actually quite adequate if he only knew it.

So what kind of support would actually help Chris? How might it relate to what we have covered in the book so far? How might the institution best 'acquire' him?

Let's look at which media we use first of all:

- Face-to-face: difficult because of Chris's transport problems.
- Phone: not at the moment.
- Computer: Chris could actually reach his local library which has good computer facilities. So we should ensure there is a friendly Web site he could visit and – more importantly perhaps – a link where he could chat with people in the same position.

Then look at the structure of the institution's offering:

Preparation: a correspondence package of diagnostic taster and preparatory materials might help Chris although it will be difficult for him to get started on it. A local 'learning workshop' might be helpful but will suffer from the same problem as an induction.

Induction: if Chris could get to the first face-to-face meeting then his problems would be over, or would they? Chris's social skills are well suited to the pub and disco: discussing concepts with a group of varying ages, backgrounds and abilities will not come easily to him. A computer induction might actually be easier and less threatening for Chris if that were a possible option. Support on a one-to-one basis initially from a sensitive and approachable tutor would certainly do the trick, but would be impossibly expensive from the institution's perspective.

Chris's main problem is that identified in the opening chapters of this book – isolation. So we should look at what support we can build on to help him:

Support from family and friends: the key might well be Chris's girl friend. If she can be encouraged to feel that her support is vital to him, then there is a good chance that he will stick at it until other support networks begin to grow. So we must make sure he has something to pass on to her about what she can do to support him.

Support from other students: one-to-one support is going to be less threatening than going into a group. So we could try to link Chris with a mentor, preferably with a background like his if possible.

Whatever support we manage to arrange for Chris, it's still going to be a chancy business. But if we can empathize with his feelings and position then we have some chance of tailoring support to meet his needs.

Retention on course

In a sense this entire book is about retention on course. If an institution has a high quality programme of student support then its student retention will be maximized – see chapter 15 for a discussion of quality in this context.

In addition it is very probable that most drop out effectively occurs at the acquisition stage, even if it does not occur administratively until later So getting the acquisition support right is the most effective on-course retention strategy. And as suggested earlier in this chapter, there may be an irreducible residual drop out rate (about 20 per cent in my institution) which is beyond our control.

However it seems clear that progress chasing and re-motivating contact is the key to in-course retention. What kind of contact should it be? That may differ from institution to institution, but there will be:

- Critical points: contacts should be made as close as possible to the critical points of a student's progress – for example:
  - start of course;
  - before first assignment;
  - return of first assignment;
  - mid-course;
  - pre-exam;
  - post-exam.
- Personal: contact should be as personal as possible, preferably from the student's direct tutor or supervisor. It should use face-to-face contact, phone or e-mail rather than a letter if possible.
- Encouraging and uncritical as far as possible.
- Informed. Not just, 'How's it going?' but, 'Have you reached the part on demand curves yet? Do you have any problems with it?'

These simple and rather obvious guidelines may be specific enough; for the institution it is a question of costing such contact and deciding on priorities. Even if a student subsequently withdraws there is evidence (Gaskell, Gibbons and Simpson, 1990) that if they were contacted by the institution, their overall satisfaction with their study experience is higher and they say they are more likely to return to study.

Macro-progress

Finally there is the question of retention over an entire programme – the micro-progress and macro-progress issue. By macro-progress I mean progress over a complete programme of courses rather than micro-progress, which is progress over individual modules. In concentrating on micro-progress it can be easy to overlook macro-progress issues. My own institution has largely dismantled its macro-progress monitoring systems on the grounds that it was not clear that they had any particular effect. Now we find an increasing number of students who, despite having completed one course successfully, do not re-register for another. Whether this is because the macro-progress system, however inadequate, has been dismantled, or whether there are other effects – greater choice, less interest in completing specific qualifications and so on – is not clear.

Retrieval

A student who has started studying and then withdrawn or failed represents a loss of investment by both the institution and the student. And given the very high levels of drop out common to almost all ODL institutions this loss can be very high – more than 50 per cent over a period of years.

Some of these students will be 'one-offs': they will have given it a try, found it's not what they wanted and have no intention of trying again. And that is often one reason given for not bothering to follow up withdrawn students. Another reason is that such students are 'failures' and not worth pursuing. The failure of course is not theirs but ours. But in many cases we have no idea what proportion of these students are indeed irretrievable: I suspect that those students who are true one-offs are a relatively small proportion of the whole.

The investment is not simply in terms of time and money either: a dissatisfied unretrieved student could be a thoroughly negative advertisement for the institution and open and distance learning generally. So it makes a great deal of sense to devote some student support effort to retrieval. Taking the customer analogy, no commercial organization with an eye to its future would allow its customers to drift away without an attempt to get them back.

The common elements of a retrieval system will be to, first, address the reasons for the withdrawal directly, and, second, make it clear that it is not necessarily the students' fault. Even if their withdrawal is because they could never find the energy to get started, we have to treat it as our fault. What did or didn't we do that failed to engage their efforts? Starting from that admittedly fundamentalist start there could be various ways of organizing a retrieval system. One might be to deal with withdrawals and failures separately.

Retrieving withdrawn students

Strictly speaking, retrieval of withdrawn students might be seen as a retention activity if done speedily. In practice by the time a student has decided to withdraw and the institution has registered that withdrawal it is probably too late to retain or restart the student. In an internal study conducted in my own institution where withdrawn students were contacted as soon after that withdrawal as possible, the number of students who were retained – that is, immediately restarted the course from which they had withdrawn – was less than 10 per cent of the number contacted. While that is not a negligible number, the main aim of a contact will be to retrieve the student in the long term. The basic text of that contact, whether it is by letter, e-mail or phone, could be along the lines of this example.

BAILING OUT AND TAKING OFF AGAIN

Dear Student,
We were sorry to hear that you have recently withdrawn from your course. This leaflet is intended:

- to help clarify your position;
- to help us find out if there is anything we can do or could have done to help;
- to assist you in dealing with any outstanding difficulties so you can restart your studies now or at some time in the future, as we hope you will.

We do hope you will find it helpful. Please don't hesitate to contact us if it raises any questions in your mind or if there are any queries you would like to discuss.

Withdrawing from your course

There are many reasons why students have to withdraw from their courses. Three important things to remember are:

1. **The university doesn't see withdrawal as 'failure' – you do not get any 'bad marks' on your record for withdrawing.** On the contrary, we realize that 'baling out' will be the best thing to do in particular circumstances. You will always be welcome back and your withdrawn course will not appear on your final record of studies when you get your degree.
2. **Do be sure that withdrawal is the right thing to do** and there are no reasonable alternatives. For example there may be sources of help that you haven't tapped or other ways round the difficulties that we could help you explore.
3. **If in the end withdrawal is the right option, then don't worry – you're in good company!** Up to half of our students have had to withdraw at some stage of their studies and have come back and continued successfully.

Did you withdraw because you felt the course was not right for you?

Inevitably some people find their course is not what they wanted. If there were particular points about the course which deterred you, do let us know – contact Student Services. If it was just simply the wrong course, do look at other courses – we would be very willing to advise you.

Did you withdraw because you didn't have the time?

Finding time is always difficult:

- Perhaps like a lot of people your circumstances changed? A new job, illness, a house move, and so on, can all make it quite impossible to stick to the best laid plans. We hope that when things have settled down you will consider starting again.
- Perhaps it took more time than you expected? Adapting to study is not easy, but it'll be easier next time. Please ask for the leaflet *Getting Behind?*
- Finding time is also sometimes about motivation and priorities. Perhaps, for very understandable reasons, there are more important things in your life at present?

Catching up

Sometimes in our experience students do give up too early when they feel they can't catch up. The way courses are organized deliberately allows for students occasionally getting behind – some parts of courses can be skimmed, assignments can be missed and so on. Discuss the possibilities with your tutor. When things are more settled for you, you will be very welcome back.

Did you withdraw because you found getting down to study very difficult?

You may have experienced 'study stress': this affects many people who return to study after some time away. Ask for our leaflet from Student Services, *Overcoming Study Problems*.

Did you withdraw because you were already worried about the exam?

Most people get stressed at the thought of exams. A little stress is probably helpful in getting your best performance. But too much stress can be disabling. We can help: ask for *Getting Through*.

Did you withdraw because of family or personal crisis and changes?

If so, we can only sympathize – the range of problems that face adult students are simply overwhelming at times.

Remember

You're right to bail out when the going gets too tough.
You can come back and restart any time when things are easier for you.
And do be sure in your own mind that you have made the right decision – talk it over with us.

How could we have helped you?

Obviously you may have reasons for withdrawal that the university could not help you with. But it may be that there was some part of the university system that did not help you as effectively as it might have done. If there was anything we did or did not do that was a cause or partial cause of your withdrawal, let us know. Contact Study Support and tell us.

Even if there wasn't anything we could have done we'd still like to hear your opinion on our courses and services, so do feel free to contact us. Your help will assist us in improving our support and will be very much appreciated.

Whatever you decide to do

We hope that you have got something interesting and useful from your time with us and we wish you the very best of luck for the future.

Some versions of this leaflet contained a questionnaire on which students could tell us a little about their withdrawal.

Retrieving failed students

A student who has persisted to the end of a course but still failed it presents a different contact issue. If the course ends with a final assessment or exam which the student has failed, having passed assessments earlier in the course, then some kind of text or contact along these lines may be helpful.

NOT THE END OF THE WORLD: FOR STUDENTS WHO HAVE FAILED EXAMS

Introduction

We're sorry to hear about your exam failure. How do you feel? It's such a personal experience that different people take it very differently. Were you:

- Depressed? That wouldn't be surprising but it's important to remember that a failed exam is not a criticism of you personally and that there's no need to contemplate giving up completely.
- Angry? That again wouldn't be surprising if you feel you've been unfairly treated for any reason. In that case you should tell us. Contact us or query your result (see below).
- Disappointed but not dejected? It's not widely known that half our students fail or withdraw from courses at some point in their studies, so it's a much more common experience than people suppose. So perhaps it's best to see exam failure as an occasional and natural hazard of being a student, understand that it's not something to be taken personally and resolve to learn from the experience.

This leaflet is designed to help you work out the best way forward from your exam failure and to cover some administrative points that might be helpful.

Did you expect to fail?

YES – you may well have come out of the exam knowing you'd failed it and why. In that case go straight to the 'Why did it happen?' section below.

NO – if you came out of the exam feeling fairly confident you'd passed then perhaps there were three possibilities. Either you were not good at assessing your own exam performance – see 'Feedback' below – or a mistake has been made – see 'Querying your result' below – or there were special circumstances that you did not tell the University about – see 'Special circumstances' below. (The next section is on administrative procedures in these cases and is omitted here – author.)

Why did it happen?

There can be many reasons for failing an exam. Here are some that might have affected you, together with ideas about how you might overcome the problem next time:

- **Inappropriate exam technique** – such as not using time effectively, misunderstanding the questions, introducing irrelevancies and so on. Did you follow instructions?
- **Inadequate revision techniques** – such as revising the wrong material, not practising exam questions, not allowing enough time and so on. If either of the above apply you might find it useful to read the book *How to Succeed in Exams and Assessments*; ask for details.
- **Exam nerves** – anxiety about exams is very natural, but excessive anxiety can adversely affect performance. Ask for the leaflet *Getting Through* from us – it's especially for students who suffer exam stress.

What now?

You've got various options:

- **Resit the exam.** You can ask to take the exam again.
- **Forget it.** Some students simply put a failed course down to experience and move on. You should remember that failed or withdrawn courses do not appear on the final record of your studies.
- **Bail out of study altogether.** Obviously we hope you won't do this unless you're sure it's the right thing for you. Very few students fail exams because of inadequate ability. There are usually other factors involved which can be put right with help.

Whatever you're thinking of doing, do contact us as soon as possible and talk it over with someone before finally deciding on your course of action.

AN EXAM FAILURE IS NOT THE END OF THE WORLD
YOU CAN GET THROUGH NEXT TIME
ASK US FOR THE HELP YOU NEED

Research

Clutterbuck (1995) says that any retention programme should be 'benchmarked and refined'. My educational analogy stretches this (rather far perhaps) into 'research'. By research I do not just mean academic research, undertaking broad studies and surveys within a theoretical framework which lead to advances in knowledge about open and distance learning. There is certainly the necessity for that; we still know very little about many particular characteristics of ODL and academic research could help us uncover much about how students learn and survive in ODL.

However, research in this context to me means something more evaluative: finding out what works well, what does not work so well and establishing ways of assessing the quality of support. Above all, such research should be carried out by the practitioners of student support – in other words it should be 'action research'.

Case studies

A tutor in an ODL scheme is worried about why turnout at her tutorials is rather low. With some very modest funding for her time from the institution, she undertakes a small survey of students and discovers that there is a variety of reasons, some of which have to do with transport and other insuperable problems. She is reassured that low attendance is not her fault and is able to amend her programme to increase attendance.

A tutor who is worried about students who can't get to her tutorials experiments with 'telephone chains' – trying to get students to pass on advice and information to each other by phone. The project is unsuccessful but at least she feels that she has established that it's probably not worth others trying this idea in the form she tried it.

A group of staff use some resources to phone some students who have withdrawn. They compare the rate at which those students returned to their courses to students who were sent a leaflet, and discover that although the return rate for phone students was higher it was probably not cost-effective.

Such action research is important for several reasons including the following.

Student support occurs best as close as possible to the student. It is often in the detail that it is most effective – the short but well-timed phone call, the note of encouragement. Student support staff need to be encouraged to reflect on their work and learn from it as they do it, in order to improve it continuously.

Such chances to reflect and learn enrich the work of staff, help to re-motivate them, and an institution whose aim is learning can ultimately only prosper if it learns itself.

Postscript

You may be wondering what happened to Chris, our main case study in this chapter. I suggested that the most important forms of support for him would be from his girl friend and other students.

In fact Chris made it to the face-to-face induction meeting but arrived late due to transport difficulties. Had he been on his own he would not have gone in the room. Fortunately he had his girl friend with him who persuaded him to join in the meeting. There he met another new student – a man from a similar background – who offered to give him a lift to the next meeting, thus bearing out my analysis. So far so good. . .

Chapter 14

Theories of student support

I embark on this chapter with considerable tentativeness. Like many practitioners of student support, I have spent too long working at the coal face of support and too little time stepped back from it, trying to understand what basic patterns, values and theories underlie my work. But without some kind of theoretical framework, no matter how simplistic, there is nothing to judge our policy and organizational developments, our structural innovations or even our changes in day-to-day working practice.

I believe that consciously or unconsciously most support practitioners do subscribe to loose theories, although they might find it hard to express these in terms acceptable to theoretical journals. In addition, I suspect that these theories probably owe much to various ideas about 'counselling' in its many different guises.

Counselling theories underlying student support

There are many different schools of counselling, but it may be helpful to distinguish two very broad categories: humanistic or person-centred (Rogerian) counselling, and behavioural therapy models.

Humanistic counselling

Humanistic or person-centred counselling revolves around a basic judgement about the 'self-directedness' of individuals and how they deal with issues in their lives, by helping individuals to clarify their feelings in such a way as to enable them to make decisions for themselves. It is drawn very much from the works of the American Carl Rogers (hence the alternative name 'Rogerian' to describe this school). The central principle of Rogerian counselling is derived from the practices of 'active listening' and 'unconditional positive regard'. As Rogers famously wrote:

> Very early in my work as a therapist I discovered that simply listening to my client very attentively was an important way of being helpful. So when I was in doubt as to what I should do, in some active way I listened. It seemed surprising to me that such a passive kind of inter-action could be so useful.

(Rogers 1951)

The theory has been much developed by later writers and practitioners, notably in *The Skilled Helper* (Egan, 1975), into a more proactive and initiative taking mode, moving a little towards the more directive modes of behaviouristic counselling.

Other schools of humanistic counselling include Fritz Perl's gestalt therapy with its emphasis on non-verbal expression and acting out of feelings. Typically, a gestalt counsellor will invite clients to act out a dialogue between them by moving from one chair to another, or using a cushion as an object of address. The philosophy is avowedly existential. Gestalt techniques are essentially psychotherapeutic and have not found many practical expressions in educational contexts as far as I know.

Behaviouristic counselling

Behaviouristic therapies tend to be much more to do with modifying people's behaviour and rather less to do with their feelings. The appeal is to people's intellect and less to their emotions.

A good example is Rational Emotive Theory (RET: Ellis, 1962), where it is held that 'activating events' in a person's life lead to 'beliefs', both rational and irrational, and these beliefs lead to 'consequences' (the 'ABC' approach). It is the counsellor's task to show clients how this process has worked in their own life and – in effect – argue with them to persuade them into changing those beliefs and hence alter the consequences.

Another example might be Eric Berne's Transactional Analysis (TA) with its division of the psyche into three states – person, adult and child – and its emphasis on the 'games' that can be played between the various states in various people.

Case study

Any theory may offer insights. I can remember one student I had been trying to help but with little success. I had offered him the opportunity to submit an assignment late, to have an extra tutorial from his tutor and I offered to make representations to the Exam Board on his behalf. Each of these offers was rejected by the student for some excellent reason and each time I would try something different.

Finally, in an insight from TA, I realized I had perhaps been drawn into a game of 'Why don't you – yes but', where every suggestion I made 'Why don't you...' was met with a perfectly valid 'Yes, but . . .'. The 'pay-off' for the student was presumably showing how hard he had tried and how useless my attempts to help were.

It even seemed worthwhile naming this particular variant so I called it 'The success-resistant student' – the person for whom success was more threatening than failure, because at least failure did not involve uncomfortable and difficult changes in his life.

Whether I was right in my diagnosis I cannot be sure. However, when I gave up on my attempts to help this student I certainly felt a lot better and it seemed to make no difference to him.

Using counselling ideas in student support

Clearly both humanistic and behavioural stances have their attractions to someone working in student support. The student-centredness, non-directional and apparently non-expert nature of Rogerian counselling is certainly very attractive to staff talking to students with difficult and inexplicable problems, and 'when in doubt, listen' is not bad advice for anyone not sure what to do.

But equally the more directive theories can be attractive, particularly those like RET or TA which appear to have some logical rationale. After all, in education we are firmly in the realm of the intellectual so what better theory than one that appeals to the intelligence of the student such as RET? Thus in practice people working in student support appear to apply an eclectic mix of theories to their work.

For example, people working with students experiencing severe exam stress may well use a mixture of humanistic and behavioural approaches. They might start by listening to students talk about their experiences and feelings about assessment. They would try to clarify those feelings and establish how they arose in the hope that students would find talking about them and understanding them a help in itself. But they would probably also work more directively: they might suggest ways of tackling stress physically such as breathing exercises or meditation or (in a behaviouristic manner) through exam rehearsal.

Such an eclectic approach still requires a range of personal qualities and skills on the part of the student support worker, as suggested in chapter 3. Underlying all the skills and qualities are the essential concepts of facilitation and reflection that seem philosophically and practically appropriate to study support in ODL.

Open and distance learning theories underlying student support

There is debate as to whether ODL constitutes a discipline in its own right and consequently whether there can be such things as theories of ODL. There is certainly a great deal of research into different aspects of ODL, and it is now taught to higher degree level in several universities.

There have been attempts to apply accepted educational theories to ODL dating back for example to Baath (1979). Such theories have often concentrated on the production of course material rather than student support. Theoretical discussions about ODL in its own right have been around issues such as:

● Is distance learning an (inferior?) substitute for conventional education or a unique mode of education in its own right? Are there things that cannot be taught by ODL (the 'brain surgery by post' criticism)? Is the quality of the educational discourse inherently poorer in ODL than other modes?
● Are open and distance learning actually very different concepts? Rumble (1989) argues that distance education systems may be open or closed but that many so-called 'open learning systems' are remarkably closed.
● Is ODL an inherently authoritarian form of education? After all, the content is usually almost entirely defined by one version of the printed word – the correspondence material that is sent to students. Students rarely have time to study outside this material. Alternatively, does it allow for student autonomy to a much greater extent than conventional education? We touched briefly on this issue when looking at the didactic–facilitative spectrum in tuition – in a system where tutors teach the material but do not write it there is no particular onus on them to defend it.
● Is ODL an anti-social form of education? Does it isolate its students, and again does that mean that it is in some sense a poor relation of more conventional methods? Peters (1989) interpreted distance study as an 'industrialized' form of teaching and learning, and stressed the structural incompatibility of that with a locally organized educational system, together with the process of alienation or isolation that can occur when students are confronted with technical artefacts instead of live human beings.

Other arguments look at specific issues in ODL such as:

● the target groups for ODL – for example do women need different approaches to support networks?

- the media that ODL uses;
- the environment, both economically and politically, in which ODL operates;
- the equal opportunities issues specific to ODL;
- and many of the other numerous facets of this rapidly developing field.

There have also been attempts to develop over-arching theories specific to ODL; for example, Holmberg's (1995) theory of 'guided didactic conversation' which attempts to involve students affectively in study by conversational manners of writing which attempt to address individual students and involve their reactions, views and experiences. Another example is Hilary Perraton (1987) who maintains that attempts to define a single theory of distance education are naive and that it is necessary to see distance education as a system of three interrelated elements: teaching, administration and assessment. Each element will require a slightly different approach to the development of theory – teaching from existing theory, administration in generalizations drawn from practice, and assessment from value judgements about quality.

There is, they say, nothing as practical as a good theory and there are many other theoretical developments that could be covered in a completely different book. Ultimately the test of any theory will be how far it can provide a framework for the setting up and testing of hypotheses about student support in ODL. We may have some way to go on that.

Chapter 15

Structures and quality in student support

Structures for ODL organizations

In writing this book I have assumed that the reader is likely to be working in one or two basic types of institution (after Rumble, 1992).

Campus-based universities (CBUs)

ODL schemes are often based on existing educational institutions where in general students come to the institution. Academic and non-academic support is largely carried out on the institution's premises even if the students study at home using distance education materials. Some students may be full time in an 'on campus' situation. Staff are often from the full-time face-to-face side of the institution and seconded to the ODL section. Such institutions enjoy flexibility but may lack the focus of specialized institutions.

Distance teaching universities (DTUs)

These are generally specialized distance learning institutions where students study largely at a distance but may meet at local 'study centres'. Academic and non-academic support is offered by local, usually part-time staff at study centres, but also direct from the institution or its regional centres. Such institutions offer national approaches and economy of scale but can find it hard to maintain as high a profile locally as CBUs. They also have to have a high administrative input into supporting and monitoring of local staff and liasing with study centres.

There are of course many hybrid possibilities: departments within institutions which have considerable autonomy and their own staff, such as the University of Wisconsin Extension; departments which have their own administrative staff but rely on their parent institution for subject specialist teaching, such as Murdoch University; and cooperative structures, where materials may be developed in one institution but are used by another institution which offers support, such as FlexiStudy in the UK. And the increasing use of the Internet may well blur distinctions between structures anyway.

Criteria for structures

While most ODL institutions fall into one of these categories there are many distinctive variations in their structures depending on a variety of factors. The most important of these will probably be:

- the characteristics of their students;
- the physical and virtual infrastructure of the areas in which they operate;
- the courses they are delivering;
- the funding regimes within which they operate.

Student characteristics

We have already looked at the different demands that different kinds of students can make for support in chapter 12. Additional factors affecting the design of a student support structure might be their physical location, ability to travel, and access to IT, all of which will probably be linked to their income levels.

Physical and virtual infrastructure

For many developing countries the information superhighway is still a distant dream. Indeed ordinary passable highways may be in short supply. There may not be a reliable postal service or it may not deliver to local addresses.

I have recently been exchanging e-mails with the Director of Student Services in a southern African country. (I am hoping that eventually my organization and his might 'twin' in some way.) The difficulties he faces are profound: an erratic postal system, a phone network that may be out of order for days at a time, a population which, while energetic and motivated, may even have difficulties getting hold of adequate supplies of paper in rural areas. In addition he has a small underpaid staff who have to spend much of their time and resources commuting by public transport over long distances to the organization's central office.

Some institutions may well find themselves attempting to serve two different kinds of infrastructure: large metropolitan areas with a reasonably good virtual network, with a large hinterland of small underdeveloped villages. Trying to satisfy both markets may be difficult and expensive.

Types of courses delivered

It may be that different kinds of courses may require different kinds of student support. On the face of it, courses that are mostly academic and knowledge based may have a different support structure from those that have skill elements such as teacher training courses. Such skill-based courses are more likely to require substantial face-to-face support contact. It is also possible that the length and level of courses will affect support strategies. A ten-week access course is likely to involve different support from a three-year Masters degree. Certainly the mode of delivery of courses will affect student support structures.

The size of the institution

Clearly there are economies of scale in courses supplied by a large distance institution with thousands of students. But such institutions may have to pay a higher price in support to maintain the identification of their students with otherwise rather anonymous structures.

The institution's funding regime

Finally there will be substantial differences between the support possible from a state-funded institution and (say) a private correspondence college which has to cover all its course production and support costs from students' fees.

These factors may interact in complex and different ways and could define various support models. Such support models could vary along a range of dimensions (IEC, 2001).

The decision where to place an institution's support services on a particular dimension may not be easy. For example the very first dimension of localized versus centralized models will provide a range of definitions and contrasts (see Figure 15.1).

Centralized models
All course production, student support and assessment are carried out from one location from which all the staff work. Many CBUs conform to such a model, but not all.

Localized models
Typically, course production and administration are centralized but student support is localized. Generally, an attempt may be made to provide support locally (in the nearest town or local call area) for both advice and tuition. Such localization is only possible where an institution covers a specific area or has very large enrolment. The UK OU is an example of the latter, where attempts are made to provide students with part-time tutors who offer support from bases at home and in local educational institutions. Such models have contrasting characteristics (see Figure 15.2).

Table 15.1   *Dimensions of support*

Support is provided locally from regional centres	Support is provided centrally from a national headquarters
Support is provided to groups of learners	Support is provided on an individual basis
Support is generalized and offered to all students	Support is specialized according to course or student needs
Support is offered face to face as well as at a distance	Support is provided only through distance media
Support is provided continuously by the same personnel throughout the programme	Support is discontinuous and provided by different people at different stages or courses
Support is organized hierarchically with individuals responsible for specific activities	Support is organized in teams which may be responsible for linked activities – and other dimensions

Perhaps the analogy ultimately is between the supermarket and the corner shop with their various advantages and disadvantages.

Costs

Finally there is cost as the bottom line as a determinant of support structures. It is beyond the scope of this book to assess the costs of the many possible different models of student support. Readers interested in the costs of ODL, particularly in developing countries, are referred to Hulsmann (2000) and Rumble (1992).

One way of reducing costs is to develop use of IT for support (see chapter 17). In this connection it is worth referring to the work of Hilary Perraton at the International Research Foundation for Open Learning (IRFOL), particularly his book *Open and Distance Learning in the Developing World* (2000). As he writes there about the impact of technology on ODL:

> Technology excites, opens some possibilities and closes others.... Today while the cost of much technology has been declining dramatically, many advances may restrict access, rather than widening it by putting more costs on the user. In much of the south courses available on computer will reach the rich or those at work in the modern sector; they will cut out the poor, the remote, and those not employed in the modern sector. This process will hurt women more than men.

Table 15.2   *Central versus local models*

Central	Local
Support can be specialized and expert	Support is general: queries which require expert advice must be referred
Support tends to be problem–centred and possibly impersonal	Support can be student–centred and personal
Staff development is relatively easy with all staff on site and available	Staff development can be difficult: staff have to be assembled locally or distance methods used
Quality assurance is relatively easy: all aspects of support including phone calls can be monitored. Standard scripts can be provided for staff to use and so on	Quality is difficult to monitor except for correspondence tuition perhaps. Support can be evaluated in retrospect by student questionnaires but not completely satisfactorily
Communications can be easy and direct with relatively little need to refer	Communications can be easy: indeed using part-time staff can provide an out-of-hours service at relatively low cost. But there will be many referrals in both directions making contact slow and liable to error
Costs are hard to compare but may be lower in a centralized system	Costs may be higher in a localized system but some support may be provided effectively uncosted by part-time staff

Appraising quality in student support

Ultimately there is clearly little point in providing a student support service unless the quality of that service is appropriate and valued by students. In addition the quality of student support in higher education institutions in the UK now also comes into the Teaching Quality Assessments process which in turn will ultimately affect funding. And it is possible that the quality of student support offers institutions some kind of 'competitive edge' where students have a choice.

So much depends on the setting up of appropriate quality appraisal mechanisms. These in turn will depend on the structures discussed previously. For example, some quality standards may be easier to establish in DTUs (such as courses whose materials may be public in a way not available in CBUs) and others more easily established in CBUs (such as student support perhaps). I have also suggested that quality standards will be easier to establish in centralized institutions and indeed may be a driving force towards centralization from senior management.

Finally, it is not clear what effect team working will have on quality standards. Will there be diffusion of responsibility through a team with no one really taking care of individual students? Or will there be collective responsibility so that individual team members will cover for each other and ensure that students' individual needs are met in some way?

One of the particular problems of a quality assurance process in ODL is the multivariate nature of the student experience. Since each service can be delivered in a variety of ways, each route may have to be assessed separately. For example:

Table 15.3 *Quality appraisal methods*

Activity	Medium	Method of assessment
Tuition	Face-to-face	Observation of a tutorial by a line manager Self-evaluation by tutor
	Correspondence	Re-marking of a selection of assignments Statistical analysis of grades awarded Measurement of speed of turnaround
	Online tuition	E-mail interactions can be monitored
	Phone	In a central system by observation or recording of interactions In a local system only by subsequently evaluating the student experience
Advising	Face-to-face	Centralized system: direct observation Local system: unlikely to be possible except by evaluating the student experience
	By correspondence	Central: copies of correspondence could be monitored Local: copies could be called in
	Online advice	Can be observed as above
	Phone	Centralized: observation and recordings Localized: difficult especially given the possibly private nature of some interactions

In addition, support may be given by different people within the institution. For example, in a localized system with a centre and regions a student may need support from different areas that may be in different locations.

Table 15.4   *Central versus regional staff (adapted from IEC, 2001)*

Central staff	Regional staff
Registry: records, fees	Student advice
Library	Tutors
Materials despatch	Tutorial organizers
Technical support: computer help desks	Coordinating staff

This raises issues for both the student seeking support and the institution giving it. Students who may be used to 'one stop shopping' – getting the information they need from one place or by one phone call – may be confused and alienated if they are passed from one place to another. But it is difficult for an institution to simplify life for the student. It is doubtful if anyone could be expert on the entire range of possible student queries from fee payment facilities, to degree regulations, to the location of a tutorial, to (even) the answer to Question 4 on this week's assignment. Even an adviser with access to a very advanced institutional Web site is unlikely to be able to track down the answer to every question. Institutions that by their nature deal with knowledge have a great deal more of it lying around than is easily manageable.

Thus appraising the quality of the support given from all these sources becomes very difficult indeed, and it may be necessary to use less immediate and indirect methods such as the following.

Questionnaires

An obvious way of appraising quality is by questionnaires, delivered either by post or increasingly with networked students by e-mail (some e-mail programs will allow the sending of electronic questionnaires that can be answered on the spot by checking the appropriate buttons).

Questionnaires have limitations, of course; they need to be designed with care and still tend to define the subject and range of answers. By definition they have to be after the event and so can present a post hoc rationalization as suggested in chapter 13.

It is also hard to find a balance between large scale multiple-choice questionnaires with satisfyingly statistical results but little sense of the individual student voice, and smaller scale questionnaires that may allow students to express comments but become correspondingly harder to evaluate. We might discover, for instance, from large scale questionnaires that (say) computer conferencing is unpopular with students, but it may need more small scale 'illuminative' evaluations to discover why.

The following is an extract from a lengthy questionnaire used to assess the quality of student services and teaching in the UK OU (Student Research Centre, UK OU, 1999). These are only three of more than 20 questions asked in the survey.

Table 15.5   *Student services support and teaching*

1 How satisfied were you with the following:	Not			Very	Not used
(Circle one only in each row)					
Information on who your tutor would be	1	2	3	4	5
Amount of teaching provided by your tutor	1	2	3	4	5
Quality of tuition you received from your tutor	1	2	3	4	5
Quality of tutor's guidance in developing your study skills	1	2	3	4	5
Availability of your tutor	1	2	3	4	5
The level of academic/professional knowledge tutors had of the subject area	1	2	3	4	5

2 How helpful was your tutor with the following:

	Not			Very	Not used
Your understanding of the course materials	1	2	3	4	5
Developing the course themes	1	2	3	4	5

3 Tutorials
a) Approximately how many tutorials/schools did you attend on this particular course?
(Circle one only)

None	1
Some	2
Most	3
All	4

b) If you did not attend all the tutorials, why was that?
(Circle all that apply)

Inconvenient times	☐
Tutorials too far away	☐
Standard of tuition poor	☐
Not on public transport route	☐
Cost of travel	☐
Offered alternative to face-to-face tuition	☐
Location/travel felt to be unsafe	☐
Decided not to complete the course	☐
Didn't feel the need/want face-to-face tuition	☐
Personal reasons	☐
Other	☐

Interviews
One way of getting at more complex issues and views is to interview students. Although the data are less statistically reliable, the more discursive nature of an interview may reveal detail missed by questionnaires. Interviews might, for instance, get closer to reasons for withdrawal.

Of course, interviews are very resource intensive and might best be used in conjunction with questionnaires.

Focus groups

There is increasing use of the focus group as an appraisal tool halfway between the axe of a questionnaire and the scalpel of the interview. Such groups usually consist of 10–15 people with a facilitator and an observer who also videos or tapes the process. A skilled leader and observer team can draw out and illuminate issues in ways that would escape a questionnaire and the recording allows conclusions to be drawn at leisure afterwards.

Focus groups can be useful for getting at the feelings behind an opinion. Here for example is an excerpt from a report of a focus group in my own institution where students explored their responses to support from their Student Support Centre and tutor.

> Contacts with the Centre lacked a personal feel. Students felt isolated in their studies and wanted information about contact people and resources: an Open Day, staff photos in brochures, pictures on the Web site were all suggested.
>
> When contacting tutors, use of e-mail was seen as more positive than telephone contact – students who had e-mail contact previously missed it when allocated to a new tutor who didn't use it.

Self-evaluation or reflection

In a local support system where there are tutors at a distance from the institution it can be important to encourage tutors to evaluate their own work. One way of doing that is through discussion by using questionnaires with their students. Table 15.6 is an excerpt from such a questionnaire at the midpoint of a course where the feedback is for the tutor's eyes only.

Related to this is the very important activity of reflection where staff reflect on an activity afterwards and ask themselves in a systematic way how they felt it went, its strengths and weaknesses and how it might be improved. See chapter 13 and the section on 'Research'.

Reports

Where you have a system that requires reports then those reports can sometimes be used to evaluate the quality of work undertaken.

I recently asked a tutor for a report on a student who had withdrawn. She replied simply that the student had not contacted her and she did not know why he had withdrawn. Clearly, she had not attempted to initiate contact herself and it took a gently worded reminder that she should be at least attempting to do so.

Of course, such evaluation is hardly systematic but can be a valuable addition to evidence gathered in other ways.

Table 15.6   *Mid-course evaluation — from your tutor*

I would be grateful if you would complete this questionnaire and return it to me as an attached e-mail document. If you prefer it to be anonymous, please return it through the post.

Please highlight or circle as appropriate

1   How helpful are the tutor group conference activities and discussions in the following areas? (1 = very and 4 = not at all):
(a) Getting help with queries about the course   1   2   3   4
(b) Understanding the course material   1   2   3   4
(c) Getting feedback on your progress through the
     course

                                                               1   2   3   4

Please expand your answers here or on a separate sheet

2   Have you read my comments on your assignment? (please be honest)

Yes/No/Partially

If yes, how well did I do the following (1 = very well and 4 = not at all well):

(a) Help you understand key concepts tested in the assignment 1   2   3   4
(b) Help you organize the content of the answer   1   2   3   4
(c) Give clear explanations of where things went wrong and
     why   1   2   3   4
(d) Help you appreciate the areas needing expansion and/or
     clarification   1   2   3   4
(e) Give you guidance as to how to improve in future   1   2   3   4

Please expand your answers here or on a separate sheet

3 Is there anything else you would like me to do to help support your studies?

Assignment monitoring

ODL institutions will need to set up assignment monitoring systems to assess both the marking standards (are grades comparable across tutors?) and the quality of the correspondence tuition (are students getting speedy, accurate and helpful feedback on their work?). Such systems may involve the re-marking of a selection of a tutor's scripts and feedback to that tutor. This will of course be an expensive and time-consuming process and it may well be that the selection will depend on the experience and previous performance of the tutor.

To give a flavour of the process here are the monitor's comments on the script comments recorded in chapter 4.

To Tutor X

From your monitor

Grading comments 'Acceptable – I feel that this is very accurate marking. I particularly like your comments – clear and concise.'

We agree very closely on the marking of this script. I have made a number of comments on the photocopied script, which I hope you will look at. You will see that, in some cases, we have awarded/deducted marks for slightly difficult things – but this is inevitable! A few main points to think about:

Could you have included a few more points/comments with questions 1 and 2 – either points of encouragement and confirmation that the student was doing well?

I marked down 1(a) more than you did. Did you try and break this kind of question down and see whether the student had addressed each point in the question?

Would it be advantageous to indicate even more – eg by subdividing each mark where the student has lost marks?

General comments: 'Very sound marking and good teaching comments. Well done.'

You will see that the monitor is as critically supportive in his comments on the tutor (using the 'feedback sandwich') as the tutor has tried to be on the student.

Complaints

Complaints are of course an important part of any quality appraisal mechanism and should be seen as vital to the institution and dealt with accordingly. That is not always easy. Few people enjoy complaining and they may need to 'psych themselves up' to do so. They then may appear more aggressive than they mean to be, student services staff on the receiving end will feel more defensive than they need and a growing spiral of aggravation can be created. Staff will therefore need a recognized administrative structure for dealing with complaints and feeding the complaint back to the appropriate part of the institution. They will need training in handling angry and distressed students and in dealing with their own resulting stress.

Many complaints arrive by e-mail or letter: people may often find it easier to complain in a way that offers a record of their case. Such complaints often involve requests for fee refunds with threats of legal action if not immediately actioned.

Replying to such a letter may be easy if the complaint seems justified. When apologizing I lay it on with a trowel as that often seems to pre-empt further correspondence. Where a complaint seems unjustified a reply can be trickier to draft. As in dealing with angry phone calls it is important to empathize with the student's feelings, acknowledge his or her absolute right to complain and the need for you to take this complaint seriously. Your aim after all is to retain the student and not to get involved in lengthy correspondence which is expensive to the institution and frustrating to the student.

This is an excerpt from a letter I had to write to a student a few weeks ago in an attempt to terminate a long correspondence which was clearly going nowhere.

Dear Ms X

Thank you for your further letter. I am so sorry that we have been unable to settle this satisfactorily for you and appreciate the frustration this may be causing. I have now looked very carefully into the issues you raise.

On the content of the course. The course is quality appraised by an external committee and I fear it would be hard to substantiate the comment that it is below the quality of other courses.

On the behaviour of the tutor. I can see that the tutor's behaviour in this case may have been disturbing to you. On investigation I think that it is possible he may have been over-zealous and possibly behaved inappropriately in the circumstances. I do profoundly apologize for any distress this may have caused.

I hope that I can now encourage you to return to your studies and continue the excellent progress you were making.

Yours sincerely

As a matter of style I find I instinctively avoid using pejorative words like complaint, allegation, rejection, and so on.

In addition, staff will need to be 'empowered' to undertake activities to remedy problems as far as possible. It may be useful, for example, to introduce the concept of 'service recovery' from the world of commerce, where staff are authorized to make modest payments to compensate customers. A student who has travelled 50 miles to get to a tutorial that was cancelled without proper warning may be satisfied by the offer of a small sum to cover her travel costs, for example.

Setting quality standards in student support

Once suitable mechanisms have been found for appraising quality, there is the issue of setting quality standards which are reasonable from the students' perspective and effectively attainable by the institution.

From the institution's perspective, there is sometimes a tendency to concentrate on the easily measurable at the expense of the more elusive: the time taken to answer the phone rather than the quality of the response when it is answered; the speed of return of marked assignments rather than the 'approachability' of the tutor.

Student charters

From the students' perspective it will be important to know what quality of service they might reasonably expect. One way of achieving this is using 'student charters' which attempt to lay down some guidelines as to what students can and should expect. A simple example is shown here (extract from *Our Commitment to Students* draft charter in UK OU).

> For you as an OU student we will endeavour to provide:
>
> 1. face-to-face, phone and correspondence tuition appropriate in both method and content to your needs;
> 2. correspondence tuition including return of assignments within four weeks of the due date and appropriate comment which explains the grade and offers adequate feedback to enable you to improve your future assignments;
> 3. counselling that provides accurate and timely academic information and advice as well as the opportunity to explore more complex issues at greater length as appropriate;
> 4. an administrative service providing appropriate and timely administrative information as well as dealing with administrative problems and failures speedily and effectively.

Charters have been criticized as often being only window-dressing or public relations. I am more sympathetic to the concept than that. I would argue (Simpson, 1992) that some students tend to blame themselves when problems arise in their studies rather than blame the institution, which may sometimes be more appropriate. Certainly, sometimes students put up with very poor service without complaining.

What a well-written charter can do is to make expected standards much clearer and encourage assertiveness among such students. Indeed, I believe I see signs of growing assertiveness among the student population which may be in part due to the widespread use of such charters. Of course such assertiveness will inevitably lead to an increase in the number of complaints from students and recourse to the legal system.

Quality assurance in student support

Moving from quality appraisal to quality assurance, where the structures and staffing of the institution are re-engineered to ensure that quality does not break down, is a key step. One important factor in that step will be the identification of where quality breakdown is likely to occur and pre-emptive steps taken to prevent that breakdown.

Quality breakdown

Quality can fail in several ways, but perhaps the most important are through organizational weakness and staff problems, although these are rather arbitrary categories. Here are some examples of breakdown selected at random from my recent files:

- I set up a meeting for new students but fail to check on the room availability and car parking arrangements, or I arrive too late to welcome them, or I am double-booked (sadly I have been responsible for all of these!).
- A student phones a tutor who is under considerable personal stress. The tutor tries to help but fails to explain his own situation and leaves the student feeling rejected by his apparent brusqueness.
- A student does not submit an assignment. A busy tutor does not spot that it is missing and the student eventually drops out.
- A tutor, irritated by what he sees as unnecessary paperwork from the institution, puts a package of 'bumf' in a file and fails to see an important note about a disabled student who needs help.
- A very unconfident student overcompensates by asking a lot of rather irrelevant questions at a tutorial. The tutor thinks that the student is rather bumptious and does not see that he really needs help.
- An adviser sends a message about a student who needs special help for her exam. However, I am away and have failed to make adequate arrangements to deal with messages. The student does not get the help she needs.
- I appoint a new tutor but fail to brief her adequately because I am busy writing a book. When the tutor runs into unexpected difficulties she resigns.

The common thread to these breakdowns is the failure to be empathic with students and staff. So when it comes to avoiding quality breakdown, it may be that the simplest question to ask again and again is, 'What will this look like, or what will happen from the student' or staff' point of view?'

Organizational structures for quality

I cannot recommend a particular structure that will be appropriate for all ODL student support systems for all time. What might be more helpful to end this chapter would be a set of rather ordinary questions about student support in any institution. Not all of these questions will be appropriate to every institution but most will be. They will not have straightforward yes/no answers but a lot of maybes or 'not very oftens' as answers may suggest areas that need looking at, and they will suggest many other questions that could be posed.

Twenty-one questions about student support

Support activities:

1. Are there systems for dealing with contacts from students by all communication media?
2. Does that system provide accurate and speedy responses by appropriate media without delay or a lot of referral?
3. Is there a proactive system of support which reaches out, particularly to disadvantaged students, using appropriate media?

4. Is there a reasonable choice of media for support so that all students can participate easily by one method or another?
5. Is there an equal opportunities policy that makes study accessible to all students regardless of physical or mental need?
6. Is the support system timely? Does it offer support at the right time, for example before and at the beginning of a course?

Support staffing:

7. Are the criteria and procedures used for selecting staff appropriate and clear?
8. Is there a staff development programme for all staff involved in student support (even if only distantly) that meets their needs?
9. Do staff have a chance to interact and reflect on that programme and feedback and influence it?
10. Is there good on-going support for staff: clear line management links, good communication and feedback and clear commitment to supporting staff as they support students?
11. Are there robust procedures for dealing with staffing problems, poor work, absences, which are supportive rather than punitive?
12. Are staff continually helped to be aware and empathic towards the problems of students, especially those with special requirements?

Materials:

13. Are there materials to cover most of the possible student problems and issues that arise?
14. Are the materials empathic, acknowledging the student's feelings, written in a friendly approachable but unpatronizing style without gravitas? Has a readability check been done on them?

Supporting students in practice. For this set of questions I shall put myself in the position of Chris (chapter 13) and ask what the institution looks like to (particularly new) students.

15. Does it look daunting and inaccessible or friendly and approachable?
16. Are the enrolment procedures complex and hard to understand?
17. What happens after enrolment? Will Chris begin to feel a part of the institution straightaway?
18. What happens when the courses start? Will Chris's sense of isolation be overcome immediately or enhanced?
19. If Chris starts but wavers is there appropriate support for him?

20. If Chris fails or withdraws is there appropriate support to get him back?
21. Are there macro-progress (progress across entire programmes) monitoring systems in place as well as micro-progress (progress within modules or individual courses) systems?

And finally an extra catch-all question.

22. Looking back at all the students who have been in the institution, have they always had the support they needed, when they needed it, within resource constraints? If not, where did the system let them down and how might it be reinforced?

Chapter 16

Staff development and appraisal for support

The success of any student support system will depend critically on the staff of the institution and their development and support. That development and support will in turn depend on what kind of staff and in what kind of institution they are working. However there are fundamental ideas that are appropriate to all staff in all institutions.

Experience, reflection and support

Student support staff will bring existing perceptions and attitudes to their ODL work. Some of these will be appropriate and some not so appropriate, such as (for example) a particular tutor's tendency to use exclusively didactic teaching methods. Changing what may possibly be deep-seated patterns of behaviour may be difficult. Kolb (1984) suggested a model that has been used extensively in ODL. This suggests that learning takes place through a cyclical process. A person:

- experiences some activity or event;
- is encouraged to reflect on that experience;
- conceptualizes the experience to develop new perspectives;
- experiments from those perspectives leading to future changes and developments.

The theory has been extended by Boud, Keogh and Walker (1996). Here the affective and possibly difficult nature of the reflection process is very important: looking back on a teaching experience that went wrong can clearly be painful. Thus those feelings must be addressed, 'by being expressed openly in a sustaining environment, for example on a one-to-on basis or within some kind of support group, so that an emotional obstacle can be removed' (Boud *et al*, 1996).

Staff development: practical approaches

The methods used for the staff development of student support staff should address these issues of reflection and support. In particular the methods used in staff development of staff in student support should mirror the methods that we would expect those staff to use with students. The methods used should be experiential, reflective and supportive.

In practice this means that staff should have a chance to experience an activity, reflect on that experience in a safe and supportive atmosphere, and then practise the results of any changes in their perceptions as a result. It is inappropriate and probably ineffectual, for example, to give a formal lecture on facilitative methods of student support.

A colleague of mine recently ran a workshop for new tutors on developing learning skills among their students. Her plan for the session was as follows: (my comments are in italics)

Session 1: snowball

1. Ask individual participants to take a few minutes on their own to think about good and bad learning experiences from their own history. They should try to identify what factors made a particular experience good or bad.
2. Join with other participants to see if they can identify common factors in their experiences.
3. Share their findings in groups of four or plenary. (This short exercise serves the purpose of getting participants to start *reflecting* on their *experience* and constructing the supportive and facilitative ambience to enable them to do so.)

Session 2: a short presentation from a tutor on his or her experiences of developing learning skills (using a colleague may encourage the feeling of a joint *supportive* endeavour).

Session 3: project group activity. In groups of three or four, to design a learning skills session for students (*experimenting* and establishing an informal *support* group that can help its members when they test their activities for real).

Session 4: plenary discussion (this allows for further *reflection* and *reinforcement*).

Session 5: farewell (it is important to have a '*consequent action*' activity at the end of any session where the participants are bound together in an informal contract to continue to experiment with new and different methods).

Topics for a staff development programme

In what follows I will assume that most staff development takes place in face-to-face sessions. Such sessions can be adapted to written and Web modes with varying degrees of success. The main issues for development are: face-to-face skills – academic and non-academic support, support values and qualities; communication skills – face to face, phone, online; boundary setting skills – referring on, inter-personal skills and so on.

Face-to-face skills

Many of the learning skills development activities in chapter 11 can be adapted for staff development sessions. For example the activity on 'Tackling the assignment' can be used almost as it stands with a group of tutors. It will then act both as a useful exercise in itself but also give the tutors a feel for the student experience.

Support values and qualities

The exercise in chapter 3 on values and responses can be used to generate reflective discussion.

Communication skills

Role plays: again the materials used in chapter 5 can be adapted for staff development. The role play activities are particularly useful, especially if recorded for playback and analysis. But role playing can be quite revealing and intimidating and needs a great deal of support.

A number of years ago I was using role play exercises with a group of my colleagues. I gave one particular pair an especially nasty exercise where a tutor was phoning his line manager because one of his students had just committed suicide. The manager was unable to answer with a simple human response but retreated into bureaucratic mode: 'We must complete the appropriate form ...'. The tutor became more and more desperate for support and the role play became a very good example of non-communication and unmet needs. But in retrospect I did not give appropriate support to the players afterwards, leaving them feeling alienated from the process and devalued by the experience.

Simulations: a less threatening way of tackling communication skills is to simulate various kinds of communication in a supportive discussion framework. For example, in my own staff development programme, for new tutors I use a 'game' called 'On course' where 'players' work in groups of four or five. In turn each player picks up a card, determined by the throw of a dice, which contains a typical student query or issue. The player says how he or she would respond to that particular issue, and the other players comment on how useful and complete they found the response and what they might have done themselves. A facilitator ensures that the discussion is apposite and supportive. The game framework means that the approach is light-hearted and informal and that the queries arise in random and unpredictable ways. The cards contain communications by various media – face to face, phone, letter, e-mail – which affect the response. Here are a few examples of student issues. Others are scattered throughout this book:

By phone: 'Sorry Jane, I'm going to be late with my assignment. Can you give me another couple of weeks?'
By letter: 'Dear Jim, sorry I've dropped out – just can't manage with the children and everything.'
By e-mail: 'Jen – I can't get my pc to download that program you sent me. Help!'

Boundary setting

The activity above also allows the exploration of boundary issues, setting limits to what staff can reasonably achieve and what they should refer on and not try to tackle themselves. Boundaries are set by various factors such as staff time, availability, skills, knowledge and priorities. Members of staff exceeding their boundaries may become stressed and give inappropriate help; staff not working up to their boundaries may be ineffective and feel disempowered. So it is important to include some boundary issues in a simulation and explore how comfortable people are in accepting the limits to student support.

For example, a tutor contacted me about a student who was facing a range of particularly difficult problems. The student was immensely grateful for this help and it was clear that the tutor had been willingly drawn in and become very involved. At the same time it was also clear that the tutor was becoming uncomfortable at the amount of time she was having to spend. It also began to look as though the student's problems were very deep-seated and well beyond the institution's capacity.

Finally, I stepped in – rightly or wrongly – to set some boundaries for the time that the tutor could spend in order to protect her (and her other students) from the time-consuming needs of this student.

Ultimately boundaries are personal. These are examples of issues that I have used with student support staff to try to define their personal boundaries.

In small groups discuss how far staff would be prepared to deal with or respond to any of the statements below. If they felt anything was outside their personal boundary how would they indicate that?

- My tutor's given me a D for this essay. I think it's at least a B. Would you have a look at it for me?
- This course has been an absolute shambles from start to finish. You'd better give me my money back or I'll sue!
- Well, you see, my husband really doesn't think I should be doing this course. (Starts to cry quietly.)
- Of course you're an intelligent woman, you know your whole organization's riddled with Marxists . . .
- You've been ever so helpful. I'm really grateful. Would you come out for a drink with me?
- Of course I cheat on assignments – doesn't everybody?
- I don't suppose you can help me – no one else has . . .
- I'm in here (prison) for a sex offence.
- What's a pretty woman like you doing working for an organization like this?

Finally there must be systems for staff to refer on issues beyond their boundaries, either to a more senior member of staff or to a referral agency. See chapter 10.

Interpersonal skills

We've seen previously that the personal qualities of support staff are important to students. For example the quality of 'approachability' in their tutors is seen as important by students. It is not easy to see how to develop qualities of 'approachability' but using the process of experience and reflection it may be possible to get tutors to be aware of its importance.

At a recent staff development day I ran a simple exercise with a group of tutors. I asked them to think of a good teacher from their recent past. What qualities did that teacher have? After a few minutes I asked them to think of a poor teacher from the past. What made that teacher a poor one? Then I asked them to draw up in pairs a list of good and bad qualities for a teacher to have. We then compared that list with a list drawn up by students from a survey and discovered that there was quite a good correlation.

I would not claim that an exercise like this would turn a naturally distant personality into a warm cuddly one. But a tutor who could remember what it was like to be a student approaching an apparently formidable tutor might be in a better position to react to his or her own students in a more friendly way.

Other skills

The other skills you may want your staff to develop may be specialized: correspondence tuition skills, phone skills, online support skills and so on. But the underlying principle of experience, reflection and support will apply to them all and can be used to design appropriate activities. So, for example, in a correspondence tuition skills exercise, tutors could compare how it would feel to receive different kinds of comments as a student.

For an online support skills exercise there is no substitute for an exercise that puts staff into a conferencing situation. It does not have to be online itself: one of the most successful computer conferencing activities I remember was a face-to-face simulation using yellow sticky pads stuck to a wall substituting for e-mails. The advantage was that the process was much faster than the online activity could be.

Staff development at a distance

In a localized system it will be necessary to carry out much staff development at a distance using the media already discussed. The most important of these are likely to be correspondence and the Internet.

Staff development by correspondence

The process of experiencing, reflecting and supporting is harder when the process is carried out at a distance by briefing materials. Attempts are certainly made: in the UK OU the main training document *Supporting Open Learners* (1997) contains 'Pauses for thought' in the main text which attempt to get the readers to reflect on their own experience. For example here is the 'Pause for thought' in a section on face-to-face tuition.

PAUSE FOR THOUGHT

It's worth thinking about each of these problems from the student's point of view. Imagine you are a distance student. Make a list of the problems that you might encounter as a result of studying in isolation from other students.

Suggestions

Your list might include some of the following:

- Not having anyone to talk to when you encounter some difficulty with the course.
- Thinking that you are the only one having difficulty with the course and therefore feeling worried and inadequate.
- Feeling the strain of having to juggle the conflicting demands of family, work and study.
- Worrying that your work is not up to standard and having no means of checking this.
- Having no one with whom to share ideas, enthusiasms and enjoyment.

Staff development on the Web

Using the Web for distance staff development has some advantages over correspondence in that material can be made interactive. Any staff development on the Web
should try to take its participants through the same process as before: experience,
reflection, experimentation and support. So, for example, the Web site should have
a chat room where staff can discuss their responses to activities and try out ideas
with the supportive help of a moderator. For example, we have recently placed
our 'On course' simulation on a Web site. Staff can bring up a student query, click
on it to get a suggested response with some supporting material, and click again to
go to a computer conference where they can discuss the response with colleagues.

Staff development and mentoring

Mentoring can be a very appropriate medium for staff development when used
to promote reflection. It works well because it sidesteps the authority of the line
manager and allows a new member of support staff to experiment and reflect
with the facilitative help of a colleague who is not in any supervisory role. Moreover,
mentoring can be conducted at a distance by regular phone calls.

Staff development courses

There are now a number of courses in distance education which contain elements
about student support. At higher degree level the two best known to me are the
UK Open University Masters Degree in Open and Distance Education and the
University of London, Institute of Education and International Extension College
MA in Distance Education. The former is an online course that may be particularly
appropriate to the developed world; the latter is a correspondence package that
relates especially well to developing world concerns. Dedicated ODL courses at
lower levels are harder to find. In the UK the NVQ system offers qualifications in
Advice and Guidance which may be appropriate across a range of staff, although
it has no option for distance education as such.

Continuing support

Once new staff have been through an induction programme of staff development
they will need an ongoing programme of support. There may be several aims to
such a programme.

Overcoming isolation

If your institution uses a localized system with local part-time staff then, like their
students, one of the characteristics of the work will be isolation. They will be

isolated both from their students and from the institution. There will not be common rooms where they can chat, notice boards to catch up on news or corridors in which to catch a head of department.

Thus anyone responsible for management of such staff needs to look at their communication routes very carefully. Do staff have easy and reliable access to their manager? If that manager goes off to an important meeting are the staff's communications dealt with in his or her absence? Are staff enabled to have good links to other staff with the same role? Do they feel part of the team that produces the courses?

Validation

If good communication systems are set up, what should be the content of the communications? My experience from being both the sender and recipient of such communication is that the line manager should be using his or her communication to encourage reflection on the part of staff and to validate that reflection. Validation is not just praise: it is acknowledging the rightness of the efforts made and the conditions under which they are made, and encouraging further reflection and experimentation and activity.

Improving quality

Where a member of staff is not working as well as he or she might, it will be necessary to examine the reasons for the poor performance. A programme of extra monitoring and support may need to be set up. But 'sandwiching' their deficiencies between validations of what they are doing well will still be a sound foundation for their improvement.

A tutor wrote to me recently: 'This student is terrified of exams and is convinced she will fail. I've spent a little time talking with her on the phone and telling her she'll be fine and she seems a little calmer now.' To which I replied: 'Thanks very much, Sheila. That sounds like a most helpful conversation. Would you have time to talk to her again nearer the exam if you think it appropriate? Perhaps you could talk about some "stress management" techniques – I'll send you some material on that. Thanks again for your helpful work.'

Thus validation is rather more than just saying 'well done' – which alas is rare enough in the educational environment, which all too often seems more committed to criticism and blame. But in addition in this example there is a very gentle suggestion about something else the tutor could have done sandwiched in between the praise.

Ultimately there is always one single simple question that will apply to everyone supporting support staff: 'Am I supporting this person in the way I expect them to support students?'

Chapter 17

Epilogue: the future of student support in ODL

The future of student support in ODL will depend on social and technical developments within the wider field of education. Most reports foresee continuing expansion in education worldwide. In the UK for example the government is currently [January 2002] hoping for an HE participation rate of 50 per cent of 18–30 year-olds by 2010.

Much of this growth is likely to be achieved by substantial growth in part-time student numbers taking 'career-friendly' modular courses locally or at a distance using open and distance learning methods. However, this growth may not be concentrated in publicly funded institutions faced with growing costs and falling subsidies. It is already apparent that there is a growth in new education-for-profit organizations or existing commercial firms that are developing education divisions, sometimes as joint enterprises with existing providers. Both examples are taking advantage of new technology to deliver courses by CD ROM and the Internet.

So the picture of further and higher education that is emerging is one of a large number of potential part-time students choosing courses from a large variety of providers face to face and by correspondence and the Internet.

One observer (Elton, 1999) has hypothesized that, at the extreme, two systems of higher education will develop. One will be a mass system delivered remotely and cheaply by the latest technology. However, the older universities (some of them already among the oldest continuing institutions in the world) will be able to attract wealthy full-time students and be able to offer face-to-face teaching on an intimate scale. There will in effect be two kinds of institution: 'Fordist', characterized by the mass production of relatively cheap single courses, and 'post-Fordist': more expensive but offering a wider range of individualized courses.

On the other hand it seems more likely that the ODL world of the millennium will be characterized by:

- greater competition from more providers in both new and established markets;
- an increasingly diverse student body with increasingly diverse needs;
- a more assertive student body more likely to demand rights and more likely to seek redress;
- pressures of funding and more direct accountability to government through quality assessment authorities requiring performance standards of various kinds;
- developments in information and communication technologies.

Student support trends

What will be the trends in student support in this scenario of competing providers, more assertive students and developing technologies? Given that the first element in the education system will be the production of courses, student support will be under very particular pressure to reduce costs – or possibly to be phased out altogether. For example at a recent conference I attended, a speaker suggested that as Internet developments went on at increasing speed, as more students familiar with the medium entered ODL, student support would become unnecessary. In any case offering student support merely increased student dependency in a vicious circle of tutor–student conspiracy.

Alternatively, student support may be seen as a competitive edge in the institution, just as some producers advertise not just the quality of their product but also the quality of the 'after-sales' service. Or, possibly, students may be allowed to purchase student support as a form of 'extended warranty' to use when they need it. Whatever the future scenario, there are some trends that do seem clear in computer and phone support.

Developments in student support using computers

I have already discussed some of the student support developments using computers and the Internet and there can be little doubt that these will continue.

Developments like these are already occurring, although they will be inhibited by the cost of computing equipment. That is certainly steadily falling, but the specification required has been rising to compensate, and the cost of local call access is not negligible for students in the UK. It seems likely that there will continue to be a need for paper versions of these materials and systems for some while yet, if not permanently. And it must be remembered that the Web is not necessarily a student-friendly place: learners can easily get lost in the complex systems and be unsure about their original purpose or how they got there (Kirkup and Jones, 1996).

Case study

It is 2005 and student A logs on to the Internet and enters her institutional password. This will bring up her personal gateway to the institution's Web site where there will be:

- Her personal details for her to amend if necessary.
- Her course material including video materials. She may not want to read this straight off her computer screen, so she may print it or perhaps transfer it to a lightweight 'e-book' or even 'electronic paper'.
- Her progress details: for example, the grades she has earned so far and what else she needs to do to pass the course. There will be reminders of where she should be up to on the course and what assignments are still outstanding. There will be copies of her marked assignments for reference, with comments from a tutor or possibly from an 'intelligent system'.
- A general study area with help on study and learning skills. There will be 'Frequently Asked Questions' about (for example) what to do if she is falling behind, diagnostic materials for skills and materials on which she can practise learning skills.
- A conferencing area where she can contact her tutor, an adviser and other students by e-mail.
- An administrative area that will contain information about regulations to be met, qualifications, rules and fees.
- A course choice area with advertisements, details and samples of future course possibilities and associated diagnostic materials.
- Links to other Internet sites that may be of interest (although I suspect that there will be few links, if any, to possible competitors).

Developments in phone services for student support

The phone will continue to be a most useful medium for student support for some time yet. It will be quicker to pick up a phone and seek support than to log on to a network, type out a query and wait for an answer. The developments seem to be in the field of making it cheaper for the institution to deal with calls. I have already mentioned my expectation that there will be increasing use of 'call-centre' solutions to student support demands. This will allow the use of less skilled and therefore cheaper advisory staff working to scripts and handling up to 100 calls or more a day. Tuition may be handled the same way, although that may be more difficult.

It is 2010. The office of Study Success Direct, a subsidiary of Global Megaversity Incorporated, is in a large warehouse in a suburb of London. From inside the huge central space there is a steady hum as 500 staff deal with calls and e-mails from students. Hunched over their computers and wearing headsets they deal with more than 100 calls a day each, 24 hours a day including Christmas. Even before calls have been answered students have been identified and their details flashed up on the support assistant's computer along with possible queries and their answers. Calls will also have been pre-directed to a particular section according to language, current course, known preferences or other criteria.

It is not inhuman; the operators are allowed one mild joke per call as long as the call length does not exceed prescribed limits. Calls are monitored at random and the quality control is very precise.

Above the operators' heads is a display: 'Total calls today 12,268: Current target 750 calls/hour: Current performance 686.'

I lied about the location: it is actually in Shanghai as labour costs are lower.

How successful this approach will be (and I argued previously that there are serious pitfalls) may depend on how far students are prepared to behave as 'customers'. Is education just a consumer durable needing servicing, or do students want a more personal relationship with the institution and preferably with one person in it? How far is such a contact important to their progress? I suspect that success in this particular competition will go to the institution that can reconcile the possible need for personal support with the economics of the call centre.

Is student support worth it?

Finally, one thing that I do expect in the near future will be reasonable and clear proof that student support works: that it is a necessary and cost-effective way of retaining students as well as an essential humanizing element of any open and distance learning system.

It may be that this proof will come from one of the new institutions that will have a stake in the cost-effectiveness of its support. Wherever it comes, I believe it will justify the achievements of many dedicated and effective people working in student support, reflected incompletely and inadequately in this book, and to whom this book is gratefully dedicated.

References

Adams, C, Rand, R and Simpson, O (1989) But what's it really like? – the Taster Pack idea, *Open Learning,* **4** (3), p 42

Asbee, S and Simpson, O (1998) Partners, families and friends: student support of the closest kind, *Open Learning,* **13** (3), p 56

Asbee, S, Simpson, O and Woodall, S (1999) Student–student mentoring in distance education, *British Journal of Access and Credit Studies,* **2** (2), pp 220–32

Baath, J (1979) *Correspondence Education in the Light of a Number of Contemporary Teaching Methods,* Liber Hermods, Malmo

Blanchfield, L, Patrick, I and Simpson, O (1999) Computer conferencing for guidance and support, *British Journal of Educational Technology,* **31**, pp 295–306

Boud, D, Keogh, R and Walker, D (1996) Promoting reflection in learning – a model, in *Boundaries of Adult Learning,* ed R Edwards, A Hanson and P Raggatt, p 32–56, Routledge, London

Carmichael, J (1995) Voicemail and the telephone: a new student support strategy in the teaching of law by distance education, *Distance Education,* **16** (1), pp 7–23

Clennell, S (1987) *Older Students in Adult Education* as reviewed by Eric Midwinter, Director, Centre for Policy on Ageing, *Open Learning,* **4** (1), p 64

Clutterbuck, D (1995) Managing customer defection, *Customer Service Management,* (7)

Dallat, J, Fraser, G, Livingston, R and Robinson, A (1992) Teaching and learning by video-conferencing at the University of Ulster, *Open Learning,* **7** (2), pp 14–22

Daniel, J (1998) *Distance Learning: The vision, and distance learning: the reality. What works, what travels?* Conference on technology standards for global learning, Utah

Daniel, J (1999) *The Global Business of HE: Technology is the answer but what was the question?* Conference speech, University of Graz, Austria

Darkenwald, G G and Merriam, S B (1982) *Adult Education: Foundations of practice,* Harper and Row, New York

Datta, S (1998) *Reading Skills of New Undergraduate Reservees,* Open University in East Anglia, unpublished

De Board, R (1983) *Counselling People at Work,* Gower Press, London

Egan, G (1975) *The Skilled Helper,* Brookes Cole, Pacific Grove, USA

Ellis, A (1962) *Reason and Emotion in Psychotherapy,* Citadel Press, New York

Elton, L (1999) Universities for the rich and for the poor, *Times Higher Educational Supplement,* 19 February

Entwistle, A and Ramsden, P (1983) *Understanding Student Learning,* Croom Helm, London

Gaskell, A and Simpson, O (2000) *What Do Students Want From Their Tutor?* Paper presented to 'Research and Innovation in Distance Education', EDEN conference, Prague

Gaskell, A and Spirit, J (eds) (2000) *Along these Lines,* internal training document, Open University in the East of England

Gaskell, A, Gibbons, S and Simpson, O (1990) Taking off and baling out, *Open Learning,* **5** (2), p 49

George, J and Cowan, J (1998) *Tutoring by Phone,* Robert Gordon University, Edinburgh

Gibbs, G (1981) *Teaching Students to Learn,* Open University Press, Milton Keynes

Henderson, L and Putt, I (1999) Evaluating audioconferencing as an effective learning tool in cross-cultural contexts, *Open Learning,* **14** (1), p 25

Holmberg, B (1995) *Theory and Practice of Distance Education,* Routledge, London

Honey, P and Mumford, A (1986) *The Manual of Learning Styles,* Honey, Maidenhead, UK

Hulsmann, T (2000) *The Costs of Open Learning: A handbook,* Bibliotheks-und Informations system der Universitat Oldenburg

IEC (International Extension College) (2001) *Module on Managing Learner Support Activities,* Cambridge, UK

Johnson, M, Mayes, R and Doolittle, M (1999) *Valuation of Admissions Advice in the OU London Region,* Open University London Region

Kirkup, G and Jones, A (1996) New technologies for open learning: the superhighway to the learning society? in *The Learning Society,* ed R Raggatt, R Edwards and N Small, p 272, Routledge, London, pp 272–91

Kirkup, G and Von Prummer, C (1990) Support and connectedness: the needs of women distance education students, *Journal of Distance Education,* Fall, **5** (2), p 29

Kolb, D (1984) *Experiential Learning,* Prentice Hall, New Jersey

Laurillard, D (1993) *Rethinking University Teaching: A framework for the effective use of educational technology,* Routledge, London

McGivney, V (1996) *Staying or Leaving the Course,* National Institute of Adult Continuing Education (NIACE), Leicester

Main, A (1980) *Encouraging Effective Learning: An approach to study counselling,* Scottish Academic Press, Edinburgh

Masie Centre, Saratoga Springs, New York 'Learning Decisions' May 2000 [Online] www.masie.com

Morgan, A (1993) Improving Your Students' Learning, Kogan Page, London

National Extension College (NEC) (1996) Open Learner, Cambridge, UK

NEC (2001a) How to Study Effectively, Cambridge, UK

NEC (2001b) How to Manage Your Time, Cambridge, UK

Open University (1997) Supporting Open Learners, Student Services, Open University, Milton Keynes

Open University (OU) (1999) Courses Survey 1998 Early Results, Institute of Educational Technology, Student Research Centre, Open University

Palloff, R and Pratt, K (1999) Building Learning Communities in Cyberspace, Jossey Bass, San Francisco

Palmer, F (1984) Seriously stressed students, Teaching at a Distance, 22, p 77

Paul, R (1988) If student services are so important why are we cutting them back? in Developing Distance Education Papers, ed D Sewart and J Daniel, 14th ICDE World Conference, Oslo

Pennels, J (2000) Teacher education for nomads in Nigeria, Open Praxis, 2, pp 46–51

Perraton, H (1987) Theories, generalisations and practice in distance education, Open Learning, 2 (3), pp 3–12

Perraton, H (2000) Open and Distance Learning in the Developing World, Routledge, London

Peters, O (1989) The iceberg has not melted: further reflections on the concept of industrialisation and distance teaching, Open Learning, 4 (3), p 3

Pichot, B (1986) The Intrapreneur's Ten Commandments Intrapreneuring, Harper and Row, New York

Robinson, B (1984) Telephone teaching, in The Role of Technology in Distance Education, ed A Bates, Croom Helm, London

Rogers, C (1951) Client Centred Therapy, Houghton Mifflin, New York

Rogers, C (1961) On Becoming a Person, Constable, Boston

Rumble, G (1989) 'Open learning', 'distance learning', and the misuse of language, Open Learning, 4 (2), pp 28–37

Rumble, G (1992) The competitive vulnerability of distance teaching universities, Open Learning, 7 (2), pp 31–45

Shepherd (2001) Keeping in Touch the Long-Distance Way, IT Training, Middlesex, UK (June)

Simpson, O (1978) Learning to listen 2 – role play, Teaching at a Distance, 13, pp 52–58

Simpson, O (1988) Counselling by correspondence in distance education, Open Learning, 3 (3), pp 43–45

Simpson, O (1992) Specifying student support services in the OU – the so-called 'student charter', Open Learning, 7 (2), pp 57–59

Stephenson, J (ed) (2001) Teaching and Learning Online, Kogan Page, London

Tait, A (1989) The politics of open learning, Adult Education, 61 (4), pp 308–13

Tait, A (1993) Key Issues in Open Learning, Longman, Harlow, UK

Tait, A (1999) Face-to-face and at a distance: the mediation of guidance and counselling through the new technologies, *British Journal of Guidance and Counselling,* **27** (1), pp 113–22

Tett, L (1993) Education and the market place, *Scottish Educational Review,* **25** (2), p 123

Thorpe, M (1988) *Evaluating Open and Distance Learning,* Longman, Harlow, UK

Thorpe, M and Grugeon, D (ed) (1987) *Open Learning for Adults,* Longman Open Learning, Harlow, UK

Visser, L (1998) *The Development of Motivational Communication in Distance Education Support* (thesis), University of Twente, Enschede, Netherlands

Wallace, J (1998) article in the *Guardian,* 16 June

Watts, F, Individual-centred cognitive counselling for study problems, *British Journal for Guidance and Counselling,* **13** (3)

Woodley, A (1987) Understanding adult student drop-out, in *Open Learning for Adults,* ed M Thorpe and D Grugeon, pp 110–24, Longman Open Learning, Harlow, UK

Wright, A (1987) Putting independent learning in its place, *Open Learning,* **2** (1), p 3

Index